W9-COB-361

Investigating Social Capital

Investigating Social Capital
Comparative Perspectives on Civil Society, Participation and Governance

Edited by

Sanjeev Prakash/Per Selle

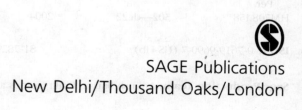

SAGE Publications
New Delhi/Thousand Oaks/London

First published in 2004 by

Sage Publications India Pvt Ltd
B-42, Panchsheel Enclave
New Delhi 110 017

Sage Publications Inc.
2455 Teller Road
Thousand Oaks, California 91320

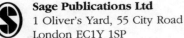

Sage Publications Ltd
1 Oliver's Yard, 55 City Road
London EC1Y 1SP

Published by Tejeshwar Singh for Sage Publications India Pvt Ltd, typeset in 10/12 Gatineau by S.R. Enterprises, New Delhi, and printed at Chaman Enterprises, New Delhi.

Library of Congress Cataloging-in-Publication Data

Investigating social capital: comparative perspectives on civil society, participation and governance/edited by Sanjeev Prakash, Per Selle.
     p.cm.
    Includes bibliographical references and index.
    1. Social capital (Sociology) 2. Civil society. I. Prakash, Sanjeev. II. Selle, Per.
HM708.I58   302—dc22   2004   2003017683

ISBN: 0-7619-9690-7 (US-Hb)   81-7829-154-1 (India-Hb)

Sage Production Team: Ankush Saikia, Rinki Gomes and Santosh Rawat

To our mothers,
Gogo Prakash
and
Maria Selle

Contents

I
Social Capital: Whence it Came

II
Empirical Approaches

III
New Directions and Cul-de-Sacs

List of Tables

List of Figures

Preface

Many people have helped make this book possible. The Norwegian Centre for Research in Organization and Management at the University of Bergen, where our project on 'Social Capital and Collective Action' was based between 1999–2001, provided an atmosphere of convivial discussion, stimulation and reflection in which to begin thinking and planning the book. Our thanks are due to many of our former colleagues at the Centre (which was terminated and integrated into the Rokkan Centre for Social Studies at the end of 2001). In particular, we wish to thank Ivar Bleiklie, director between 1999–2001, and Åse Netland, administrator, for unstinting support and the enviable ability to carry out difficult administrative tasks with graceful ease. Maila Solheim organized and formatted the manuscript for the publisher in her usual efficient style. *Tusen takk*!

The major part of this book is based on papers presented at the 'Investigating Social Capital' workshop that was held in Solstrand in May 2000 with financial support from the Norwegian Power and Democracy Project. We are grateful to them. We thank each of the participants at the Solstrand workshop (including those whose papers did not make it to the book) for their comments and stimulating presence. The chairs of the workshop sessions, Agnar Sandmo, Dietlind Stolle, Irene van Staveren, Paul Dekker and Steve Rayner, helped ensure that discussions took place in an orderly and effective manner. Our thanks to each of them as well.

Finally, we dedicate this book to our mothers, Maria Selle and Gogo Prakash, who (as our friend and colleague Ric Uslaner* tells it) helped us develop an early appreciation for the complex non-linearities involved in instituting trust in strangers. Needless to state, without their formative contributions this book, and so much else, would not be possible.

Sanjeev Prakash/Per Selle   **Bergen, April 2003**

*In his absorbing paper to the Solstrand Workshop, 'Bonding with Friends: Moralistic Trust and Civic Engagement', as well as in his recent book, *The Moral Foundations of Trust*.

Acknowledgements

We acknowledge the following publishers for permission to include material originally published by them in this volume. The papers with their complete citations are mentioned below:

Chapter 9. Putting Social Capital to Work: Agency and Development by Anirudh Krishna. Originally published in *World Development*, vol. 29, no. 6, as Moving from the Stock of Social Capital to the Flow of Benefits: The Role of Agency, pp. 925–43, 2001, reprinted with permission from Elsevier.

Chapter 11. Social Capital and Economic Development: A Plea for Mechanisms by Gaute Torsvik. Originally published in *Rationality and Society*, vol. 12, no. 2, pp. 451–76. Copyright © Sage Publications Ltd. Reprinted by permission of Sage Publications Ltd, London.

I
Social Capital: Whence it Came

1

Introduction:
Why Investigate Social Capital?

Sanjeev Prakash/Per Selle[1]

A book about social capital and civil society in India, Scandinavia, the Netherlands and Italy may seem to require some explanation. After all, even a cursory survey of country data tables reveals that, by all the usual yardsticks, these countries and societies have little in common. Why, then, choose cases marked by widely differing political and social institutions, levels of education, income distribution, demographic patterns and general aspirations for a comparative study of social capital?

There are several reasons for this book, and most of them are concerned with the state of the current debate on social capital. Among democratic countries where associational participation—one of the more widely accepted indicators of social capital—has been the subject of sustained research, the Nordic countries and the Netherlands report the highest rates for membership of formal associations. Separate research on India suggests it may have among the lowest rates for formal associational participation.[2] The typical Scandinavian and Dutch form of civic participation in broad-based organizational clusters, as well as new developments such as the rise of 'passive' membership, provide a marked complement to the multiplicity of local networks and organisational forms that flourish in contemporary India. There are notable differences between the cases in this book and the mainly American and Italian examples around which much of the early social capital literature within political theory has revolved (Putnam 1993, 1995). It is perhaps time to re-evaluate some of the key assumptions that underpin this literature. For instance, in a chapter for this book, Mario Diani uses an innovative relational approach to examine detailed data on associational membership in Lombardy, Northern Italy, thus raising compelling questions about previous studies of this supposedly 'high social capital' region. Our selection of cases is neither accidental nor random, and provides valuable material for a broad, comparative study of social capital. This is all the more so because, in many senses, the study of social capital seems to have reached an impasse in recent years.

More than a decade after general interest in social capital as an explanation for the differential achievement of countries in institutionalizing civil society, democratic governance and economic development was initiated, the accusation that the term means many different things to different people rings truer than ever before (Narayan and Pritchett 1997; Fine 1999). A major reason for this state of affairs is a persisting lack of clarity about what social capital is, and what it is not. Despite the initial efforts of the late James Coleman to identify 'certain aspects of social structure by their functions' in facilitating various actions of individual or corporate actors (Coleman 1988; 1990), there remain some rather large gaps in the conceptual articulation of the social-capital idea.[3]

Few scholars would now dispute that defining something mainly by its functions risks confusing causes with effects.[4] Social capital is generally understood to mean the social structures and networks necessary for sustaining collective action, the supposed normative contents of these structures (such as trustworthiness and reciprocal relations), as well as—frequently—the outcome of collective action achieved through such structures. It makes sense here to distinguish between stock and flow, where a given stock or quantity of assets deployed in a productive way provides a stream of benefits or interest over time. Which is the stock and which is the flow here, and which are the variables necessary for realising beneficial outcomes from social capital? Such distinctions might give more substance to the explicit analogy with forms of economic capital. Unfortunately, methods to separate and measure these aspects of social capital in any consistent form remain contentious and are not generally agreed upon (but see Krishna, this volume, for an innovative effort in this direction).

Robert Putnam's influential version of social capital (Putnam 1993, 1995, 2000) involving the combination of trust, norms and networks of civic engagement has raised even more difficult and critical methodological questions. In considering horizontal relations within voluntary associations as the main sources of differentiation in endowments of social capital and the relative extent of civic networks in Northern and Southern Italy as well as across the USA, Putnam builds on Tocquevillean assumptions that seem particularly limited and narrow when transferred to countries and contexts other than the USA. A major issue here is the extent to which voluntary associations are the primary basis for the development of social networks and civic trust in comparison to other associational forms like extended families, neighbourhood groups, traditional caste associations, class factions, common-property managing organizations, social movements and so on. Recent writers have begun to dispute the claim that a simple count of formal associational memberships provides a useful or adequate picture of the level of civil society and generalized trust within any society (Rudolph, Dekker, this volume; Newton 1999; Foley and Edwards 1999). Though the need for sustained research on the role of voluntary associations in facilitating civil society, democratic participation and economic development— a primary arena for contemporary social capital studies—remains vital and compelling, the widening application of the social capital idea to complex arenas of society and governance has tended to increase the level of conceptual confusion instead of clarifying underlying frameworks.

In this book we offer a set of empirical and conceptual analyses of the contexts, causes and consequences of social capital in an attempt to achieve a basic modicum of clarity and consistency. We believe this is best done by constructing a broad comparative perspective and by analysing different cases and contexts to test the robustness of underlying explanations. For this reason, we have not limited the ambit of this book exclusively to societies in the North or the South, or to democracy, civil society and economic development in isolation. Instead, we present a range of analytical studies that span disciplinary and thematic boundaries to search for viable explanations and hypotheses. While our studies do not adopt a single methodological framework in approaching their quite different analytical aims (a difficult if not impossible task), they explore a variety of cases and methods to produce an extended evaluation of some of the key assumptions of the social capital idea.

The Need for Intermediate Mechanisms

Any new work on social capital must address a number of interrelated conceptual issues. For instance, should normative values and attitudes such as trust and reciprocity as well as the more objective aspects of social networks and structures be considered independent components of social capital, or should we in some senses consider them to be interdependent variables subject to verifiable degrees of correlation? Given that different kinds of trust—in close friends and family, in local institutions, across generations, in 'weak' and 'strong' ties, in labour unions and social movements, in political institutions, in strangers or in wider social frameworks—reveal little or no correlation across sectors and countries (Foley and Edwards 1999; Newton 1999; Diani, this volume), what type of trust should we consider relevant in different contexts? More critically, where data supports alternative conclusions, should we take this sort of social trust to arise essentially from the experience of 'overlapping' associational membership[5] and 'bridging' ties (as Robert Putnam has suggested) or should we instead consider alternate causal mechanisms that involve levels of pre-existing trust or distrust[6] in the possibilities and outcomes of associational membership (Stolle this volume, 2001; Diani, this volume)? And should we attempt to consider the institutional structures that supposedly arise from social capital and trust as somehow separate from their normative content, and their implications for social welfare and the common good?

Many of the contributors to this volume are concerned with the specific mechanisms that explain the formation and performance of social capital. They find a variety of different mechanisms that serve to facilitate or obstruct social capital, depending on the institutional context and the kind of social capital involved. This in itself should not be surprising. What is in fact surprising is that there should be so little analysis of underlying mechanisms in the development of a concept explained primarily through its functions. Such a condition makes it extremely difficult to distinguish between different causes for the same effect and different effects from the same causal process, sometimes turning the task of identifying essential relationships into a matter of personal conviction rather than of theoretical

clarity. Clearly, more attention to the specific intermediate mechanisms that relate the causes and consequences of social capital could
serve to test the validity of alternate explanations and hypotheses.

For both James Coleman and Robert Putnam, social capital arises
from interactions achieved through membership in social networks
and voluntary associations. For Coleman it is 'multiplex' relations
(similar in some ways to Putnam's overlapping memberships) and
the 'closure' of social networks that provide the conditions necessary for developing trustworthiness (Coleman 1988: 105–9). Both
explanations range conspicuously from micro-to macro-levels in their
scope. While Coleman is consciously innovating a conceptual entity in sociology that, like economic axioms, can 'make the micro-
macro transition from pair relations to system' (Coleman 1988: 98),[7]
Putnam argues that the experience of extended face-to-face interaction between citizens in associations (he stresses horizontal relations and overlapping memberships) leads to the development of
'generalized trust' and civil society, phenomena that operate over
appreciably larger scales (Putnam 1993, 2000).

The contributors to this volume contest these hypotheses, finding little evidence that trust can be 'generalized' evenly or sym-
metrically across a society. Nearly all of them agree with Susanne
Rudolph; that the consequences of membership in different types
of associations—political or social, deliberative or interest-based,
hierarchic or egalitarian, voluntary, ascriptive or 'intentional'—need
to be further analysed and differentiated in terms of their impact on
civil society.

> We need criteria of distinction ... Not all associations are the same; not
> all have the capacity to generate mutuality and cooperation. Those that
> are able to generate internal solidarity may succeed in ways that make
> members feel sympathy only with each other and insulate them from
> civic others ... Associational life, in other words, can make members
> appreciate each other even while making them self-regarding and paro-
> chial. It can generate a form of group selfishness that results in ethnic
> conflict and civil war, as in Bosnia and Bihar. What are the conditions
> and mechanisms that translate the social capital generated by associa-
> tional life from inside to outside and that makes social capital available
> for strengthening the pursuit of the public good?

In general, the contributors to this book offer perspectives that treat
trust and social capital as complex processes that cannot be
decontextualised. Some of them find that where trust does expand

beyond local or intimate ties, it does so within specific institutional or sectoral contexts (Diani, Caulkins). Others find that social trust develops in relation to the performance of political institutions, especially of local government (Stolle, Caulkins). Some argue that widespread transformations in technology, society and human mobility are changing the forms of social capital in the modern world, requiring us to conceive of it in new ways (Hadenius, Tranvik). Yet others suggest that recent developments in organizational society, especially in the countries of the North, such as growth of passive membership or 'cheque-book participation', are not at all negative in their implications for civic engagement as implied in earlier studies (Wollebæk and Selle). In analysing detailed data for associational membership in Lombardy, part of the high social capital regions of northern Italy that were the subject of Putnam's initial study (Putnam 1993), Mario Diani provides a context-dependent explanation for civic participation that is very different from Putnam's explanatory scheme. All our contributors seem to agree that the field of social capital studies needs to be opened up from the formulation of simple generalized statements to the articulation of coherent, testable frameworks focusing on the highly differentiated contexts, particularities and consequences of different types of associations, social structures and forms of trust.

Part of the criticism levied at theorists of social capital is that they attempt to reduce the manifold complexities of trust to an unviable general scheme. Trust is not a new theme in empirical research, and the elusive nature of its sources has been referred to in several studies (Gambetta 1988; Hardin 1993; Moore 1999; Humphrey and Schmitz 1998; Seligman 1997). For instance, Moore (1999), after Hardin (1993), distinguishes between trust arising from 'character assessment' and 'incentive assessment' and develops a preliminary taxonomy of nine categories of trust. He cites the *World Values Survey*, which found that average levels of trust were higher among people in industrial countries than in developing countries,[8] but is sceptical of any inference about a causal sequence that runs from trust to development. Such survey methods, he argues, provide valuations of trust that have little basis in the revealed preferences, actual behaviour or even the mental states of individuals.

Moreover, the *World Values* data provides no evidence about causal relationships. After all, the opposite causal sequence—that the institutional environment that underlies economic development based on markets and enterprise, including reliable enforcement of contract, better policing and access to formal legal institutions, also provides for higher levels of mutual trust among individual and corporate actors—has long been understood by students of political economy. Rothstein (this volume), in an engaging account that ranges from the film *The Godfather* to conflagrations in Swedish discotheques, develops the argument that the fair and impartial functioning of political institutions—especially those concerned with the maintenance of justice and order—is central to the development of generalized forms of trust and social capital. It makes little sense to trust 'most' people when they are generally known to bribe, threaten or corrupt the impartiality of government institutions and local authorities in order to extract special favours. But, if trust is also to be the *cause* of strong civic institutions and 'good governance', then we are getting close to tautology.

Like many others, we see social capital as a field principally involving explanations from political theory and sociology. We do not see it as originating in economics or being utilised in that discipline in any extensive or central sense. This is not only because of the rational choice assumptions of neoclassical economic theory which the social capital idea refutes;[9] nor simply due to the lack of specification of intermediate mechanisms, which at least one economist compares to a conceptual 'black box' (Torsvik, this volume); nor because of a multiplicity of variables that are weakly correlated, if at all, across contexts and cultures. It is also because the term 'social capital' appears to be inaccurate from an economics perspective.

The basic explanation given for the development of social capital from social ties and networks is a functional one, in that social capital supposedly arises as an *unintended* consequence of individual actions meant to achieve other purposes.[10] In most cases, individuals are not motivated to develop social ties or friendships primarily because they expect to derive personal advantage from them. Instead, such social relationships have an intrinsic value that stems from the interaction itself. With few exceptions, this is precisely what gives social networks their value in monitoring others' actions (Arrow 2000) or developing over time the trustworthiness, reliability and institutionalised collective endeavour that are the bedrock of robust institutions (Solow 2000).

However, to the extent that this is a functional explanation, it sits uneasily with the economic notion of 'capital'. Unlike forms of capital in economic analysis—physical, financial or human—investments in social capital do not come about as a deliberate or intended result of decisions to forgo some aspect of present consumption in order to derive a future benefit (Arrow 2000).[11] As many observers have noted, this is what gives social capital its characteristic propensity to increase with use—'the more you draw upon it, the more you have'. To speak here of 'investment' in a form of capital, implying fungibility and intentionality, is unwarranted.[12]

Another reason this conceptual area does not appear entirely suitable for an economics approach is that the measurement of social capital presents severe methodological problems. As mentioned earlier, in many cases it is not clear whether what is being measured is a stock of assets, a flow of benefits or some proxy variables (a wide variety of proxies is frequently used, particularly by political scientists). As at least one well-known economist has pointed out, investment in the development of social capital does not seem amenable to direct quantified measurement, even in principle, because of the elusive nature of efforts expended in building social networks (Solow 1997, cited in Adler and Kwon 1999). For these reasons we find the term 'social capital', understood *sensu stricto*, misleading and capable of generating unproductive confusion. Perhaps less harm is done if it is borne in mind that the term is used metaphorically rather than in any formal, rigorous or technical sense.

Scale, Embeddedness and Exclusion in Conceptions of Social Capital

There are substantive differences between explanations of social capital developed within sociology and political theory. We will compare them by examining approaches taken to three aspects of social capital—scale, embeddedness and exclusion—within these disciplines.

The literature on social capital ranges widely across scales, from the individual and the class faction in Bourdieu (1986) through the family and community in Coleman to regions, provinces and even countries in Putnam and in Fukuyama (1995). Each version can be said to involve assumptions about the typical operation of mechanisms, such as frequent face-to-face interaction in Putnam (1993) or in Ostrom (1998). Do these widely different scales involve similar or different mechanisms for the action of social capital within and across networks or groups? What is the relevance of scale for a conceptual refinement of the social capital concept?

Second, most models of social capital see it as a *relational* resource, in the sense that it exists not as a property of individuals but
in their relations with other individuals and entities. A critical issue
here is the extent to which social capital can be transferred from
one context to another. To what extent is such fungibility affected
by the way in which social capital is embedded in social relations
and organizations? Can aspects of embeddedness be related to levels of scale and closure, or to some specific qualities and types of
social capital? For instance, will 'denser' communities or networks,
or those endowed with the strong ties and thick trust of 'bonding'
social capital, be able to transfer less or more social capital across
contexts than those possessing the weak ties and thin trust of 'bridging' social capital? Much of the evidence so far has pointed to the
advantages that weak ties and bridging social capital may have in
this respect, but which factors determine the limits of such fungibility? If, on the other hand, social capital is embedded in *particular*
organizational contexts (as suggested by Diani as well as Wollebæk
and Selle, both in this volume) then transferring it may be a very
different matter. The nature of embeddedness raises a number of
complex issues for research and policy.

Finally, right from the initial delineations of Coleman and
Bourdieu, we know that the development of trust involves a closure of networks, for 'reputation cannot arise in an open structure,
and collective sanctions that would ensure trustworthiness cannot
be applied' (Coleman 1988: 107–108). In this view, network closure
serves to develop norms of trustworthiness, but also to keep some
people out. Put another way, the facilitation of transactions among
certain interest groups may have adverse consequences for other
groups, such as the consequences of political bargaining among
elites for socially marginalized and disadvantaged groups. Though
clearly not all situations are of this sort, this is a problem that is
particularly acute over larger scales, such as access to public goods
or the distribution of the benefits of formal institutions in democratic polities. Social capital thus has negative as well as positive
consequences. While occasionally referred to in the literature, this
issue has critical unexplored implications for policies to benefit disadvantaged, poverty stricken, socially excluded or vulnerable groups.

Network sociologists working on social capital lay relatively greater
emphasis on embeddedness, distinguishing between types of networks (eg., egocentric, 'whole network') or ties and relations (weak/

strong, value homogenous/crosscutting). For most sociologists, norms, values and trust are endogenous to social structures or specific to a central actor's network. Thus sociological definitions of social capital are often couched in social structural terms. Pierre Bourdieu, for instance, represents social capital as 'the sum of the resources, actual or virtual, that accrue to an individual or a group by virtue of possessing a durable network of more or less institutionalized relationships of mutual acquaintance and recognition' (Bourdieu and Wacquant 1992: 119).

On the other hand political theorists, particularly those working from a perspective of civic or political culture, focus mainly on interactions within voluntary associations and civil society, or on aspects of state-society relations. Most of them approach social capital in terms of the norms, values or attitudes of individual actors, following the 'civic culture' argument of Almond and Verba (1963) or Tocquevillean notions of associational democracy. The main emphasis here is on a scale transition from individual attributes to the evolution of institutions at various scales, rather than on aspects of embeddedness or closure. As Foley and Edwards (1999) point out, this disciplinary trajectory has led most political scientists to approach social structures and institutional density as sources or outcomes of social capital, and not as forms of it.

The differing conceptions are evident in the indicators used within each discipline to measure social capital. Sociologists in general use some measure of social structure such as networks, ties or aspects of institutional density. Political scientists often approach social capital by measuring and aggregating individual attitudes such as levels of social or institutional trust. For political scientists, these individual attitudes and norms are the essential evidence and measure of social capital. Aggregating such individual-level measures to derive an average for a group, however, tends to overlook key relational and distributional aspects that may influence processes of embeddedness, power and exclusion within the behaviour of groups, and thus affect substantive outcomes. While sociological methods may not capture all relevant aspects of social capital, they have the advantage of directing attention to the relational dimensions of social capital which, for Coleman, 'inheres in the structure of relations between actors and among actors', and not 'in the actors themselves or in physical implements of production' (Coleman 1988: 98).

In this respect, while Bourdieu's conceptual delineation of social capital is often considered complex and difficult to adopt for empirical purposes, his understanding of its measurement is direct and consistent: 'the volume of social capital possessed by a given agent ... depends on the size of the network of connections he can effectively mobilise and on the volume of the capital (economic, cultural or symbolic) possessed in his own right by each of those to whom he is connected' (Bourdieu 1986: 249).

This book offers a sample of the wide range of methods used to assess social capital; from organizational cluster analysis (Caulkins) and contextualised approaches (Diani) to stream-of-benefits assessment (Krishna) and attitudinal surveys (Dekker and Stolle). Dekker investigates the survey approach for consistency and finds little value in the individual questionnaire techniques used for assessing levels of social and political trust. He notes that there is little correlation between such measurements of generalized trust and the actual existence of social networks. These findings provide room for some scepticism about the utility of survey techniques, particularly for measuring civic or public forms of trust.

Bridging Social Capital and the Sources of Civil Society

Just as somewhat different notions of embeddedness and autonomy, or integrity and linkage, permeate the two disciplinary streams, so do related distinctions between thin/thick trust and weak/strong reciprocity. Recognition has grown across both disciplines of the value of *bridging* social capital (that is, crosscutting ties and institutional linkage). Bridging social capital is increasingly being seen as a necessary condition for civil society, economic development, good governance, inter-firm relations and success in other arenas (Woolcock 1998; Van Deth, et al. 1999; Wall, Ferrazzi and Schryer 1998; Burt 1992). This interest in crosscutting ties revisits Mark Granovetter's analysis of the 'strength' of weak ties in economic sociology (Granovetter 1973)[13] and has now become central to neo-Tocquevillean analyses of civil society and political culture. The essential mechanism for the creation of bridging social capital is exemplified by Putnam: a plethora of bounded associations involving frequent face-to-face interaction among individuals of similar disposition (implying the existence of strong embeddedness and bonding social capital) socializes general habits extending to association with strangers or those of different disposition, thus endowing a society with high linkage, strong autonomy and a civil society.[14] Putnam's basic explanation brings together a number of things—including aspects of scale, embeddedness and exclusion—in a very different way than in sociological explanation. At one level there is a striking transition across scale here, from micro-level interactions among individuals to civil society and governance, phenomena that are usually understood as being situated at larger scales. Sociological understandings of social capital, even those involving crosscutting linkages across networks, remain at relatively smaller scales than this 'bottom up' explanation of the formation of civil society. However, to an extent the explanation remains heuristically incomplete: it models how individual, micro-level interactions aggregate and influence institutions at larger scales, but largely ignores the ways in which macro-level phenomena, such as rapid changes in political institutions, influence micro-level interactions and behaviour.[15] Though Putnam's explanation of regional differences in Italy does involve a role for macro-level political institutions, he sees this role primarily in terms of the relatively benign historical effects of the medieval city states in Northern Italy in contrast to the oppressively exploitative Norman kingdom of the South—that is, as a remote, path-dependent process incapable of rapid transformation or induced change.

At another level, the explanation involves a relationship between different kinds of embeddedness. The principal contention here is that, across a certain threshold, quantities of strong horizontal ties tend to produce bridging or crosscutting linkages as a 'spillover' or externality. The implication is that dense networks of strong ties across a given social structure will result in the widespread production of weak ties. Rudolph and other authors in this volume contest this hypothesis, citing a variety of cases and associational contexts where it fails. These authors argue that strong embeddedness of this type often has the opposite effect—of civic conflict or war— even where groups possess high capacities for *endogenous* trust. They suggest we need a more appropriate and precise taxonomy of associations in order to discover the consequences of different associational forms (Rudolph, this volume).

Perhaps the most unusual thing about Putnam's explanation is its treatment of exclusion. As mentioned earlier, in Coleman's early description of social capital, network closure is seen as a necessary condition for the development of trust and reputation (Coleman 1988, 1990). Associations possessing so-called 'bonding' social capital (involving the high embeddedness and thick trust of strong communities and bounded groups) imply a level of closure that results in the effective exclusion of persons with dissimilar interests, persuasions or dispositions. Clearly, it is hard to conceive of a network or association that is infinitely inclusive and open to all.[16] Yet Putnam sees the accumulation of such bonding social capital as the source for a conception of civil society that is generally benign and inclusive of all citizens. In other words, we are asked to believe that denser supplies of associations based on bonding social capital (that is, with strong ties and network closure at the micro-level) are the key to *reducing* some of the negative effects of this form of social capital—social exclusion, inequality and segregation—at a macro-institutional level.

Enough has been said elsewhere about public and private forms of social capital—those that possess high social or civic utility and those that primarily benefit the individual, respectively—for these issues to require extensive comment here. However, we will mention two issues in passing. The first, the distribution of social capital, is one that is often ignored. Measurements of social capital based on survey techniques aggregate individual attitudes into indicators of the average level of social capital prevailing within a society, region or other unit of analysis—a measure of social capital *per capita*. As noted earlier, this is a rather problematic way to evaluate a relational resource. Like any other aspect of power and relationality, what is most important about social capital is not its average level but its distribution across a society or population. Who has social capital in a particular context, and to what extent compared to others, appear to us to be more critical issues than the fact that a given society appears—on average—to possess a lot (or a little) of it. To see social capital as a relational resource is one thing, to see it as an evenly distributed, collective good is quite another. Perhaps one of the more misleading aspects of current theorizing is that social capital is so often represented as a public goods type of resource that is evenly distributed and available to all, when this is not the case in most empirical contexts.

Another problem stems from the notion of civil society itself. Ideas and models of civil society prevalent in different parts of the world at different times have shared little in common. The 'liberation theology' of 1970s Latin America was very different from the 'resistance against the state' version of 1980s Eastern Europe or many developing countries in Asia, and both are different from the sphere of social autonomy and democratisation of the 1970s German

Greens or Putnam's benign model of cooperative, trusting citizens in the 1990s (Rudolph, this volume; Edwards and Foley 2001). However, scholars often seem unaware of models of civil society other than those of their own conception—as if theirs were the only plausible or practical kind. As Edwards and Foley put it

> Competing concepts of civil society ... almost invariably bear the marks of the political struggles within which they were born. Considerable overlap in the sorts of social actors identified as central to 'civil society' among these conceptions gives the notion an air of universality—suggesting that, if only we could come to agreement about just who and what is included under its umbrella, we could achieve a comprehensive theory of state-society relations. Yet, the real purchase of the notion of civil society today is polemical and normative and tied closely to the debates that currently shape it (Edwards and Foley 2001: pp. 2–3).

Despite these drawbacks, we believe the introduction of civil society into the debate on social capital is a potentially challenging one and constitutes a significant contribution from political theory. Because civil society—at least in principle—is inclusive of all citizens, its introduction challenges analysts of social capital to approach issues of scale, closure and embeddedness consistent with a comprehensive theoretical mapping of their subject. Nevertheless, whether social capital can, howsoever construed, provide credible explanations for the roots and origins of civil society remains an open question.

Alternate Approaches to Social Capital

One way to approach this area is suggested by a recent study of conflict between Hindus and Muslims in India. In a recent book, Ashutosh Varshney (2002,2001) argues that the links between theories of civil society and ethnic and religious conflict are crying out for serious attention. Varshney asks why certain Indian cities have suffered from chronic levels of conflict between Hindu and Muslim groups while others have experienced relatively peaceful coexistence. He analyses the incidence of this conflict in relation to the structure of civic ties in 28 Indian cities and towns over a 46-year period (1950–95). Varshney's data shows that in towns and cities where strong intra-group ties (similar to bonding social capital) flourished within Hindu and Muslim groups but inter-group (or bridging) ties between the two communities were weak, there were regular incidents of violence and conflict. On the other hand, in towns and cities where extensive bridging ties connected members of Muslim and Hindu groups in common networks, such ties served to reduce or prevent serious incidents of violent conflict. This was particularly true, notes Varshney, where bridging ties developed through common membership of formal organizations such as trade unions, professional/business associations, NGOs, recreation clubs and sports clubs, rather than through participation in informal or everyday networks. Varshney suggests that the actual pattern of such bridging ties originated in local institutional histories that are fairly recent.

Significantly, there is no relationship asserted here between the existence of strong group-or intra-community ties and the development of civic networks across communities and groups. To put it another way, Varshney argues that the existence of strong-bonding social capital does not necessarily lead to civil society or bridging social capital, but frequently to civic breakdown and violent conflict. Another point Varshney makes is that formal, organized associations involving members from both groups appear more important for maintaining civic order and peace as compared with more informal, everyday interactions. Varshney suggests that while the latter kind of interactions may be effective in smaller contexts such as villages and small towns, formal associations are indispensable at larger scales, such as in the metropolises and large towns that were the subject of his study. Varshney's study also raises some intriguing conceptual questions. For instance, is there a trade-off between strong-bonding social capital and the emergence of bridging social capital? Is it possible that bridging ties will be established not because of the existence of bonding ties, but at the cost of weakening bonding ties?

One might venture that the answer will depend, at least in part, on the normative contents or purposes of the group within which bonding ties are developed, and not on the form of institutional structures alone. We know from past work in economic sociology that networks of 'weak' ties, which underlie the exchange of information necessary for well-functioning markets, require actors to develop a degree of autonomy from embeddedness in strong ties and proximate groups. In other words, there is often a trade-off between the demands of strong groups or bonding ties and the development of crosscutting and bridging linkages (cf. Granovetter 1992; Polanyi 1992).[17] If this is so, it seems at odds with Putnam's

explanation of the development of bridging ties. Such contradic-
tions suggest there are areas where social capital theory may be
distracting analysts from appreciating the relevance of older, well-
established conceptual frameworks and explanations.

Other political scientists have challenged Putnam's methods and
findings in seeking micro-institutional explanations for phenomena
that are apparently better explained at larger scales. Historical insti-
tutionalists such as Theda Skocpol and others disagree with his
stress on generalized social trust as the essence of democracy, arguing that liberal parliamentary regimes and democracies grew out of
centuries-long struggles among social groups that were rooted in
organised conflict and *distrust* (Skocpol and Fiorina 1999). More
recently, Skocpol has shown from historical evidence that civic interaction within American voluntary associations has not been exclusively
or specifically at small scales, but instead has nested across local,
state and national scales in a way that mirrors the structure of government (Skocpol, Ganz and Munson 2000). She has also suggested that
large-scale economic and political changes have affected civic engagement in America in a way that Putnam's analysis does not capture.

Some commentators have criticised Putnam for ignoring politics
and political structure (Tarrow 1996; Foley and Edwards 1999; Edwards
and Foley 2001), while yet others contend that the broad relationships between economic development and 'good' governance that
are among Putnam's main concerns are better approached through
macro-institutional analysis (Arrow 2000; Hall and Jones 1997). Ben
Fine's is perhaps the severest of these criticisms on the use of micro-
level data to arrive at macro-level conclusions:

> The crudity of such studies cannot be over-emphasised: they speculate
> about a few causal relations and then seek to demonstrate their validity
> through a statistical exercise ... Such studies have the explicit aim of
> leaping from the individual to the social by the use of macro-structural
> indicators and statistics to avoid both conceptual issues and the causal
> mechanisms and processes by which the social is reproduced (Fine
> 1999: 6).

The contributors to this volume take less sceptical views of social
capital than this, concentrating on civic communities, voluntary
organizations and governance, and particularly on certain aspects
of local government. These include the universal delivery of essential services (Stolle); or partnerships between local government and
voluntary associations in developing projects with local communities

(Caulkins); or the impartiality of agencies responsible for maintaining justice and order (Rothstein); or the presence of 'agency' to provide pathways for channelling existing stocks of social capital into institutionalized collective action (Krishna).[18] While conventionally understood factors such as group fragmentation, conflict, leadership, and the need for benefits from collective action are certainly important, the successful deployment of social capital often depends on a reciprocal relationship between such factors and institutional processes at intermediate or meso-levels (Krishna, Stolle). A constant feature running through most of these studies is that local government is the aspect of government citizens most often come into contact with, and its reliability, predictability, trustworthiness, and ability to give balanced attention to the equal claims of all citizens is a key to the creation of bridging or linking forms of social capital as well as broader forms of trust and trustworthiness.

Peter Evans, in a multi-country analysis of the role of state-society 'synergy' in economic development, suggests that even where local supplies of social capital are plentiful the achievement of positive development outcomes requires the presence of institutional resources at larger scales (Evans 1996). Foremost among these Evans identifies as robust, coherent bureaucratic structures with sufficient connectedness to local organizational society to provide responsive support and the possibility of larger arenas for collective action. Evans associates the success of East Asian economies such as Taiwan and South Korea with these broad factors, contrasting them with the functions of regulation and bureaucratic insulation that characterize South Asia's bureaucracies.

The other major factor that Evans identifies for effective 'synergy' between state and society is political competition, though he points out that this must be constrained by commonly accepted ground rules that channel political energies into building broad-based mobilisation and trust in government structures. Evans suggests that incentives arising from political competition are hard to actualise in the absence of adequate administrative structures (Evans 1996: 1,127). Evans' conclusions are broadly supported by several contributors to this volume, including some who dwell on the positive effects of the strong, socially embedded bureaucracies of Scandinavia, as well as others who stress the effects of political competition and alliance across groups and castes in India.

Our contributors approach the role of local government in fostering civic or crosscutting forms of social capital in three broad ways: (*a*) through effects on the institutional environment, (*b*) in building a context for the development of linkages across groups in civil society, and (*c*) by facilitating networks that activate existing stocks of social capital in the community. The first aspect is explicitly discussed in the chapters by Rothstein, Stolle and Diani, and by Hadenius in his discussion of institutional preconditions. Many aspects of the institutional environment these authors discuss, such as the enforcement of rules and reliable, impartial policing, are relevant at the scale of local government. Caulkins, Stolle, Wollebæk and Selle, as well as Hadenius in his discussion of social preconditions, treat the second aspect, building a context for linkages between groups and associations in civil society, though in somewhat different ways. The third aspect, including connectedness and access to local politicians (which Krishna refers to as an aspect of what he terms 'capable agency'), is also referred to by several other authors including Rudolph, Wollebæk and Selle, and Diani.

While social capital is often understood in terms of social structures and norms that are relatively independent of government, most contributors to this book believe there is a critical relationship between bridging or civic forms of social capital and aspects of governance, particularly local governance. This does not necessarily mean that these 'public' forms of social capital arise directly from the action of states, but rather that there is interdependence between such bridging forms of social capital and the performance of government. Readers familiar with the literature on common property resource (CPR) management will note that this argument resonates with some discussions that have recently taken place in that field. For instance, Oran Young has argued that most contemporary CPR institutions are not entirely traditional and self-contained, but instead comprise of complex mixes of local arrangements and various interventions stemming from the policy initiatives of modern states. For Young, this makes the formulation of any 'universal' principles for CPR institutions a problematic prospect (Young 1995). Rather than merely the direct action of government, it is the complex interstices of state and society that we need to investigate for the basis of the synergistic or adversarial relations that influence state-society interactions at larger scales.

Such conclusions about the strong role of government might seem particularly Scandinavian, especially given the mix of studies in this volume. We would argue, however, that this avenue of social capital studies is relevant for countries in processes of economic transition or development, particularly in rural areas where institutional density is usually thin and where local government often constitutes the single potentially impartial institution that can act as the focus and guarantor of trustworthiness and institutional interaction. Clearly, given the diverse and burgeoning interest in social capital at present, these issues require broader and more sustained investigation and research. What our studies also suggest, in general, is that more plausible arenas for analysing the processes that give rise to social capital and the associated socialization of norms of trust and fairness lie at an intermediate level, in meso-level dynamics and processes that are rooted in specific institutional histories.

Organization of the Volume

Axel Hadenius sets the stage for the volume with an analysis of the general relationship between social capital and democracy. Hadenius asks broad questions. Are there certain kinds of organizational structures and social practices that help or hinder democracy? How are citizens schooled and socialised in democratic participation and practice? What roles do popular organizations, parliaments, NGOs, trade unions, social movements and other forms for organized interaction play in democratic functioning, and how are those roles changing, evolving and being transformed in modern democracies?

Susanne Rudolph challenges standard Western notions of associations and civil society. From long-term observation of associations in the world's largest democracy, she argues that we require a comprehensive taxonomy of associational forms as well as a more refined understanding of the relationship between associations and normative ideas of civil society in order to make sense of how social capital works across cultures and polities. Rudolph suggests that we should dispense with the simple dichotomies of early modernization theorists in order to appreciate the role of new organizational forms, such as intentional associations and 'paracommunities', in relation to social capital in India or other developing countries.

Paul Dekker investigates the degree of correspondence between two empirical approaches to social capital: one based on social structural variables as developed mainly by sociologists, the other based on personal norms and values as developed mainly by political scientists. Drawing on data from a recent survey of volunteering and civil society in the Netherlands, he finds that results from the two approaches show little or no correlation. Dekker concludes that the 'trust, norms and networks' approach used by some political scientists not only contradicts Coleman's original conception of social capital, but also appears to have weak empirical foundations. While extensive studies are needed before we can arrive at robust conclusions, Dekker's study raises interesting questions about the conceptual foundations of a frequently-used empirical method for assessing social capital.

Bo Rothstein discusses the problem of social trust in relation to the overall institutional environment. Rothstein argues that it makes little sense to trust 'most other people' in civic domains if they are engaged in bribing and threatening government institutions in order to extract personal favours. While cross-country data do not show any reliable correlation between general social trust and trust in institutions, Rothstein suggests those categories are too broadly constructed to capture specific relationships. Using data from Swedish national surveys, he shows that despite declining levels of trust in politicians and political parties there is a robust correlation between trust in other people and trust in certain institutions, most notably the courts, police and parliament. According to Rothstein, the most viable causal link runs from the trustworthiness of institutions responsible for ensuring justice, order and fairness to the trust individuals invest in each other.

Mario Diani uses a network sociology approach to examine a central issue in theoretical and empirical research on social capital: the transferability or 'fungibility' of social capital. Whether social capital and trust accumulated in one associational domain can be transferred to other contexts is a critical issue for confirming the neo-Tocquevillean thesis that overlapping membership and cross-cutting ties produce 'generalized' social trust. If correct, it would also go some way in justifying the analogy with economic capital. Diani draws on primary data from an earlier study of associational membership in Lombardy (one of the 'high social capital' regions of Italy in Putnam's 1993 study) to show that social capital and trust accumulated in one associational context cannot necessarily be transferred to other contexts. How trust changes over time and across associational contexts is a complex, 'context-dependent' issue. Diani discovers little evidence for generalized trust or bridging social capital from his analysis. Significantly though, he finds that the Lombards have the highest trust in virtually the same institutions as the Swedes studied by Rothstein: the police, the courts and parliament (Lombards also display a high regard for the Catholic Church, but this is a sentiment that the protestant Swedes understandably do not share).

Doug Caulkins applies a different approach to explore a related issue. Drawing on his long-term research of voluntary organizations in Volda, a West Norwegian coastal community, he examines how overlapping memberships are structured into organizational clusters reflecting ideological and political affiliations. He finds little evidence in Volda of true crosscutting ties that span network cleavages and value-homogenous groups. His main point is that dense overlapping memberships can exist without creating bridging social capital. Caulkins offers an alternate explanation for the sources of civic trust, suggesting that the threads of trust that link Volda's civic community are reinforced and sustained by agencies of the local government which involve all groups in discussions about local affairs, and which are relatively impartial in providing the funding, trust and legitimacy necessary for local groups to pursue their projects.

Dietlind Stolle explores regional differences in social and institutional trust using an approach that differs from both that of Diani and Caulkins. Using sample surveys from two regions of Sweden, one in the north and the other in the south, she finds substantial variations in levels of social trust and trust in institutions. She suggests that the main explanation for this variation is the performance of local governments, particularly in the delivery of basic services and the universality of treatment of all citizens. In marked contrast to the southern region of Gnösjo, the remoter parts of the northern region of Kiruna not only suffered from the ineffective delivery of basic services, but its citizens also reported widespread problems in gaining access to local politicians as well as problems of low civic connectedness. Stolle shows that these problems are correlated with a low level of general social trust in Kiruna. She argues that the most credible causal link runs from trust in institutions, particularly everyday aspects of local governance, to trust in other people. Like Caulkins and Rothstein, she considers the role of local government to be critical for the growth of social trust and civic forms of social capital.

While Stolle studies variations in social trust in relation to local government performance, Anirudh Krishna attempts to hold the quality of governance constant in order to explore another key aspect of social capital. Krishna studies 60 villages in Rajasthan, India, to discover how social capital affects development performance. All 60 villages were covered by the same government programme for watershed development with comparable levels of provision and efficiency. However, the villages performed very differently in achieving development goals. Krishna finds that, apart from the grassroots associations and local networks that constitute resources for local collective action, another set of factors, which he terms 'capable agency', explain this divergence. Krishna includes in the idea of 'agency' various aspects of social and political connectedness, such as the presence of effective local councils, active politicians, and caste associations that reach outside the village to influence decision-making at higher levels. While government may provide similar development programmes and opportunities to different communities, the availability of wider networks substantially affects the quantum of access and benefits that will actually be experienced by communities. Krishna's thesis about the effects of agency (which can be compared to linking or bridging forms of social capital at meso-level scales) affirms a reciprocal relationship between local governance and the broader, more civic forms of social capital.

Dag Wollebæk and Per Selle investigate a relatively new development in organizational participation, the rapid growth and implications of 'passive' membership. Do members who take little active part in their associations, often doing nothing more than signing a cheque once a year, play any part in developing social capital, civic ties or the activities of their associations? Drawing on a comprehensive survey of organizational participation in Norway, they find that passive members have an important role to play in modern societies. They also find that the social and political connectedness, as well as the multiple organizational memberships made through passive membership, are valuable for both members and organisations, and that the boundaries between 'active' and 'passive' membership are not as clear and straightforward as is often assumed. These results make Wollebæk and Selle question Putnam's thesis that face-to-face interaction within voluntary organisations is a sufficient or a necessary mechanism for building social capital and civic trust.

Gaute Torsvik brings an economist's perspective to bear on the claim that social capital is an explanandum for regional differences in economic success. He contends that definitions of social capital and their relationship to different types of trust are not clear enough to be testable in terms of this claim. While accepting that trust is important for economic production, he argues that policy makers need to be sensitive to the specific mechanisms and institutional contexts that link trust and production. As an example he takes institutional contexts based on two different types of trust, arising from repeated play and pro-social motivation, to demonstrate how optimal policies will differ in each case. Torsvik suggests that understanding the causal relationships between trust, social capital and economic development is necessary not only for theoretical purposes, but also for making sound policy decisions.

Finally, Tommy Tranvik explores new information and communication technologies (ICTs) such as the Internet as sources and sites for social capital. Do the dense communication networks made possible by the Internet have a positive impact on social and political connectedness, or are they (as television supposedly is) a retreat from social engagement? Certainly, many voluntary organizations have begun to make extensive use of such technologies for communication, advocacy and recruitment purposes. Tranvik suggests that as communication technologies change, so will forms of civic engagement and social capital. Because social and technological change go hand in hand, we need to understand better both the potential and the pitfalls of emerging ICTs for social and organizational change.

In closing, let us note that there are many ways in which we could have organized such a volume. If we have chosen to interweave strands representing the experience of different societies, and to combine conceptual and empirical material instead of arranging our chapters in more conventional fashion, this is because we want our readers to appreciate something of the diversity and complexity that characterize the debate on social capital and civil society today. No simple answers exist for the complex questions and manifold uncertainties that are involved in this debate. However, we hope that the present volume will succeed in stimulating our readers with a new and refreshing set of perspectives on a critical and unfinished discussion.

Notes

1.   Senior Researcher at the Centre for Development Studies and Professor in the Department of Comparative Politics, respectively, University of Bergen, Bergen, Norway.

2. *World Values Survey 1991* reported that the percentage of adult popu-
    lation with membership in at least one association was: Iceland 90 per
    cent, Sweden 85 per cent, Netherlands 84 per cent, Norway 82 per cent,
    Denmark 81 per cent, Finland 77 per cent, United States 71 per cent,
    Italy 43 per cent (for selected countries; cited in Blomkvist 2001). Recent
    research on India suggests that only 13 per cent of the population
    participated in one or more formal associations over a similar period
    (Chhibber 1999). It should be noted that roughly 25 per cent of India's
    population was urban in 1991, and that there are few associations in
    most rural areas (but see Rudolph, this volume, for a discussion on
    why membership in formal associations may not be a suitable basis for
    cross-country comparisons).

3. Coleman's definition has the virtue of being less limited than those
    proposed by many others: 'Social capital is defined by its function. It is
    not a single entity but a variety of different entities, with two elements
    in common: they all consist of some aspect of social structures, and
    they facilitate certain actions of actors—whether persons or corporate
    actors—within the structure ... Like physical and human capital, social
    capital is not completely fungible but may be specific to certain activi-
    ties. A given form of social capital that is valuable in facilitating certain
    actions may be useless or even harmful in others ... Unlike other forms
    of capital, social capital inheres in the structure of relations between
    actors and among actors. It is not lodged either in the actors themselves
    or in physical implements of production' (Coleman 1988: 98). For a
    comparison of different definitions of social capital, see Adler and Kwon
    1999. While it differs in significant ways from the present use of the
    term in the English language literature, it is not out of place here to
    acknowledge Pierre's Bourdieu's earlier (1986) efforts within French soci-
    ology to develop an original interpretation of 'social capital' (within a
    taxonomy of forms of 'symbolic capital'). In Bourdieu's conception,
    social capital provides individuals and groups unequal access to re-
    sources through asymmetric networks of relationships. For further dis-
    cussion of Bourdieu's conceptualisation and some of its implications,
    see the section below on scale, embeddedness and exclusion as well as
    the chapter by Diani (this volume).

4. At least half of Coleman's analysis in the earlier paper as well as most
    of the data he presents there deals with the correlation between paren-
    tal expectations and involvement in children's education on the one
    hand, and the educational achievement of children on the other. One
    could argue that this is an area where intentional explanation seems to
    fit better than the explicitly functional one that he applies. We will
    reflect further on these aspects of explanation later in this introduction.
    To be fair to him, Coleman did state in the same paper: 'Although ... social

capital constitutes an unanalyzed concept, it signals to the analyst and to the reader that something of value has been produced for those actors who have this resource available and that the value depends on social organization. It then becomes a second stage in the analysis to unpack the concept, to discover what components of social organization contribute to the value produced' (Coleman 1988: 101). We believe it is this second stage of the analysis, more specific and contextual as well as relating specific causes to consequences, that scholars of social capital need to engage in now.

5. By 'overlapping membership' Putnam refers to a situation where a given set of individuals are able to interact over multiple associations of which they are members.

6. Diani (this volume) describes how levels of pre-existing trust *as well as distrust* in other people's abilities or motivation to contribute to the creation of collective goods influence individuals' decisions to participate in social groups and networks. See also Oliver 1984, and Stolle and Rochon 1998.

7. Though the examples Coleman discusses explicitly in that paper (family and local community) do not go beyond the small-scale (see note 4 above).

8. The World Values Survey in the 1980s and 1990s was based on the responses of randomly selected samples of people in 40 countries. It included the following question: 'Generally speaking, would you say that most people can be trusted or that you can't be too careful in dealing with people?' (Moore 1999: 80). Similar questions have been used in most survey-based assessments of generalized trust.

9. At least in a network sociology sense of trust and norms being endogenous to social structure, and even—to many observers—in Coleman's articulation of social capital as part of a 'rational choice sociology' where norms and related sanctions become part of the individual's matrix of opportunity costs.

10. The use of functional explanations in the social sciences is the subject of a broad, continuing debate that has involved some major figures of 20th century social science. While we cannot enter into that debate here, the reason we consider the basic explanation of social capital to involve a functional element should be clear from this section. Readers interested in functional explanation are referred to the writings of (especially) Robert Merton 1957; Arthur Stinchcombe 1968; Jon Elster 1979 and 1989; Russel Hardin 1980; and many others, as also the able summary in the discussion on Elster in Thompson, Ellis and Wildavsky 1990.

11. Coleman (1990) includes 'intentional organization'—implying direct investment of social capital—in his later description of forms of social capital (though he does not develop any associated implications). Does intentionality to associate, say, for purposes of asserting a common

identity, mean the same thing as deliberate 'investment' of trust or other relational assets? See Rudolph's (this volume) argument for the inclusion of intentional organizations in any classification of associational forms. For a more detailed comparison of social capital with financial, physical and human capital, see Adler and Kwon 1999.

12. It may be useful to reflect on the distinction between resources, assets and capital in this context.

13. Other aspects and forms of social capital have been traced back much further, to Marx, Weber and Durkheim; see Swedberg 1987; Portes and Sensenbrenner 1993; Woolcock 1998.

14. Though Caulkins (this volume) suggests that crosscutting ties can exist without producing bridging social capital. Using an organizational cluster analysis approach, he examines a case where dense overlapping ties between members of voluntary organizations have the effect of producing larger but bounded value-homogenous groups, clustered spatially and along political party formations, but with little overlap across these formations. Based on this analysis, Caulkins disputes Putnam's claims about overlapping memberships being the basic source of bridging social capital with its beneficial consequences for civil society as a whole. Dekker (this volume) takes up some related issues.

15. This kind of feedback is suggested by James Coleman's (1986) own 'macro-micro-macro' model for conceptualisations of collective action. The model involves situating micro-level phenomena in their context because, as Peter Hedström and Richard Swedberg explain it, 'proper explanations of change and variation at the macro-level entails showing how macro states at one point of time influence the behaviour of individual actors, and how these actions generate new macro states at a later time. That is, instead of analyzing relationships between phenomena exclusively at the macro-level, one should always try to establish how macro-level events or conditions affect the individual (Step 1), how the individual assimilates the impact of these macro-level events (Step 2), and how a number of individuals, through their actions and interactions, generate macro-level outcomes (Step 3), (Hedström and Swedberg 1998: 21–22).

16. Bourdieu's understanding of social capital 'mainly as a powerful mechanism of social closure' (see Diani, this volume, note 3) adequately captures this aspect, though it may risk overstating the case.

17. Political sociologists of the 1950s and 1960s such as the Norwegian Stein Rokkan (1970) have said much the same thing.

18. Krishna's notion of capable agency might fall within Bourdieu's understanding and definition of social capital, though it appears to be outside Putnam's conception of it as 'trust, norms and networks of civic engagement' (see Bourdieu's definition from Bourdieu and Wacquant 1992, cited in the section on scale, embeddedness and exclusion, above).

References

Adler, P., and Kwon, S. 1999. 'Social Capital: The good, the bad, and the ugly'. Unpublished web manuscript *(http://www.worldbank.org/poverty/scapital/library/adler.htm)*.

Almond, G.A., and Verba, S. 1963. *The Civic Culture: Political Attitudes and Democracy in Five Nations*. Princeton: Princeton University Press.

Arrow, K. 2000. 'Observations on Social Capital', in P. Dasgupta and I. Serageldin (eds.), *Social Capital: A Multifaceted Perspective*. Washington, D.C.: The World Bank, pp. 3–5.

Blomkvist, H. 2001. 'Traditional Communities, Caste and Democracy: The Indian Mystery' in P. Dekker and E. Uslaner (eds.), *Social Capital and Participation in Everyday Life*. London: Routledge.

Bourdieu, P. 1986. 'The Forms of Capital' in J. Richardson (ed.), *Handbook of Theory and Research for the Sociology of Education*. New York: Greenwood Press, pp. 241–58.

Bourdieu, P., and Wacquant, L. 1992. *An Invitation to Reflexive Sociology*. Chicago: University of Chicago Press.

Burt, R. 1992. *Structural Holes: The Social Structure of Competition*. Cambridge, Massachusetts: Harvard University Press.

Chhibber, P. 1999. *Democracy Without Associations*. Ann Arbor, Michigan: University of Michigan Press.

Coleman, J. 1986. 'Social Theory, Social Research, and a Theory of Action'. *American Journal of Sociology* 91: pp. 1,309–35.

Coleman, J. 1988. 'Social Capital in the Creation of Human Capital'. American Journal of Sociology 94 (supplement): S95–S120.

Coleman, J. 1990. *Foundations of Social Theory*. Cambridge, Massachusetts: Harvard University Press.

Edwards, B., and Foley, M. 2001. 'Civil Society and Social Capital: A Primer', in B. Edwards, M. Foley and M. Diani (eds.), *Beyond Tocqueville: Civil Society and the Social Capital Debate in Comparative Perspective*. Hanover, New Hampshire: University Press of New England.

Elster, J. 1979. *Ulysses and the Sirens: Studies in Rationality and Irrationality*. Cambridge: Cambridge University Press.

Elster, J. 1989. *Nuts and Bolts for the Social Sciences*. Cambridge: Cambridge University Press.

Evans, P. 1996. 'Government Action, Social Capital and Development: Reviewing the Evidence on Synergy'. *World Development* 24(6): pp. 1,119–32.

Fine, B. 1999. 'The Developmental State is Dead: Long Live Social Capital?'. *Development and Change* 30(1): pp. 1–19.

Foley, M., and Edwards, B. 1999. 'Is it Time to Disinvest in Social Capital?'. *Journal of Public Policy* 19: pp. 669–78.

Fukuyama, F. 1995. *Trust: The Social Virtues and the Creation of Prosperity.* London: Penguin.

Gambetta, D. 1988. *Trust: The Making and Breaking of Cooperative Relations.* Oxford: Basil Blackwell.

Geertz, C. 1992. 'The Bazaar Economy: Information and Search in Peasant Marketing', in M. Granovetter and R. Swedberg (eds.), *The Sociology of Economic Life.* Boulder, Colorado: Westview Press.

Granovetter, M.S. 1973. 'The Strength of Weak Ties'. American Journal of Sociology 78: pp. 1,360–80.

Granovetter, M.S. 1992. 'Economic Action and Social Structure: The Problem of Embeddedness', in M. Granovetter and R. Swedberg (eds.), *The Sociology of Economic Life.* Boulder, Colorado: Westview Press.

Hall, R.E., and Jones, C.I. 1997. 'Levels of Economic Activity across Countries'. *American Economic Review (Papers and Proceedings)* 87(2): pp. 173–77.

Hardin, R. 1980. 'Rationality, Irrationality and Functionalist Explanation'. *Social Science Information:* pp. 755–72.

Hardin, R. 1993. 'The Street-Level Epistemology of Trust'. *Politics and Society* 21(4): pp. 505–30.

Hedström, P., and Swedberg, R. 1998. 'Social Mechanisms: An Introductory Essay', in P. Hedström and R. Swedberg (eds.), *Social Mechanisms: An Analytical Approach to Social Theory,* Cambridge: Cambridge University Press, pp. 1–31.

Humphrey, J., and Schmitz, H. 1998. 'Trust and Inter–Firm Relations in Developing and Transition Economies'. *Journal of Development Studies* 34(4): pp. 32–61.

Merton, R. 1957. *Social Theory and Social Structure.* Glencoe, Illinois.: Free Press.

Moore, M. 1999. 'Truth, Trust and Market Transactions: What Do We Know?' *Journal of Development Studies* 36(1): pp. 74–88.

Narayan, D., and Pritchett, L. 1997. 'Cents and Sociability: Household Income and Social Capital in Rural Tanzania'. Washington, D.C.: The World Bank.

Newton, K. 1999. 'Social and Political Trust in Established Democracies', in Pippa Norris (ed.), *Critical Citizens: Global Support for Democratic Governance.* Oxford: Oxford University Press.

Oliver, P. 1984. '"If You Don't Do It, Nobody Else Will": Active and Token Contributors to Local Collective Action'. *American Sociological Review* 49: pp. 601–10.

Ostrom, E. 1998. 'A Behavioural Approach to the Rational Choice Theory of Collective Action'. *American Political Science Review* 92(1): pp. 1–22.

Polanyi, K. 1992. 'The Economy as Instituted Process', in M. Granovetter and R. Swedberg (eds.), *The Sociology of Economic Life.* Boulder, Colorado: Westview Press.

Portes, A., and Sensenbrenner, J. 1993. 'Embeddedness and Immigration: Notes on the Social Determinants of Economic Action'. *American Journal of Sociology* 98(6): pp. 1,320–50.

Putnam, R.D. 1993. *Making Democracy Work: Civic Traditions in Modern Italy*. Princeton: Princeton University Press.

——. 1995. 'Bowling Alone: America's Declining Social Capital'. *Journal of Democracy* 6(1): pp. 65–78.

——. 2000. *Bowling Alone: The Collapse and Revival of American Community*. New York: Simon & Schuster.

Rokkan, S. 1970. *Citizens, Elections, Parties*. Oslo: Universitetsforlaget.

Seligman, A. 1997. *The Problem of Trust*. Princeton: Princeton University Press.

Skocpol, T., and Fiorina, M. 1999. 'Making Sense of the Civic Engagement Debate', in T. Skocpol and M. Fiorina (eds.), *Civic Engagement in American Democracy*. Washington, D.C.: Brookings Institution Press.

Skocpol,T., Ganz, M. and Munson, Z. 2000. 'A Nation of Organizers: The Institutional Origins of Civic Voluntarism in the United States'. *American Political Science Review* 94(3): pp. 527–46.

Solow, R. 1997. 'Tell me again what we are talking about'. *Stern Business Magazine* 4(1).

Solow, R. 2000. 'Notes on Social Capital and Economic Performance', in P. Dasgupta and I. Serageldin (eds.), *Social Capital: A Multifaceted Perspective*. Washington, D.C.: The World Bank, pp. 6–10.

Stinchcombe, A. 1968. *Constructing Social Theories*. New York: Harcourt, Brace and World.

Stolle, D. 2001. 'Getting to Trust: An Analysis of the Importance of Institutions, Families, Personal Experiences and Group Membership', in P. Dekker and E.M. Uslaner (eds.), *Social Capital and Participation in Everyday Life*. London: Routledge.

Stolle, D., and Rochon, T.R. 1998. 'Are All Associations Alike? Member Diversity, Associational Type, and the Creation of Social Capital'. *American Behavioural Scientist* 42: pp. 47–65.

Swedberg, R. 1987. 'Economic Sociology: Past and Present'. *Current Sociology* 35(1): pp. 1–215.

Tarrow, S. 1996: 'Making Social Science Work Across Space and Time: A Critical Reflection on Robert Putnam's *Making Democracy Work*'. *American Political Science Review* 90: pp. 389–97.

Thompson, M., Ellis, R., and Wildavsky, A. 1990. *Cultural Theory*. Boulder, Colorado: Westview Press.

Van Deth, J., Maraffi, M., Newton, K. and Whitely, P. 1999. *Social Capital and European Democracy*. London: Routledge.

Varshney, A. 2001. 'Ethnic Conflict and Civil Society: India and Beyond'. *World Politics* 53(3): pp. 362–98.

Varshney, A. 2002. *Ethnic Conflict and Civic Life: Hindus and Muslims in India*. New Haven, Connecticut: Yale University Press.

Wall, E., Ferrazzi G., and Schryer, F.: 'Getting the Goods on Social Capital'. *Rural Sociology* 63(2): pp. 300–322.

Woolcock, M. 1998. 'Social Capital and Economic Development: Towards a theoretical synthesis and policy framework'. *Theory and Society* 27(2): pp. 151–208.

Young, O. 1995. 'The Problem of Scale in Human/Environment Relationships', in R. Keohane and E. Ostrom (eds.) *Local Commons and Global Interdependence: Heterogeneity and Cooperation in Two Domains*. London: Sage.

2

Social Capital and Democracy:
Institutional and Social Preconditions

Axel Hadenius

Points of Departure

Democracy presupposes the existence of democrats, of persons both
willing and able to shoulder the responsibilities entailed by popular
government. It requires citizens with an interest in the political process, and a preparedness to take part in it. It presumes a will—and
a real capacity—to formulate one's demands and to make one's
voice heard. Such participation must take place, of course, in accordance with the rules of the democratic game. Democracy involves
competition and the dissemination of opinions. At the same time,
however, it presumes the peaceful and ordered resolution of political disputes. Even as we express our opinions and pursue our interests, we must show respect for the ideas and demands of others.

When we seek more precisely to delineate the characteristics
which democratic citizens ought to exhibit, we find that two dimensions bear distinguishing from each other: the one bears on traits
possessed by each one of us as individuals, the other on such qualities as we share with other members of the various collectives of
which we are a part. We may thus distinguish between individual-
related and group-related characteristics. In modern research on
political attitudes and resources, 'human capital' is the term used in

reference to the individual level, and 'social capital' pertains to the collective level.

Where human capital (i.e., the individual dimension of citizenship) is concerned, we find, first of all, certain attitudes associated with democratic citizenship. These include a substantial interest in political matters, and a desire to participate and to exert influence. Citizens should therefore feel a closeness to, and a trust and confidence in, the political institutions that represent them. People should furthermore feel confident in their own capacity to make their voice heard in the political process. They should be open and tolerant in their basic political attitudes, and rational and deliberate in their approach to issues. But attitudes are not everything. There must also be opportunities—real resources. On the individual level, it is a question of political competence (in a broad sense); of being well-informed, able to take initiative and capable of establishing the contacts requisite to the exercise of influence. Sufficient time is necessary as well. Economic resources can be important too.

Where social capital (i.e., the collective dimension of citizenship) is concerned, it is not individuals who are of interest, but rather the relations *between* them. Here too we must distinguish between attitudes and real resources. The former have to do with our feelings of trust in, and affinity for, a certain circle of people. They involve identifying with a larger unit, and feeling solidarity and responsibility towards it. Real resources, by contrast, are a question of the instruments which have been devised in order to achieve coordinated collective action. They relate to the patterns of collaboration that have been established between people. These can be of various sorts. They may be loose and informal networks, or fixed and solid organizations.

Organization and cooperation are of importance in several ways. The first is the most obvious. Collective action makes for a strength *vis-à-vis* other actors in society that private individuals find hard to achieve on their own. Organizing is therefore an effective way to exert influence. This is an external consequence. But there are internal consequences as well. People are affected by the experience of working together with others on an orderly basis. We may call this the socializing effect: we are influenced in various ways by the environment—in this case the organizational environment—of which we are a part. Regular interaction between people reinforces identity and promotes mutual affinity. Emotional bonds become stronger.

This we can call the identity—creating effect. The forms under which cooperation takes place are also important. The working procedures used within an organisation affect people's attitudes and behaviour. If the internal life of the organisation is democratic and energizing, this affects those taking part: they are schooled in democracy. They acquire skills and values which are beneficial in the political sphere too. We may call this the educational effect.

Where democracy is concerned, two of the three aspects mentioned above are crucial: the external aspect (that bearing on the exertion of influence), and the internal educational aspect. The effect of the other internal aspect—the identity-creating element—is more indirect. We shall furthermore see that its effect differs in relation to each of the two primary aspects. Indeed, the type of identity-formation which is advantageous in the one case can be a drawback in the other. A latent contradiction is illustrated thereby. The very conditions which enhance a group's external capacity can also hinder the development of an internal educational effect.

The External Effect: Exerting Influence

Participating in an organized collective makes it easier to exert influence. In his famous study of democracy in the young United States, Alexis de Tocqueville attached great importance to the rich and varied organizational life found in the new republic. These abundant organizational networks facilitated collective action and served as forceful agents of popular power. 'An association,' he wrote, 'unites the energies of divergent minds and vigorously directs them toward a clearly indicated goal' (1969: 190). A modern researcher in this area, Michael Bratton, puts the point in the following way: 'Power—the ability to secure compliance to one's will—is difficult for individuals to obtain when acting alone. To mount a credible bid to exercise power, individuals must combine with others; thus power is accumulated and exercised in the context of political organization' (1994: 233).

Taking part in an organized network reduces our uncertainty about how others will behave—an uncertainty that would otherwise reduce our propensity to act. This applies particularly when the action in question is associated with risk. 'When protesting politically,' Robert Bates points out (1994: 23), 'it is safer to be a member of a crowd. The implication is that coordination is essential to the politics of reform. Knowing that others have acted or will act decreases the perceived risks of acting.'

Joining an organization can be seen, then, as tantamount to entering into a compact which guarantees a certain commonality of preferences, as well as a shared preparedness to act. We know there are people around us who share our interests and values, and upon whom we can rely to act in our support, if such be needed. This increases our disposition to step forward and express our opinions and demands. The larger the network in which we participate, the stronger the 'social support' available to us. This is a question partly of the number of people involved, and partly of organizational upscaling. Organizational upscaling involves the extension of linkages upward and outward, so that local associations are connected to each other regionally and nationally; international connections can be, important too. The wider the geographical reach of the networks, the better the support they can offer (other things being equal).

Organizations can also provide access to a range of resources—of an economic and professional nature—which individuals would find difficult to acquire on their own. The strike funds administered by trade unions are a classic example; these exist in order to provide economic protection in the event of industrial conflict. Organizations may also offer legal support to their members, as well as various kinds of training. They may furthermore have leaders and functionaries charged with defending the interests of members on a regular basis. In a large part this reflects economies of scale. Services of this kind are easier to provide the larger the organization is. Quantity matters, in other words.

But there is also a qualitative aspect to this. Through activities of an extended duration, a fund of experience—an organizational memory—is created, which makes it easier for the organization to interact with its surroundings. This memory enables the organization to defend the interests of its members more effectively. As mentioned earlier, the time factor is an important component here. It plays in two ways. Organizational memory is a function of repeated interaction with other actors in the environment; such repeated interaction, of course, takes time. But the ability to act effectively *vis-à-vis* other actors depends on internal coordination as well: the ability to make the different units of the organization act in unison. An organization which is divided internally finds it hard to act forcefully *vis-à-vis* other actors. This capacity for internal coordination is a function of the degree of cohesion and confidence prevailing within the organization. This too is something that normally takes time to build up.

This leads us to another interesting parameter: the identity-creating function. Organizations are not just aggregates of individual preferences; they do not simply mirror the private wishes of their members. They play an active role, rather, in constructing the identities held by their members. Persons who form part of a fixed collective—and thus interact regularly with a group—find their preferences affected in a certain way. They develop joint interests and a sense of community (March and Olsen 1989). A strong normative identity strengthens the affinity which members feel with their organization. It increases their motivation to participate and to work for the common interest (Tarrow 1994: 22f.).

The duration of enrollment plays a role here too. Long-term membership in an organization reinforces the process of socialization into the culture and norms of the unit. Interaction over a long period strengthens group identity. It also increases the capacity of members to 'screen' their leaders and to hold them accountable. Viewing this interaction as a principal/agent relationship, we could say that, with the passage of time, the principals stand a progressively better chance of selecting agents that share their goals and are competent and reliable (Moe 1984). In all, the feeling of collective identity and trust is boosted. This enhances the external capacity of the organization in question.

Faithful and long-term members, in other words, are an asset. They increase cohesion and effectiveness *vis-à-vis* outside actors. Ideally, moreover, the members are associated only with this single organization, to which they belong virtually from the cradle to the grave. This guarantees a strong identity and a solidarity with the collective in question. Organizational encapsulation—whereby members have but minimal ties with other groups—is therefore an advantage. It makes the organization stronger.

The Internal Effect: Democratic Education

When Tocqueville described the democratic vitality of the American republic, he attached great importance to the wealth of organizational networks. These popular associations facilitated collective action, and served as powerful agents of civic influence. This contributed to political pluralism. In addition, however, de Tocqueville stressed something else. The civic spirit and active political culture which he found in such abundance among common people in the young United States was, as he saw it, the result of a process of learning and socialization. Through their participation in self-governing organizations, citizens had been schooled in a democratic process. Through mutual interaction and intercourse, they had acquired an array of political resources—and developed more democratic attitudes as well. In the language of modern institutional theory, the preferences of citizens had been endogenously formed—through the interaction created by the organizational context of which they were a part (March and Olsen 1989). John Stuart Mill considered this dynamic and fostering function to be the strongest justification for democratic decision-making: only through popular responsibility and participation in public affairs, he argued, can a suitable civic spirit grow forth. In addition, democratic practice serves to advance certain skills that can be used politically. Tocqueville and Mill have inspired those modern researchers who stress the democratic merits of popular participation. Carole Pateman (1970) and Benjamin Barber (1984) may be mentioned as influential exponents of this school of thought.

It is an advantage, then, if organizations forming the framework for collective action are themselves democratically structured. It is desirable that they be characterized by pluralism and openness in their internal life, and that they provide developed procedures through which members can hold their leaders accountable and take part in the running of affairs. In this way, associational involvement can have a socializing and fostering import: it can advance the democratic skills, and shape the preferences, of those taking part.

If participation is to have such an educative effect, the internal life of the organizations must be characterized by democratic decision-making, free debate and a diversity of opinions. There must be internal arenas within which groups of members (and mid-level leaders too) can gather independently to discuss matters, to spread information and to act in common. Only in this way can the openness and pluralism needed for a functioning democracy be maintained. The goal of democratic socialization indicates, moreover, what type of identity-formation should take place. If tolerance and understanding in social life are to be furthered, it is desirable that we come into contact with people of a variety of backgrounds and sorts—culturally, religiously and socially speaking.

Our organizational connections should not, therefore, be too exclusive and dense. Our affiliations should be characterized, as Mark Granovetter (1973) puts it, by a multiplicity of weak ties, so that an overlap is created between different segments of society. What Granovetter has in mind is the phenomenon known in group theory as crosscutting membership (or multiple affiliations). This means that, as citizens, we participate in many varied communities, and so associate with persons whose identity partly differs from our own. This requires that organizations apply, in general, a fairly open policy in respect of the admission of new members, and that they refrain from any ambition to enclose their members totally (Lipset 1960; Gellner 1994; Newton 1999).

The desirability of this state of affairs is commonly thought to reside in the fact that social intercourse helps to dampen conflict. When we participate in several different contexts, we are confronted with a broad array of people from backgrounds other than our own. At the same time, we are socialized into a greater number of identities—each of which is therefore weaker. As a result of the cross-influences generated by multiple affiliations, we become more understanding and tolerant of the views and behaviour of others. Thus we learn how to handle and to cope with the divergent preferences arising from pluralist processes. What is more, with a broadened sphere of interaction a gradual harmonization of preferences can come about. Through social intercourse we become more integrated; we widen our public sphere; we extend our sense of belonging, responsibility and trust. This makes it easier to apply democratic procedures for decision-making on an overarching societal level (Lipset 1960; Offe 1997; see also Hadenius and Karvonen 2001).

The important thing, from this perspective, is to counteract organizational encapsulation: the separation of people into closed circles of interaction. Where strong patterns of encapsulation prevail, people are constrained from making contacts outside of their own group. They socialize with the same kind of people in all the different areas of their life. Patterns of this kind may indeed reinforce cohesion within the group, and strengthen feelings of community and solidarity. Where the external capacity of the group is concerned, such patterns can be seen as an asset. Where the interests of democratic education are concerned, however, they are most definitely a drawback.

In other respects too, these different democratic criteria can come into conflict with each other. Where external capacity is concerned, internal cohesion is an advantage. This speaks for centralization, as well as for limits on internal debate and opinion-formation. United and forceful action *vis-à-vis* outside actors is difficult, namely, if there are several different arenas for decision-making within the organization—arenas which are partly independent of each other, and within which a multiplicity of conflicting wills can come to expression. Centralization can lead to limits on internal democracy in several ways. It was Robert Michels who discovered this tendency. Thus his famous dictum: who says organization says oligarchy.

Where external capacity is concerned, furthermore, large, formally structured units constitute a strength. They make possible an accumulation of economic and professional resources, together with an extension of organizational contacts (both nationally and internationally), thus making for greater effectiveness. Internal democracy, on the other hand, usually develops better within units that are smaller and more informal. Organizations of this kind tend to exhibit a lesser degree of professionalism and a less pronounced division of functions between the leaders and the followers. They leave more room for—and normally have a greater need of—active participation on the part of their members. Such associations have a more limited repertoire as a rule; at the same time, however, the members of such organizations find it easier to get involved, and to gain insight into organizational operations (Dahl and Tufte 1973; Diamond 1999).

Michel's pessimism regarding the degeneration of organizational life in democratic respects has certainly proved to be exaggerated. There is no 'iron law' (as he put it) that leads infallibly to elite rule. What he points to, one could say, is a possible tendency. There can be a contradiction, undeniably, between different values within associational life; between external influence on the one hand, and internal democratic education on the other. Some sort of balance must be struck.

Institutional Preconditions

Popular organizations develop more easily within a framework of democratic political rights. Building up strong organizations is arduous and protracted work. It is harder still if the process is continually impeded and interrupted. France may serve as an example. Free association was forbidden in that country for a century (up to the early 1900s). This handicap left its mark long thereafter. For a long time, parties and other organizations were unusually weak in France, and indeed they remain so today. A similar pattern can be seen in South America. Incessant military coups—and subsequent periods of dictatorship—have obstructed the development of parties and organizations in that region (Tarrow 1994; Hadenius 2001).

Democracy is more than just freedom of association. It also involves organs of representation like parliaments and similar assemblies. Arenas for contact and interaction between different social groups are thereby created. In all periods the existence of such organs has promoted the formation of group identities which have supplied a basis for political organization. 'The English Parliament aided in the formation of an interlocal *national* bourgeoisie,' Brian Downing remarks (1992: 31). The examples are many in which political organizations have had their roots in parliament. Groups of parliamentarians have formed political clubs, which then built organizations for gaining popular support. Even parties established in the opposite manner—so-called outsider parties, which have come into being through a bottom-up process—have in many instances had an existing parliament as a rationale for organizing. They have been formed, that is, to lend force to the demand for broader parliamentary involvement (Duverger 1954; Shefter 1977; Gallagher, Laver and Mair 2001). Success tends, moreover, to breed success in this field. Organizations with political influence generally find it easier to attract members (Hadenius and Uggla 1996).

Political participation can also have significant spread effects. Tocqueville emphasized the importance of participation as a source of democratic vitality in the young United States. He particularly stressed the stimulating effect of local self-government. By taking part in local government, American citizens learned the practice of democracy. This habituated them to resolving conflicts and to holding leaders accountable, and gave rise to feelings of identification with the public organs. Citizens were included in the political sphere in a natural way. Furthermore, the civic skills acquired through participation in local public affairs could be utilized in other settings also. This yielded resources for the exercise of influence at higher political levels, and gave a strong impetus to civic organizing. The close connection between local government and free associational life was, in de Tocqueville's view, a fundamental feature of American democracy. In Robert D. Putnam's well-known study of Italy (1993), moreover, the socializing impact of decentralized political activity is found to be decisive. The regions faring best, democratically speaking—those marked by high levels of social capital—shared a common history of popular participation in local decision-making. Regions that performed poorly, on the other hand, tended to have a legacy of autocracy and centralization.

The existence of organs for popular influence on the local level makes it easier for ordinary people to become involved. In this way, democratic experiences are generated which can have important effects on the larger environment. Decentralized decision-making stimulates the development of local organizational networks. This contributes to the emergence of political and civic organizations with vital local roots. This in turn strengthens opportunities for the exertion of influence from below with such organizations.

Another important precondition is the existence of a rule-governed state apparatus. This institutional feature sets the stage for the development of trust and reciprocity among political actors. It also affects the formation of popular organizations and the legitimacy of the democratic game.

The existence of a functioning system of rules makes long-term cooperation possible. This has an important implication: when there is little trust between actors, a large increment is needed of the 'external support' which institutions can give.

If you do not trust each other, you must put trust in institutions. Trust in institutions enhances interpersonal trust (Brehm and Rahn 1997; Rothstein 2000). In societies with strong tensions between different segments, it is particularly important that the legal and administrative structure upheld by the state be of a fixed and rule-governed kind. If this is not the case, the risk is great that segmental interaction will intensify old animosities.

Institutions must be built which counteract tendencies towards discrimination and group favouritism. This is a question of how the legal and administrative bodies function, and most fundamentally, of how the law-enforcing units—such as the police and the military—operate (Diamond 1999). When confidence in these institutions is lacking, disastrous spirals of uncertainty and hostility between groups can be set in motion (Hadenius and Karvonen 2001).

What is more, a state characterized by the virtual absence of functioning legal and administrative rules (a so-called 'soft state') affects the character of popular networks in society. When people cannot rely on the existing system of rules, they have to count on personal contacts. This is the logic of clientelism. This form of organization has normally accompanied the 'soft state'. Clientelist arrangements presuppose a state which leaves substantial room for corruption and personal favours. It is the spoils yielded by state position that are the very 'fuel' of clientelism. Such a system is based on particularism: you only enjoy a favour if you have the right contacts. It also presupposes dependence and subordination. Clientelism is a system built on political bossism. It is a strongly hierarchical system affording few opportunities for the exertion of influence from below. It is a form of organization with little democratic content (Hadenius 2001).

Another feature of the soft state is the fact that it contributes, as a rule, to a low level of political legitimacy. Corruption, nepotism and the like are generally regarded by citizens with contempt. On account of both its mode of operation and its inadequate performance, such a state inspires very little popular trust (Della Porta and Vannucci 1997; Diamond 1999). The consequence is that many groups in society—especially those keen on reform—turn their back on established political institutions. Instead of cooperating with the state organs (and thus running the risk of becoming politically captured and dependent), they strive for isolation and autonomy. Many of the new social movements in Latin America and India have such an orientation. Strong local roots, non-hierarchical structures and a preference for popular participation often distinguish such associations. At the same time, these organizations assume a role of critical outsider *vis-à-vis* the political and administrative establishment (Escobar 1992; Kohli 1990). This is understandable. But it is not desirable. Democracy is weakened when popular organizations turn their back on the state, on parties and on elections.

Social Preconditions

Organizations provide a regularized form for cooperation between people. It is well-known that the existence of certain conditions in society makes such cooperation easier to achieve. It may be said, as a general matter, that continuous interaction promotes cooperation. As Robert Axelrod (1984) has shown through game-theoretical experiments, repeated play generates a fundamental incentive. Interaction under the shadow of the future—i.e., in the knowledge that we shall meet again—makes us less inclined to cheat or to take advantage of each other (for we know we can get paid back in the same coin the next time around). In addition, regular contacts within a group have the advantage that the actors involved gain better information about one another. They come to know each other's preferences and behaviour, and learn whom to and whom not to trust. They may furthermore be affected by each other's values and cultural patterns. A convergence of preferences may thus eventually take place (North 1990).

It is therefore important that there be arenas and meeting-places where people can come together. The more frequently such meetings take place, and the longer they proceed, the better are the conditions for the creation of mutual understanding and cooperation. It has accordingly been easier, as a rule, to create strong organizations in occupations where people work close to each other and where staff turnover is low. Stronger organizations have typically emerged, for example, among industrial than agricultural workers. (The former, after all, work in factories in large teams, while the latter do their work in groups which are smaller and more spread out.) Conditions for organizing have been especially favourable in mining and mill towns, where workers both live and work in close proximity to each other, and where mobility tends to be low. Where substantial geographical mobility prevails, by contrast, it has been harder to create strong organizations. The same applies in the case of social and cultural mobility. A static society—wherein people are divided into stable segments based on class, language, religion, etc.—is advantageous from an organizational point of view. Such a society encourages the formation of distinct group identities. It is not to be wondered at, from this perspective, that the degree of organization—the amount of social capital—tends to diminish in the ever more open and mobile society of the post-industrial era (Putnam 2000).

The strong organizations found in many industrial countries have been built on collective loyalties of long standing. It is loyalty, according to Hirschman (1970), that prevents members of an organization from leaving it, notwithstanding their displeasure with the policies pursued. The members of such an organization identify strongly with it, and they have firm confidence in its leadership. The establishment of such bonds results in a strengthened external capacity. An organization of this kind can serve as an effective offensive instrument—a tool for mobilizing support and publicizing demands. It is also equipped to function as an effective actor within a game of negotiation. This may consist of protracted piecemeal engineering, and it may sometimes require the organization in question to take a step backward in order to be able to move forward later. Such a game can demand much of the trust and patience of members. An organization without a stable fund of loyalty will find it hard to play.

Trade unions have been the classic example. They have often held a monopoly within their area of recruitment; seldom has there been any room for competitors. Keeping new organizations out has often been in the interests both of the established trade unions and of the employers. Membership in such bodies, moreover, has usually been of a stable and long-standing character. Such members have a firm identity, and a high degree of loyalty to their organization. The internal structure of such associations have typically been markedly hierarchical in character. The leaders have been able to mobilize their faithful followers on behalf of various demands. But they have also been able, when necessary, to discipline their followers and to hold them back. This has made such organizations into forceful negotiating partners. On account of their organizational resources and their cohesive membership, they have often been able to play an important role in political life—both in their own right, and more indirectly (i.e., by serving as a support and recruitment base for political parties). These elite-dominated organizations have proved, in other words, to be strong organs for the exertion of influence. At the same time, however, they have offered their members scant opportunities for participation (Inglehart 1997).

The more recent organizations—or 'social movements', as they are often called—tend to have a different character. They are looser associations. People join and leave them at a more rapid rate. Membership in them is briefer. They are also more partial in nature. Those taking part in them have a more limited commitment. The organization man of contemporary society exhibits an increasing similarity to the 'modular man' depicted by Ernest Gellner:

> Modular man is capable of combining into effective associations and institutions *without* these being total, many-stranded, underwritten by ritual and made stable through being linked to a whole inside set of relationships, all of these being tied in with each other and so immobilized. He can combine into specific-purpose, *ad hoc*, limited associations and institutions without binding himself to any blood ritual. He

can leave an association when he comes to disagree with its policy, without being open to an accusation of treason (1994: 100).

Modular man is an individual with relatively flexible and partial organizational affiliations. He can join associations of various sorts, and he can also leave them. When he does sign up, moreover, he only does so in a limited sense. The activities of the organization embrace just a part of his life. He has other identities too.

This leads to a different pattern in the internal life of organizations. Loyalties become weaker. In exchange, however, there is more room for the exercise of influence through the methods pointed out by Hirschman (1970): exit and voice. Exit means that one protests by leaving the organization. If, however, such a measure (or the threat thereof) is to have any real effect, there must be other associations capable of competing with the old, or substituting for it in one way or another. An exit into 'exile' typically has little effect. If established organizations are able to prevent competitors from arising, an important prerequisite for the exertion of influence by members is absent. Not just the exit option is weaker, but the voice option too. If there are no competing organizations of any importance, the risks associated with exclusion become substantially greater, and the expression of criticism becomes correspondingly more cautious. In short, leaders can acquire a very 'safe' and powerful position in organizations where the exit option is highly restricted.

A looser organizational commitment and a greater multiplicity of affiliations make for less hierarchical and more member-directed organizations. The leaders of such organizations are more dependent on short-term support from their members; they cannot rely on deep-rooted loyalties of long standing. Besides, there are other associations of a broadly similar character to turn to for those who might so wish. The opportunities for achieving encapsulation, in other words, are small. This makes such organizations less effective where the exercise of influence on a long-term basis is concerned. Such organizations find it hard, in particular, to function as effective negotiating partners, for they lack the requisite capacity to discipline their members.

As a rule, the new social movements which have emerged in our time have a relatively narrow activity repertoire: they are usually restricted to mobilizations of an expressive and short-term nature. At the same time, however, they are more democratic internally. They leave more room for participation and the exercise of influence by members. With increased mobility, moreover, there is greater interaction between people from different social groups. This promotes understanding and tolerance (Tarrow 1994; Cooper 1996; Inglehart 1997). The social capital of today's society is accordingly changing. Connections of the fixed, traditional kind are being weakened. Links between people are becoming looser and more varied. Where the effective defense of different social groups' interests is concerned, these are unfavourable developments. On the other hand, where democratic education is concerned, the changes we are witnessing are to be welcomed.

References

Axelrod, R. 1984. *The Evolution of Cooperation.* New York: Basic Books.

Barber, B. 1984. *Strong Democracy.* Berkeley: University of California Press.

Bates, R. 1994. 'The Impulse to Reform in Africa,' in J. Widner (ed.), *Economic Change and Political Liberalization in Sub-Saharan Africa.* Baltimore: The Johns Hopkins University Press.

Bratton, M. 1994. 'Peasant–State Relations in Postcolonial Africa: Patterns of Engagement and Disengagement', in J. S. Migdal, A. Kohli and V. Shue (eds.), *State Power and Social Forces: Domination and Transformation in the Third World.* Cambridge: Cambridge University Press.

Brehm, J. and Rahn, W. 1997. 'Individual-Level Evidence for the Causes and Consequences of Social Capital', *American Journal of Political Science* 41: pp. 999–1,023.

Cooper, A. H. 1996. 'Public-Good Movements and the Dimensions of Political Process: Postwar German Peace Movements', *Comparative Political Studies* 29: pp. 267–89.

Dahl, R. and Tufte, E. 1973. *Size and Democracy.* Stanford, CA: Stanford University Press.

De Tocqueville, A. 1969. *Democracy in America.* Garden City, N.Y.: Anchor Press.

Della Porta, D. and Vannucci, A. 1997. 'The "Perverse Effects" of Political Corruption', *Political Studies* 45: pp. 516–38.

Diamond, L. 1999. *Developing Democracy. Toward Consolidation.* Baltimore: The Johns Hopkins University Press.

Downing, B. M. 1992. *The Military Revolution and Political Change: Origins of Democracy and Autocracy in Early Modern Europe.* Princeton, N.J.: Princeton University Press.

Duverger, M. 1954. *Political Parties: Their Organization and Activity in the Modern State.* London: Methuen.

Escobar, A. 1992. 'Culture, Economics, and Politics in Latin American Social Movements Theory and Research', in Escobar, A. and Alvarez, S. E. (eds.), *The Making of Social Movements in Latin America.* Boulder, Colorado: Westview Press.

Gallagher, M., Laver, M., and Mair, P. 2001. *Representative Government in Modern Europe.* New York: McGraw-Hill.

Gellner, E. 1994. *Conditions of Liberty: Civil Society and its Rivals.* London: Hamish Hamilton.

Granovetter, M. S. 1973. 'The Strength of Weak Ties', *American Journal of Sociology* 6: pp. 1,360–80.

Hadenius, A. 2001. *Institutions and Democratic Citizenship.* Oxford: Oxford University Press.

Hadenius, A. and Karvonen, L. 2001. 'The Paradox of Integration in Intra-State Conflicts', *Journal of Theoretical Politics* 13: pp. 35–51.

Hadenius, A. and Uggla, F. 1996. 'Making Civil Society Work, Promoting Democratic Development: What Can States and Donors Do?', *World Development* 24: pp. 1,621–39.

Hirschman, A. 1970. *Exit, Voice, and Loyalty: Responses to Decline in Firms, Organizations, and States.* Cambridge, Massachusetts: Harvard University Press.

Inglehart, R. 1997. *Modernization and Postmodernization. Cultural, Economic and Political Change in 43 Societies.* Princeton: Princeton University Press.

Kohli, A. 1990. *Democracy and Discontent: India's Growing Crisis of Governability.* Cambridge: Cambridge University Press.

Lipset, S. M. 1960. *Political Man: The Social Bases of Politics.* New York: Doubleday.

March, J. and Olsen, J. P. 1989. *Rediscovering Institutions: The Organizational Basis of Politics.* New York: The Free Press.

Moe, T. M. 1984. 'The New Economics of Organization', *American Journal of Political Science* 28: pp. 739–777.

Newton, K. 1999. 'Social and Political Trust in Established Democracies', in Norris, P. (ed.) *Critical Citizens. Global Support for Democratic Government.* Oxford: Oxford University Press.

North, D. C. 1990. *Institutions, Institutional Change and Economic Performance.* Cambridge: Cambridge University Press.

Offe, C. 1997. 'Micro-aspects of Democratic Theory: What Makes for the Deliberative Competence of Citizens', in Hadenius, A. (ed.) *Democracy's Victory and Crisis.* Cambridge: Cambridge University Press.

Pateman, C. 1970. *Participation and Democratic Theory.* Cambridge: Cambridge University Press.

Putnam, R. D. 1993. *Making Democracy Work: Civic Traditions in Modern Italy*. Princeton, N.J.: Princeton University Press.

————. 2000. *Bowling Alone: The Collapse and Revival of American Community*. New York: Simon & Schuster.

Rothstein, B. 2000. 'Trust, Social Dilemmas and Collective Memories', *Journal of Theoretical Politics* 12: pp. 473–97.

Shefter, M. 1977. 'Party and Patronage: Germany, England, and Italy', *Politics and Society* 7: pp. 403–51.

Tarrow, S. 1994. *Power in Movement: Social Movements, Collective Action and Politics*. Cambridge: Cambridge University Press.

3

Is Civil Society the Answer?

Susanne Hoeber Rudolph[1]

Is civil society the answer? In an era of transition to market economies and political democracies, civil society is said to provide the
social capital, the trust, the cooperation and the legitimacy that make
market relations and pluralist politics possible. Civil society is cel-
ebrated as a panacea, a silver bullet, that can cure the ills afflicting
post-modern societies, states and economies. When policy makers
discuss the possibilities of democracy and market economies in the
states of the former Soviet empire, they inquire into the vigour of civil
society. Students of the Middle East investigate anxiously whether Saudi
Arabia, Yemen or Kuwait do or do not have a robust civil society. Can
China make a transit to democracy minus a vigorous civil society? Is its
market economy spawning a civil society? Is the relative success of
democracy in India partially explained by the robustness of its civil
society, its NGOs and caste associations as well as its formal organizations?

The British theorist, John Keane, provides an apt summary of
current positive thinking about civil society:

> The emerging consensus that civil society is a realm of freedom cor-
> rectly highlights its basic value as a condition of democracy; where there
> is no civil society there cannot be citizens with capacities to choose
> their identities, entitlements and duties within a political-legal frame-
> work (Keane 1998: 114).

Civil society is defined variously by different theorists, but a minimal definition would include the idea of a non-state autonomous sphere, empowerment of citizens, trust-building associational life and interaction with rather than subordination to the state. A review of the literature and debates suggests, however, that Western history and institutions disproportionately define the terms of the debate. The imaginary landscape of many theorists in this debate is Rome and Greece on the one hand, and 18th century Europe on the other. Participatory communication is said to have taken place in the fourth century *polis* and in the 18th century coffeehouse.

The most exotic landscape addressed by many Anglo-American theorists is that of Eastern Europe. 'Bringing civil society back in' got a new lease of life after the collapse of communism in Eastern Europe and the Soviet empire, with the people there attempting to establish democracy and markets in its place. The difficulties experienced were attributed to the fact that the previous regimes had decimated civil society.[2] The absence of civil society was said to affect not only the robustness of democracy, but also the possibilities of markets. When Russian market behaviour deteriorated into vicious warfare, it was recalled that the 'other' Adam Smith argued in *The Theory of Moral Sentiments* that the 'social passions'—sympathy, willingness to cooperate—are preconditions for self-interested exchange, and that 'barter and truck' in turn strengthen the social passions, enabling cooperation (Smith 1759/1982).[3]

But when the debate about civil society in Europe or America reaches out to the East or South of Istanbul, Western mainstream liberal theorists tune out. Scholars from, or of, the South take over; scholars whose metier is the Middle East, East Asia, South-East Asia, Africa and Latin America. The discussion about civil society in the 'South' moves on a different track from debates in the 'North', where most liberal theorists remain innocent about Southern societies and histories.[4]

I wish to bridge this gap by starting a conversation that joins the Northern and Southern discourses on civil society.[5] I take as my departure empirical accounts dealing with society and politics in South Asia. These accounts raise significant theoretical questions about the positive relationship between democracy and civil society. The discourses I would like to challenge feature undifferentiated conceptions of associational life,[6] treat all associations as if they were the same and advance arguments that suggest their consequences for democracy are uniformly positive. A more fine-grained and complex taxonomy of associations, and a more critical perspective on their impact on democracy, might generate subtler evaluations of the meaning and consequences of civil society. What follows is an effort to move the discussion in this direction.

How Associations Constitute Civil Society

The idea of associationalism is central to the concept of civil society. Associations empower citizens who in isolation cannot confront the state as agent and participant, nor create consequences within society. It is by being part of social collectivities that citizens can resist, escape or influence state and society. The emphasis on associationalism has a long genealogy in the history of political theory. Montesquieu held that freedom depended on intermediary associations, social forms that would mediate between individuals and the state. Intermediate associations enhance the force of individuals and limit the state by interposing social groupings between the state and vulnerable individuals. Marx followed Montesquieu when he argued that a basic feature of the Asian mode of production was the absence in Asia of intermediate social forms that could resist. He envisioned myriad Asian villages as solopsistic, self-contained social isolates dispersed at the bottom of an empty social space. Without intermediate associations between them and the state, they were unable to resist the force of Oriental despotism.[7] Marx returns to this vision of disarticulate units in his representation of European and Asian peasants. Peasants are simply 'homologous magnitudes, much as potatoes in a sack form a sackful of potatoes'. In such a society, he writes, 'the members ... live in similar conditions, but without entering into manifold relations with one another.' (Marx, n.d., II: 415). They are seen as being incapable of associationalism.

Another way of understanding the significance of intermediate associations for democratic society is to start with Francis Fukuyama's 'tray of sand' metaphor (Fukuyama 1995). The vision of a sandpile, of a society composed of so many atomized, isolated individuals appears in several thinkers. The image conveys individuals without social identities or solidarities. The metaphor has a pre-democratic and a democratic version.[8] The pre-democratic version focuses on the levelling wrought by the absolute state. Where monarchs succeed in destroying feudal solidarities, the local hierarchical associations of a master and his dependents, or where the solidarity of citizens acting as urban communes or guilds are smashed, nothing remains to hold individuals together. Monarchs are then free to act tyrannically because the atomized population will be supine, without the capacity to unite in resistance—a state Max Weber called 'passive democratization'. The post-democratic version of the metaphor of the sandpile imagines that democratic society is a mass society in which all individuals will be equal, but equally powerless. In Weber's words:

> The most decisive thing ... is the levelling of the governed in opposition to the ruling and bureaucratically articulated group, which in its turn may occupy a quite autocratic position ... (Weber, in Gerth and Mills, 1946a: 226).

In the 19th century the intrepid traveller and French theorist, Alexis de Tocqueville, wrote two books. One pictured the destruction of intermediary associations in France first by the monarch, then by the revolution (de Tocqueville 1955), and expressed despair at the tyrannical conditions that would necessarily follow. The second book sees him travelling to America to find out whether the absence of feudal forms of association in that country had left America as a tray of sand, as an unmediated mass society vulnerable to tyranny. de Tocqueville was 26 when he came to America in 1831 to write his classic *Democracy in America*. He was euphoric to discover that America was not after all what he had expected, a featureless society of isolated individuals:

> Americans of all ages, all stations in life, and all types of dispositions are forever forming associations. There are not only commercial and industrial associations in which all take part, but others of a thousand different types—religious, moral, serious, futile, very general and very limited, immensely large and very minute ...

Such associations have, he concludes

> An effect on the inner moral life of those who participate, enhancing their sympathies and understanding for fellow humans, and they have an external effect, nurturing their engagement with a wider community of purposes and making common purposes more effective (de Tocqueville 1969: 514–15).

Let me underline two passages in this last quote from de Tocqueville because disputing their claims is one of the agendas of this paper.

de Tocqueville claims that the associational experience has an effect on *the inner moral life of those who participate*; that is, the experience

of participating in cricket teams, *sampradayas*, choral societies and
political clubs builds in members a sense of fellow feeling and effica-
ciousness, a capacity to trust and influence others. It builds what James
Coleman and Robert Putnam, taking their cue from de Tocqueville,
later on came to call social capital. de Tocqueville also claims that
associations will have *an external effect, nurturing their engagement
with a wider community of purposes.* He claims that associational
experience will engender in members an interest in, and a capacity
to cooperate in, pursuit of the general or common good, to participate in the larger community, and to eschew 'free rides'. The argument is that the intimate negotiations which make members of an
association respect and trust each other will carry over, so the argument
goes, to the mutual respect and tolerance required to run community
affairs as well as local and regional self-government. It is this second
claim that I want to challenge, not necessarily to deny its validity
altogether, but to emphasize its weaknesses.

How Associations Constitute Social Capital

At a 1999 conference on 'Democracy and Social Capital in Segmented
Societies', participants from Sweden, South Asia and South Africa[9] swam
in the vocabulary that has come to structure the discussions of civil
society: civility, incivility, social capital, trust, collaboration/coop-
eration, public sphere, public good, and the like. They were particularly focused on the idea of social capital, an idea given
common currency these days in American social science discourses
by James Coleman (1990) and Robert Putnam (1993). Coleman sees
social capital as a set of institutionalized expectations that lead other
social actors to reciprocate by making collaborative moves. Putnam
writes:

> Social capital here refers to features of social organization, such as trust,
> norms and networks, that can improve the efficiency of society by facili-
> tating coordinated action (Putnam 1993: 169).

Where does social capital come from? Putnam's book suggests that
social capital can have a historical and a contemporary dimension.
On the historical side, he asks us to look at examples in Italian
history. His account distinguishes Northern and Southern Italy as
arenas that have generated and not generated social capital, respectively. These different heritages, he argues, spring from different

histories. The Northern Italian tradition is one of social capital generating states, featuring participatory city states dating back to the 12th century. This stands in contrast with the heritage of the Neapolitan-Sicilian South, the country of feudal oppression and monarchical absolutism, where 'any glimmerings of communal autonomy were extinguished as soon as they appeared' (Putnam 1993: 123).

One of Putnam's answers to where social capital comes from is from historical experience. But he also has a contemporary answer. The social capital that provides the basis for democracy is generated by the rich web of non-political associations that characterize modern North Italian society. Such associations are missing in the South. Putnam used a census of Italian associations to provide quantitative evidence. The count included amateur soccer clubs, choral societies, hiking clubs, bird-watching groups, literary circles, hunting associations, rotary clubs, and more. The array emphasizes that it is sociability in general, not political sociability in particular, which is said to create the habits of exchange and collaboration on the basis of which cooperation for the public good and democratic participation become possible.

Putnam suggests, then, as does Tocqueville, a causal relationship between the social capital constituted by the practice of associationalism and the capacity for civic participation and self-government.

The Relationship of Civil Society and Democracy under Conditions of Inequality: Three Studies

I want to insert some interruptions into this causal chain on the basis of a series of Indian field studies reported at the above-mentioned Agora Conference at Uppsala. Scholars and activists who evoke civil society do not always imagine it in similar ways. Some imagine it as obstreperous and challenging. Some imagine it in pianissimo, gentle and mannerly. Some see it as the arena in which activists organize resistance to the state. Others see it as a place where the natural human potential for aggression is reined in by artificial conventions that gentle the temper and sweeten manners (Keane 1998: 115). The resistant strand has been emphasized especially in connection with the revolutions in Eastern Europe: 'against the state, in partial independence from it' (Taylor 1990: 95). What such theories of civil society, and its derivative, theories of social capital, do not squarely confront is the fate of these mannerly and cooperative conceptions when placed in the context of highly unequal societies in the grip of radical social change, which is the condition of many countries in the South. How does social capital, understood as networks of trust, cooperation and participation, fare under conditions of social revolution? The Indian studies reported at the Agora conference were carried out in such contexts. Their findings challenge not only exclusively benign readings of why and how associational experience produces social capital and cooperation, but also Northern conceptions of the nature of associations.

Four North Indian Villages

The first challenge is to the claim that informal associations provide models and habits of collaboration and reciprocity that lead individuals to cooperate and that enable them to act effectively in formal political processes. When do such consequences result? And when does the associational experience sharpen social conflict by creating or strengthening social divisions? What happens when competing associations come into conflict over scarce resources or when the strengthening of one group challenges the dominion of other groups? Sudha Pai, a scholar at Delhi's Jawaharlal Nehru University, who with her students studied four North Indian villages summarizes the problem:

> Our study shows that social capital exists but *within* and not *between* segments in rural society. Group ... identities have the potential to create strong reservoirs of social capital within segments, but they do not facilitate—and in fact inhibit—the creation of a more broad-based ... social capital, which has the capacity to ensure responsive democratic government (Pai 1999: 26).

Pai, in other words, confirms the first of Tocqueville's propositions, that associations have an *internal* effect upon the 'inner moral life of those who participate', even while questioning the second, external consequence that associations can be counted on to 'nurture engagement with a community of common purposes'.

There is a reason for this lack of fit between Tocqueville's second specification and the reality of social history in North India. The discourse of social capital, with its emphasis on cooperation and collaboration, is not sensitive to negative effects in situations of social conflict.[10] Conflict over resources and status can tear apart a social fabric based on traditionally legitimated equilibria. Conflict under conditions of rapid social change hardly engenders the trust that is a basic component of social capital. Should we declare the concept of social capital incapable of handling rapid social change?

Pai's study focuses on *dalits*, ex-untouchables in Uttar Pradesh, India's most populous state. She examines their mobilization within a still steeply hierarchical social structure in response to the opportunities created by the 73rd Constitutional Amendment (1992). It led to the founding of a new, well-endowed level of local government and provided for the reservation of seats for *dalits* in local government councils. At the same time the state government in the capital city, Lucknow, moved into the hands of a *dalit* Chief Minister, Mayawati, a leader of the newly-founded dalit dominated party, the Bahujan Samaj Party (BSP). The new chief minister specifically channelled state development funds into villages with *dalit* pluralities or majorities. The *panchayats*, as the local government councils are called, became the arena for the continuing social revolution that has affected all levels of Indian government over the past decade.

The new *dalit* militancy generated several arenas of conflict, e.g. upper castes versus OBCs (other 'backward' classes). The ability of landowning, upper-caste Rajputs and middle-caste Jat farmers to control, disrespect and abuse *dalits* was limited from above by the presence of the dalit chief minister and from below by *dalit* representation on the newly constituted *panchayats*. Apart from a brief period of cooperation,[11] the OBCs or backward classes have started contesting against the politically ambitious *dalits*. Pai, in summing up the consequences of mobilization, says about the *dalits*,

> In positive terms social capital in the form of communal solidarity has united them, making them conscious of their special problems, bringing them together for joint social and political action against the upper and middle classes and providing them collective mobility upwards .... However, in negative terms, such activities have divided them from other groups of their own *dalit* community such as the *balmikis* and *musahars*, and sections of the rural poor such as the MBCs (more backward classes) with whom they have much in common in economic terms (Pai 1999: 27).

Pai's main finding is that strengthening the 'inner moral life of those who participate' may not translate into 'engagement with a wider community of purpose'.

Two Himalayan Villages

My second challenge to the all light and no shadows undifferentiated view of associationalism targets the assertion that associationalism and social capital on the one hand, and the exercise of democratic choice and the working of democratic institutions on the other, are positively related. The argument hypothesizes that associationalism, civil society and social capital 'cause' democracy. In the Indian cases, on the contrary, the causal arrows in the relationship between democracy and associationalism sometimes run in the reverse direction, and the effect is negative, not positive. The practice of democracy—elections, party activity—and its exercise through governing bodies may have disruptive effects on social capital. Democratic competition may devastate older lines of collaboration and solidarity. Niraja Jayal, whose research team investigated two Himalayan villages in the Garhwal region of Uttaranchal state in north India, observes:

> The field work ... suggests that the establishment of democratic institutions at the local level, and the channelizing of development funds and programmes through these, have set in motion processes that tend to deplete—rather than enhance—the pre-existing reserves of social capital (Jayal 1999: 8–9).

Jayal's story of local self-government and communal effort in the two villages provides a strong positive account of villagers self-organizing for conservation of forest resources and other community purposes. In one of the communities, forest resources had been 'completely denuded as a result of over-exploitation by the villagers themselves', but a community mobilization under the auspices of the Gandhian-style Chipko Movement took measures that, over a 20-year period, restored those resources. A series of voluntary organizations among young people and women were invigorated by the regional propaganda and campaigns of the Chipko Movement.[12] Such voluntary associations operated by majority decision or consensus and imposed fines or sanctions 'that suggest norms of fairness and reciprocity' (Jayal 1999: 20). Here the transfer of the social capital built by particular associations transferred to a larger political sphere. The research villages built strong conventions of local self-government.

But Jayal also tells a negative story. Community collaboration at the local level and 'external linkages' can be negatively correlated. External linkages can disrupt local initiatives and organization via state action and party-oriented activity. For example, state agencies funded conservation activity through forest *panchayats*, and the Uttar Pradesh (UP) government enacted the Forest Conservation Act of 1980. These moves 'weakened the sense of community and introduced a more cavalier attitude towards the forest which now came to be seen as government property' (Jayal 1999: 23). Such stories are not particular to the villages Jayal studied. The reports of Indian voluntarism from Andhra Pradesh to Bihar are rife with stories about how the entry of government undermines self-help activity.[13] Substituting government bureaus and processes for community initiatives can destroy voluntary associations. The spirit of routine and rationalization contradicts the spirit of voluntarism. Because the coexistence of bureaucracy and NGOs generates competition about who controls the action, official connections and status create a distance across which the trust and cooperation generated by social capital fails to stretch.

The very process of democratic decision-making, the electoral machinery of a democratic state driven by partisan mobilization, proved destructive in both Jayal's Himalayan villages and Pai's UP localities.

> Election (says Jayal) lies at the root of the schism in this divided community ... because it ... decides who controls development expenditure and therefore opportunities for material advancement (Jayal 1999: 25).

Well-established conventions of community decision-making and implementation did not transfer smoothly to democratic decision-making. Instead, local habits of cooperation were disrupted by electoral competition and by the impact of higher governing bodies.

A Village in Orissa

My third challenge is to that part of the social capital argument that assumes continuities and cumulation of social capital. Bishnu Mohapatra summarizes the cumulation argument:

> The more the stock of social capital a society has, the easier it becomes for its citizens to undertake group activities and sustain collective practices. Embedded within such activities is a pedagogy, a process of learning about mutuality that gets reinforced with every act of cooperation. (Mohapatra 1999: 3).

But the social process may not be unilinear or progressive. It may zigzag or regress. Memory may be disrupted, social cumulation cease. Robert D. Putnam's Italy-based historical account bears on the question of continuities and discontinuities of social capital. He suggests that the virtuous Italian North had republican and participatory traditions from the 12th to the 14th century, when the tradition yielded to Renaissance oligarchy and tyrannies. Participatory governance did not revive until the 19th century. What happened to the accumulated social capital in the intervening 500 years? When he tells us that the 12th century traditions of self-government, despite the 500-years respite, generated social capital that helps explain the North's talent for local self-governance in the 20th century, he suggests that social capital can be put in mothballs. Dan Levine, who applies the concept of social capital to the accumulation of participatory skills by liberation Catholic organizations in Latin America in the 1960s, has a more modest version of the mothball theory of social capital. He records the decline of liberationism in the 1990s and speculates that social capital may recede but not vanish, waiting in the wings to be reactivated, to revivify political practice sometime in the future (Levine and Stoll 1997).[14] We are left with a question. If social capital declines and goes underground, what are the conditions for its return?

Mohapatra addresses the question of discontinuity. He records a veritable rollercoaster of positive communitarian and negative conflictual moments in Talajanga village in Puri district of Orissa, all occurring in rapid succession in the 1990s.[15] Upon initial encounters between 1994 and 1996, Talajanga presented a smiling face, a locale remarkably virtuous as a participatory arena. Five non-formal committees, one for each locality of the village and unanimously elected, looked after yearly festivals in the localities, fined individuals for serious breaches of civility, non-payment of loans and disobeying committee decisions. Four of the committees—excluding the one for the *dalit* community (!)—constituted a *charisahi* committee, that is, a committee for the four localities. Meeting 38 times between 1994 and 1996, it appeared to provide a sturdy and respected vehicle of collective life in the village. It convened meetings that were attended by most of the villagers. 'Cases are heard, arguments and counter-arguments are made and the committee and sometimes a few recognized arbitrators deliberate until a solution is found.' But this benign communitarianism was recent and temporary. Until 1994 the village had been afflicted by violent conflicts between two of its localities, conflicts that were aggravated by a murder and the state assembly elections of 1990 (Mohapatra 1999: 10). In 1998, four years later, the benign arrangements were again on the verge of expiration. An incident between a boy and a girl had escalated, leading to a murder, and to ill feeling between localities. Villagers said the *charisahi* had lost legitimacy. But there was some sign of the transfer of social capital. A new association, launched by young people after feeling excluded by the older organization, had begun to fill the communitarian niche occupied by the older *charisahi* committee by taking patients to the hospital, offering relief in time of disaster and so on (Mohapatra 1999: 14).

How should we read such an account ? Do we explain the discontinuity as a failure of collaboration? Do we call it failure to build a durable civility? Or do we recognize it as a sign that particular civil society forms have waxing and waning careers? Perhaps the supersession by a village-wide association controlled by young people of a village body controlled by elders suggests that cooperation continues, but in new forms and with new players? How do we theorize continuity and discontinuity?

One way to theorize the problems raised by the scholars I have cited is to reflect on the nature of social revolution in India. We are accustomed to using the term 'revolution' for the events of Paris in 1789 and the events of Russia in 1917, when revolutionaries seized the state and used it to decimate their opponents and to attempt to transform the society. Revolution is thought of as an apocalyptic moment. Social revolution in India is a different kind of affair. It is a revolution taking place both within, and on the margins of, the constitutional framework. Legitimately elected local *panchayats* and a legitimately elected *dalit* chief minister like Mayawati collaborate to reallocate resources, especially status resources, to a segment of the oppressed. At the same time, encounters between caste and class groupings erupt into violence and mayhem, caste wars and massacres. India appears to pursue its social revolution not through an apocalyptic moment but at a low boil, over extended time, through constitutional and extra-constitutional channels.

This analysis suggests one context in which to understand the disrupted and intermittent processes by which Indian associations and communities accumulate and use social capital. The processes are often disrupted by harsh confrontations of unequals trying to become equals, and by challenges to established hierarchies by new forces trying to displace or replace them.

Distinguishing Types of Associations

Some of the conceptual problems posed by the study of associational life in India can be addressed by recognizing that not all associations are the same. Some are unfriendly to democracy while constituting part of civil society—Montesquieu's intermediate associations, the medieval Catholic Church. Some are uncivil—drug cartels, mafias. Differentiating types of associations might produce better assessments of their effect on democracy. To differentiate among associations I address three types of questions: (*1*) Are associations political or non-political, and if political, are they deliberative or interest-oriented? (*2*) Are they hierarchial or egalitarian? (*3*) Are they voluntary or 'natural' (ascribed)? Such differences may be consequential for the relationships between associations and democracy.[16]

Why does it matter whether associational life is political or non-political? Jurgen Habermas, in his well-known discussion of the public sphere, says it matters; that political associations are the pre condition for deliberative communication. Putnam on the other hand says it doesn't matter. In his analysis, choral societies and bowling leagues too are the source of social capital. Habermas' definition of associations relevant for the public sphere is narrowly constrained. He is suspicious of associations that might represent an organized expression of the private sphere, particularly of private interest, because it would negate the requirement of deliberating on 'matters of general interest'. There is, for Habermas, a 'weakening of the public sphere', even 'refeudalization' of society, when associational life becomes 'a field for competition among interests in the cruder form of forcible confrontation' (Seidman 1988: 232). For Habermas the 18th century coffeehouse, the political club and the journal of opinion are political associations that made 'public' what monarchs and aristocrats had kept secret and private. They deliberate on the general interest rather than representing the private. This emphasis on a vision of the political that entails deliberative communication rather than a struggle among interests reflects Habermas' attachment to a continental civic virtue tradition from Machiavelli through Rousseau and Arendt.[17] It takes its inspiration from an imagined *polis* derived from Athens and republican Rome. The tradition embraces a 'definition of man as citizen where, following Aristotle, man's, (and now presumably woman's) telos was to be found in, and only in, the sphere of political activity'.[18]

Unlike Habermas, Tocqueville, Weber and Putnam take *both* private and social associations as creating the moral capacity to act and nurturing the habits of collaboration. Putnam argues both sides of the question. He tells us that the local self-government of 12th century Northern Italy created trust, suggesting political sociability as a critical factor in creating the habits and conventions required for cooperation. On the other hand, like Tocqueville before him, he argues that non-political associations have political consequences, because they create friendships, networks and lines of communication that generate cooperation across spheres and domains. Soccer teams, bridge clubs and rotary clubs generate civility—mutual respect, and human ties that clear the path for shared conceptions of the common good.[19] Among political associations, Tocqueville, Weber and Putnam, more than Habermas, would regard interest associations as plausible agents of the social capital required for a viable civil society.

A second way to differentiate associations is to ask whether they are hierarchical or egalitarian. Do members stand in dependent, clientelist relations to patrons? Are they habituated to comply with, and act on, the directives of those in authority? Or are they egalitarian, i.e. do members participate in formulating goals and carrying out purposes? Do members share power and status? Hierarchical associations are not likely to create the sort of psychological and moral preconditions that generate the social capital considered a precondition for democracy. In his use of Italian society as the arena of examples, Putnam excluded Catholic associations from those relevant for the formation of social capital.[20] He did so, he said, because they were hierarchically organized and negatively correlated with democratic participation.[21] On the other hand, observers of Latin America's liberation Catholicism see it as a more participatory and egalitarian phenomenon, one which is generative of social capital. Presumably Edmund Burke's 'little platoons', 18th century social formations centred on a great local lord who mobilized his 'interest', that is, his dependent tenants and craftsmen, would hardly qualify as builders of social capital relevant for democratic participation.[22] Nor would the *Rashtriya Sevak Sangh*, the Hindu nationalist social organization that is structured on Leninist-style principles of leadership. In other words, not all forms of associations qualify for social capital formation.[23]

Reconceptualizing Associational Life: Intentional Associations

The third question is, are associations voluntary or ascribed, i.e., based on choice or birth? Associations have often been distinguished by the use of such dichotomies.[24] They have a provenance in German sociology. Weber distinguished between church and sect (born into one, admitted by qualification into the other), Toennies between *gemeinschaft* and *gesellschaft* (one organic, affective; the other contractual, rational). Tocqueville approximated these distinctions in his contrast between voluntary and natural associations. These more or less synonymous terms—ascribed, primordial, natural—relate to family, lineage, religion, ethnicity. Modernization theory in the 1960s tended to expel such inherited identities from the realm of civil society. Voluntary associations were a realm of freedom, ascribed associations a realm of unfreedom. Voluntary associations were said to allow individuals to choose their identities, ascribed associations to impose them. Ascribed associations were considered incompatible with civil society because they were considered impervious to individual choice.

Edward Shils, an important creator of modernization theory dichotomies, has much in common with Habermas. Shils thought 'civility' signified 'a solicitude for the interest of the whole society, a concern for the common good ... '. Because ascribed associations were incapable of being concerned with the common good, they could not be a path to civil society. The public spirited citizen is one 'who thinks primarily of the civil society as the object of his obligations, not of the members of his family, or his village, or his party, or his ethnic group, or his social class, or his occupation' (Shils 1992: 1–15, cited in Keane 1998: 114–15). Even as Habermas seeks to exclude interest associations from his normative understanding of the political, Shils excludes both ascribed and interest associations from his realm of the 'civil'.

This call for a civil society based on a self-transcending, affililation-transcending public ethic is surely appealing. But Shils' suggestion would elicit from David Hume or the authors of the *Federalist Papers,* James Madison and Alexander Hamilton, the objection that a political system has to be based on a 'realistic' conception of human nature. An objection from quite different quarters, the multi-cultural and communitarian theorists of the 1990s, would be that the unmarked self, 'unencumbered' by family, ethnicity or interest that Shils imagined was implausible (Sandel 1984: 81–96). Michael Sandel speaks of individuals as always 'members of this family or community or nation or people, as bearers of this history, as sons and daughters of that revolution, as citizens of this republic' (Sandel 1982, cited in Seligman 1997: 117–18).[25]

Voluntary and ascriptive do not exhaust the conceptualizations of associational life. The dichotomy precludes hybrid or constructed forms of association.[26] Constructivist interpretations of ethnicity, for example, have exposed the synthetic nature of most categories previously considered primordial. Until 20 years ago, most observers believed that the people living in what is now Greece were Hellenes, the same who had participated in the *polis* in the 4th century and fought the Peloponnesian war. But the modern Greeks only learned they were Hellenes at the beginning of the 19th century, when a talented poet and humanist, Adamantiius Koeros, informed them about 'who they truly were'. We accept that Slobodan Milosevic's media control made a major contribution to the idea of an exclusivist Serb identity, freshly differentiating it from that of peoples among whom the Serbs lived and with whom they had a shared culture. We came to entertain the idea, in the 1990s, that nationalities which we had thought of as primordial were instead the 'imagined communities' that Benedict Anderson introduced us to 20 years ago, creations of the print media by humanists, historians and poets.

Understanding that communities are imagined or constructed rather than primordial and innate opens the way to recognizing a hybrid form of association, what Lloyd Rudolph and I have elsewhere called intentional associations (Rudolph and Rudolph 2001). What appear in the first instance as ascribed identities, such as Serb (a national identity), Yadav (a caste identity) or Christian (a religious identity), can be reinforced or rejected by acts of choice. Intentional associations can combine with their biological givenness or specificity a cultural and psychological act of social and political choice. This means that an ascribed ethnic identity like Serb, a caste identity such as Yadav or a religious identity such as Christian can be the result of intention as much as birth, can be created as much as inherited; not a biological attribute, but a cultural construction, and a social and political choice.

If we look at practice, we find hybrids, associations that blend ascriptive and voluntary features. Take that quintessentially ascribed identity, caste, as it manifests itself in and out of India among Hindus as well as adherents of other religions such as Christianity and Islam. We know that caste self-transformed in the course of the 19th century and earlier, changing both its internal meaning and external standing. Local *jatis* joined with like *jatis* in their regions to create larger intentional self-help associations on the basis of inherited ritual structures, what Lloyd Rudolph and I in a 1960s book called paracommunities. The caste associations became vehicles of self-organization for social reform and for political participation (Rudolph and Rudolph, 1967). Caste, a vehicle for maintenance of a hierarchical society, was converted via caste associations into a means for the more numerous lower castes to mobilize and participate in ways that challenged ritual hierarchy. No one was born into a caste association; he or she had to become active within it by an act of choice, including having to shape its social and political goals.

Caste associations are intentional associations. The adjective conveys that those who participate in them have *chosen* their ascriptive identity. Caste associations are very much like ethnic groups in America. The Polish, German, Irish and Latino clubs and associations in all major cities are made up of members who have chosen to identify with them. Designating such clubs and organizations as intentional associations challenges the ascribed-voluntary dichotomy, opening space for a third, hybrid category. It also overrides the distinction between realms of freedom and unfreedom sought to be superimposed on this dichotomy.

What are the implications of this renegotiating of a dichotomy into a trichotomy? First, associations that draw on inherited identities and solidarities need to be taken into account as associations that may generate social capital. They clearly create collaborative and cooperative conventions. And they can and do mediate between individuals and social wholes or individuals and the state. Whether they do so in ways that enable horizontal egalitarian exchanges, or in hierarchical ways that smother the engagement of lower participants, is a matter of investigation rather than as *a priori* decision. Thus, in evaluating religious sociability, about which partisans of civil society are uneasy, Putnam does not count Catholic solidarities in contemporary Italy as generative of social capital. Weber on the other hand counts 16th century Protestant sects as generative of habits of self-government. These are distinctions that provide a more fine-grained definition of social capital and civil society.

Conclusion: Is Civil Society the Answer?

This chapter began with the question, 'Is Civil Society the Answer?' It went on to ask how well civil society works as a precondition for democracy when transplanted from its origins in the self-referential North to the different historical, social and political contexts of the South. I have tried to answer these questions in several ways. One was to confront civil society theory with several micro-studies by Indian colleagues. They suggest *inter alia* that the relationship between civil society and democracy can be negative as well as positive.

Another was to create a finer taxonomy of associational categories that would permit differentiated evaluations of their practical and normative relationship to civil society: political/non-political; hierarchical/egalitarian; ascriptive/voluntary. This taxonomy placed particular emphasis on the hybrid form of associational life, more evident in the South than the North but present in both, the 'intentional association'. This form is neither voluntary nor ascriptive, and blurs the distinction, important to civil society discourses, between arenas of freedom and choice and arenas of unfreedom and determinism.

If we are to use the concept of civil society at all, and populate it with social capital-generating associational life, we must be able to specify what type of associations are likely to generate habits of mutual trust and collaboration. Not all associations are likely to do so, and we need criteria of distinction. Putnam confesses that soccer clubs in the Italian South may be more hierarchical than those in the Italian North, and hence less suitable as pedagogies of collaboration. Not all associations are the same; not all have the capacity to generate mutuality and cooperation. Those that are able to generate internal solidarity may succeed in ways that make members feel sympathy only with each other and insulate them from civic others. Associations may nurture, as Tocqueville said, 'the inner moral life of those who participate, enhancing their sympathies … for fellow humans', without, however, 'nurturing their engagement with a wider community'. Associational life, in other words, can make members appreciate each other even while making them self-regarding and parochial. It can generate a form of group selfishness that results in ethnic conflict and civil war as in Bosnia and Bihar. What are the conditions and mechanisms that translate the social capital generated by associational life from inside to outside, and that makes social capital available for strengthening the pursuit of the public good? If civil society is to be the answer for making democracy (and markets?) work, and work better, more and better answers to this question will have to be found.

Notes

1. William Benton Distinguished Professor of Political Science, University of Chicago. This essay was first presented on 2 August 1999 as a lecture

in the series sponsored by the Sri Lanka Ministry of Foreign Affairs to celebrate the Golden Jubilee of Sri Lankan independence. The revision has profited greatly from Lloyd Rudolph's critical reading and suggestions about concepts, analysis and evidence.

2. See for example Timothy Garton-Ash's series of articles in the *New York Review of Books* in 1998. See also Havel et al., 1985.

3. For a leading example of revisionist readings of Smith, see Griswold, Jr., 1999. See also Dubin, Ph.D. in progress.

4. Commenting on the bias among mainstream European theorists against incorporating an understanding of plural societies, Gurpreet Mahajan notes, 'In fact, even today most liberals are unsympathetic to the idea that the public realm should reflect diverse cultural values and ways of life. A least in part, this response is shaped by the historical context in which this ideology evolved in Europe' (Mahajan 1998: 1).

5. For other initiatives along these lines, see for example the following Agora conference participants: Chatterjee, 1997; Mahajan, 1998; Chandhoke, 1995.

6. An important example of lack of differentiation is the array of associations that Robert D. Putnam features in his discussion of social capital-generating forces. He admits many different types into his definition of what counts as an association—formal, informal, political, unpolitical—but assumes they are the same in the social consequences they generate. All are depicted as promoting the social capital, the habits of cooperation, requisite for democratic government. 'Neighbourhood associations, choral societies, cooperatives, sports clubs, mass-based parties and the like' all 'represent intense horizontal interaction. The denser such networks in a community, the more likely that its citizens will be able to cooperate for mutual benefit.' (Putnam 1993: 173).

7. Perry Anderson gives this view an ancient lineage, tracing it to Aristotle's view of the natural despotic inclinations of 'barbaric peoples'. See Anderson, 1974: 465.

8. 'Men are all equal in a republican state; they are also equal in a despotic state; in the first, because they are everything; in the second, because they are nothing.' (Charles de Secondat, Baron de la Brede et de Montesquieu 1961, I: 81). Montesquieu's view of the democratic condition is patently more optimistic about democratic equality than Weber's and Tocqueville's.

9. 'Democracy and Social Capital in Segmented Societies: The Third International Agora Conference', Vasasalen, Uppsala University, Sweden, June 17–19, 1999.

10. Putnam obviously believes that social conflict is compatible with the building of social capital. After examining various measures of political fragmentation and social conflict he concludes: 'none of these investigations ... offered the slightest sustenance for the theory that social and political strife is incompatible with good government.' (Putnam 1993: 117).

11. The short period of cooperation in 1993, when Mulyam Singh Yadav, Uttar Pradesh's leading OBC leader, and Kanshi Ram, head of the *dalit Bahujan Samaj Party*, joined forces to defeat the Hindu nationalist and then upper-caste *Bharatiya Janata Party*, soon ended.

12. The villagers created a *van suraksha samiti* (save the forest association), formulated rules of use, and self-enforced them, partly through the agency of a mahila mangal dal (women's association) (Jayal 1999: 13–15).

13. Mahesh Barenwal reports from Bihar that government built schools are neglected by local villagers—not cleaned, not repaired—on the principle that they are government responsibility (dissertation in progress, oral report 1998, Department of Sociology, University of Chicago). An Andhra woman activist featured at the 1996 meeting of the Association of Indian Women in Jaipur reported the decline of (effective) women's anti-liquor movements when the N.T. Rama Rao government passed legislation and set up (ineffective) government sanctioning mechanisms (author's notes from meeting).

14. As the title suggests, Levine and Stoll are concerned that very promising social solidarities generated by liberationism petered out. On the other hand, they and other observers note that many caught up in liberationist Catholic activity migrated to Protestant evangelical movements. The question is whether this had any consequences for governmental participation—or was a substitute for it.

15. The group's shifting experience suggests the limitations of a one-time snapshot of a fluid social reality, and the revealing quality of investigations over time.

16. For that view of civil society which sees its prime importance in establishing a non-state space, a sphere autonomous of the state, the differences I am about to discuss are less important. For Tocqueville and Montesquieu, 'intermediary classes' were a bulwark against 'despotism', whether they were hierarchical and elite, popular and democratic, ascribed or voluntary (Montesquieu was sure that non-western 'despotisms' had no such bulwarks). But for most 20th century writers, equality and horizontal forms of organization and patterns of participation are as important as the preservation of a non-state space.

17. Partha Chatterjee, who has no special affection for the civic virtue tradition, also argues for a narrow definition of civil society/public sphere, preferring to follow Hegel and Marx in restricting it to bourgeois society and to a highly rationalist, contractualist definition. This allows civil society to function as a 'pure model of origin—the institutions of modernity as they were meant to be'. However, unlike Habermas and others he does not eliminate 'traditional' society from consideration, as he searches for a conceptual space between the state and the private sphere in which to park non-bourgeois associations (Chatterjee 1997: 31). However, others have less restrictive definitions: 'In India, the meaning, if not

the terminology, of civil society has been widely used to delineate the
upsurge of popular movements against the state'. (Chandhoke 1995: 28).

18. For a helpful discussion that seats the concept of trust in an intellectual
genealogy of the Western canon, including the civic virtue tradition,
see Seligman 1997: 108–9.

19. Weber too sees associational life as composed of non-political organizations: 'The Protestant Sects' depict the transfer of the autonomous
religious organizational forms of 17th and 18th century Protestant religious congregations to 20th century social groups (Weber, in Gerth and
Mills, 1946).

20. But Daniel H. Levine points out that the associations spawned by the
Latin American popular church are more communitarian and egalitarian (Levine and Stoll 1997: 63–103). See also Levine, 1981.

21. 'Organized religion, at least in Catholic Italy, is an alternative to the
civic community, not a part of it ...Vertical bonds of authority are more
characteristic of the Italian Church than horizontal bonds of fellowship.
At the regional level all manifestations of religiosity and clericalism ...
are negatively correlated with civic engagement.' (Putnam 1993: 107).

22. Although they would qualify as components of Montesquieu's and
Tocqueville's tyranny-resisting intermediate classes.

23. Putnam confesses in a footnote, 'Lacking micro-level information on
status and power within secondary associations in various parts of Italy,
we are forced to assume that across all regions social ties within, say,
soccer clubs, are equally horizontal and thus equally effective as social
capital. In fact, we suspect that soccer clubs and other voluntary associations are socially more hierarchical in the less civil, less successful
areas'. This is dangerous talk, threatening to reverse the causal arrow
so that associations become the dependent variable—dependent on
larger social conditions (Putnam 1993: 245, n.69).

24. De Tocqueville used the dichotomy, voluntary and natural; Talcott Parsons' pattern variables included ascribed and achieved. These usages
express subtle differences of meaning and reflect different cultural and
philosophical presuppositions that will not, however, be explored here
(see Parsons and Shils 1951: 77).

25. Seligman sums up the dichotomy as it affects the communitarian debate:
'For the liberal-individualist (or universalist) tradition which emerges
out of the idea of civil society, the model of solidarity is one of acts of
exchange between morally autonomous and agentic individuals, for
the communitarian tradition, or that of republican citizenship, it is one
most often rooted in primordial or ascriptive criteria' (Seligman 1997:
117). This paper does not address the significant difference between
communitarian and multiculturalist discourses: for the communitarians
difference plays an adjectival or modifying role that equips individuals
with a point of view within a unitary political community, while for

multiculturalists difference has a defining, ontological significance and entails a pluralist political community.

26. A recent study by Pradeep Chhibber implicitly excludes not only hybrid forms of association but also informal and non-political ones (see Chhibber, 1999). Chhibber claims that India has the lowest level of associational life among all democracies. This conclusion is based on a 3,000 person sample in six states in 1991 (in English? in four different languages?) that found, among other things, that 'Few Indians profess membership in religious or caste associations'. Associations are defined as organizations that 'help mobilize voters by defining issues that are salient to voters' (Chhibber 1999: 183). The formulation suggests that the author's survey instrument cued respondents toward formal political association. That way of asking about membership may account for the view that India is a 'democracy without associations'. It is unlikely that participants in the annual Durga *puja* societies that proliferate in the Kolkata *mohallas* and elicit intense community participation would volunteer such membership if asked 'whether (they) were members of an association'? (Chhibber 1999: 17, note to Table 3). Chhibber's view contrasts with the stress now common among India-oriented social scientists on the unprecedented proliferation of NGOs in the last 20 years, and their consequences for policy outcomes. For a critical appraisal that critiques Chhibber's lack of theorizing 'association', see Chandhoke 2000: 55.

References

Anderson, P. 1974. 'The Asiatic Mode of Production', in *Lineages of the Absolutist State*, London: Routledge.

Chandhoke, N. 1995. *State and Civil Society: Explorations in Political Theory*. New Delhi: Sage.

Chandhoke, N. 2000. 'When is an Association not an Association?' *The Book Review*, XXIV, 1–2, January–February: 55.

Chatterjee, P. 1997. 'Beyond the Nation? Or Within?', *Economic and Political Weekly*, January 4–11.

Chhibber, P. 1999. *Democracy Without Associations: Transformation of the Party System and Social Cleavages in India*. Ann Arbor: Michigan University Press.

Coleman, J.S. 1990. *Foundations of Social Theory*. Cambridge, Massachusetts: Harvard University Press.

Davis, D. et al. 1995. *Urban Spaces in Contemporary China*. Cambridge: Cambridge University Press.

de Secondat, C., Baron de la Brede et de Montesquieu. 1961. *De L' Esprit des Lois, I.* Paris.

de Tocqueville, A. 1955. *The Old Regime and the French Revolution* (transl. by S. Gilbert). Garden City, N.Y.: Doubleday Press.

_____. 1835 reprint 1969. *Democracy in America.* Garden City, New York: Anchor Press.

Dubin, F.F. (forthcoming). 'Introduction. Cosmopolitanism and Commerce: Globalizing the Adam Smith Problem', Ph.D. in progress, Department of Political Science, University of Chicago.

Fukuyama, F. 1995. *Trust: The Social Virtues and the Creation of Prosperity.* New York: Free Press.

Gambetta, D. 1993. *The Sicilian Mafia: The Business of Private Protection.* Cambridge: Harvard University Press.

Gerth, H.H. and Mills, C.W. 1946. 'The Protestant Sects and the Spirit of Capitalism', in H.H. Gerth and C.W. Mills (eds.), *From Max Weber.* New York: Oxford University Press.

Griswold Jr., C.L. 1999. *Adam Smith and the Virtues of the Enlightenment.* Cambridge: Cambridge University Press.

Havel, V. et al. 1985. *The Power of the Powerless: citizens against the state in central-eastern Europe.* Armonk, New York: M.E. Sharpe.

Jayal, N.G. 1999. 'Democracy and Social Capital in the Central Himalayas: A Tale of Two Villages', unpublished manuscript, Uppsala Conference on 'Democracy in Segmented Societies', Uppsala University, Sweden.

Keane, J. 1998. *Civil Society: Old Images, New Visions.* Stanford: Stanford University Press.

Levine, D.H. 1981. *Religion and Politics in Latin America: The Catholic Church in Venezuela and Colombia.* Princeton: Princeton University Press.

Levine, D.L. and Stoll, D. 1997. 'Bridging the Gap Between Empowerment and Power in Latin America,' in S. H. Rudolph and J. Piscatori (eds.), *Transnational Religion and Fading States.* Boulder, Colorado: Westview Press.

Mahajan, G. 1998. *Identitities and Rights: Aspects of Liberal Democracies in India.* Delhi: Oxford University Press.

Marx, K. (n.d.). 'The Eighteenth Brumaire of Louis Napoleon,' in *Selected Works, II.* New York: Free Press.

Mohapatra, B. 1999. 'Social Connectedness, Civility, and Democracy: A View from an Orissa Village', unpublished manuscript, Uppsala Conference on 'Democracy in Segmented Societies', Uppsala University, Sweden.

Mortara, A. (ed.) 1985. *Le Associazzioni Italiane.* Milan: Franco Angeli.

Pai, S. 1999. 'Social Capital, Panchayats and Grassroots Democracy: Politics of Dalit Assertion in Two Districts of Uttar Pradesh', unpublished manuscript, Uppsala Conference on 'Democracy in Segmented Societies', Uppsala University, Sweden.

Parsons, T. and Shils, E. 1951. *Toward a General Theory of Action*. Cambridge: Harvard University Press.

Putnam, R. D. 1993. *Making Democracy Work: Civic Traditions in Modern Italy*. Princeton: Princeton University Press.

Rudolph, L.I. and Rudolph, S.H. 1967. *The Modernity of Tradition: Political Development in India*. Chicago: University of Chicago Press, and Mumbai: Orient Longman.

Rudolph, L.I. and Rudolph, S.H. 2001. 'Living with Multiculturalism in India: Universalism and Particularism in Historical Context', forthcoming in R. Schweder, M. Minow, and H.R. Markus (eds.), *The Free Exercise of Culture: How Free Is It? How Free Ought It to Be?*. New York: Russell Sage.

Sandel, M. 1982. *Liberalism and the Limits of Justice*. Cambridge: Cambridge University Press.

Sandel, M. 1984. 'The Procedural Republic and the Unencumbered Self', *Political Theory*, pp. 81–96.

Seidman, S. (ed.) 1988. *Jurgen Habermas on Society and Politics: a Reader*. Boston: Beacon Press.

Seligman, A.B. 1997. *The Problem of Trust*. Princeton: Princeton University Press.

Shils, E. 1992. 'Civility and Civil Society', in E.C. Banfield (ed.), *Civility and Citizenship in Liberal Democratic Societies*. New York: Paragon House, pp. 1–15.

Smith, A. 1759/1982. 'The Theory of Moral Sentiments', in D.D. Raphael and A.L. Macfie (eds.), *Glasgow Edition of the Works and Correspondence of Adam Smith, Vol. I*. Oxford: Oxford University Press. (Reprinted Indianapolis, Indiana: Liberty Press, 1982).

Taylor, C. 1990. 'Modes of Civil Society', *Public Culture* 3, 1: pp. 95–118.

Wasserstrom, J.N. and Perry, E.J. 1991. *Popular Protest and Political Culture in Modern China: Learning from 1989*. Boulder, Colorado: Westview Press.

Weber, M. 1946a. 'Bureaucracy', in H.H. Gerth and C. W. Mills (eds.), *From Max Weber*. New York: Oxford University Press.

Weber, M. 1946b. 'The Protestant Sects and the Spirit of Capitalism', in H.H. Gerth and C. W. Mills (eds.), *From Max Weber*. New York: Oxford University Press.

4

Social Capital of Individuals:
Relational Asset or Personal Quality?

Paul Dekker[1]

Introduction

According to Foley and Edwards (1999: 141), the watershed in social capital research is between 'those who operationalize the concept principally in terms of norms, values and attitudes and those
who choose a more social structural operationalization, invoking
social networks, organizations and linkages'. This gulf has professional roots: political scientists write most of the time about norms
and values, while sociologists are more interested in networks and
organizations. There is a difference in scale related to this; sociologists prefer the smaller scale of real organizations and concrete,
often even 'egocentric', networks, and political scientists the more
diffuse and abstract traits of larger collectives, such as municipalities, regions and even nations. Related to this is a distinction in
focus: some look at the private advantages of resources that are
available through networks, others at social capital as a public good.

My primary concern in this chapter is with social capital as a
collective or public good. For both godfathers of the present debates,
James Coleman (1988) and Robert Putnam (1993, 1995, 2000), this
kind of social capital is a compound of trust, networks and shared
norms.[2] My starting point is, once again, the now most popular

description of social capital by Putnam. In his book about Italy, the concept 'refers to features of social organization, such as trust, norms and networks, that can improve the efficiency of society by facilitating coordinated actions' (Putnam 1993: 167), and in *Bowling Alone* seven years later it 'refers to connections among individuals—social networks and the norms of reciprocity and trustworthiness that arise from them' (Putnam 2000: 19). The way Putnam defines social capital hardly changes over the years, and neither do his positive associations of social capital with benefits for the community, the larger society and for politics. It is only a small step from 'networks' to 'networks of civic engagement' (1993: 171), and from 'norms of reciprocity and trustworthiness' to 'civic virtue' (2000: 19). Putnam has been criticized for having focussed almost exclusively on the benign societal and political effects of social capital. Actually, Putnam more than once acknowledges that social capital is not necessarily 'praiseworthy'; that it may have exclusively individual benefits or even negative effects for other people and society. His focus on ('praiseworthy') public social capital is an intentional one.[3]

Independent of who or what is the beneficiary of social capital, this capital is never an object of pure private ownership. It might be inherent in networks, embodied in institutions or just 'in the air', but it is always something collective. The wording 'social capital of individuals' in the title of this chapter can mean very different things: close to private ownership is accessibility of social capital for private use by the individual (e.g., some helpful people around, knowledge); somewhat different is social capital as a positive condition for individual behaviour that cannot be privatized (e.g., reliability and safety, low transaction costs) and completely different is the connectedness of individuals to communities with high levels of social capital for common undertakings. In the latter case the individual might not primarily be the beneficiary of social capital, but more of a contributor to it. In the case of social capital as a public good, we have to measure the 'social capital of individuals' by indicators for the integration of individuals in networks that contain social capital, their support for the norms that belong to a collective with social capital, their behaviour that manifests and helps to generate social capital, etc.

The 'norms' attributed to social capital well illustrate the importance of the distinction between 'private' and 'public' social capital. At the macro-level, the average support for civic values, norms or reciprocity, pro-social attitudes etc. according to surveys can be good indicators for social capital in a society.[4] At the micro-level, the same indicators are fine to show the individual connectedness with, or the support of, social capital as a public good. But in the case of social capital as an individual resource there is a different situation. It is the situation we know as the free-rider problem in collective action theory: the best situation for me is that people around me strongly support civic norms so I can exploit them and my egoistic deflection of social behaviour has no negative consequences.

Table 4.1 combines the distinction between private and public social capital with the networks/culture distinction of Foley and Edwards (1999) that was mentioned at the beginning. The cells suggest phenomena to be investigated for different conceptualisations of social capital.

My interest is to investigate the relationships between a broad range of potential indicators within and between the two cells on the right-hand 'public good' side of the table. I consider the 'networks, trust and norms' complex of Putnam not so much as a definition, but more as a hypothesis. This hypothesis of strong inter-relationships will be tested at the individual level. There will be no further discussion in this chapter of the collective character of social capital or its effects on the social, political and economic performance of a society. The chapter merely deals with individuals and draws exclusively on survey-data variables that indicate their (possession of/connectedness with) social capital. It does so in a very empirical and inductive way: are there any eye-catching combinations of indicators? How strong is the relationship between the social capital of networks

Table 4.1 Issues to investigate at the crossing of dimensions of the use of 'social capital'

Inherent in ↓ is social capital as →	Individual or group resource	Public good
Networks and organizations	Personal relationships, available assets in networks, networking	Social cohesion, bonds, social and political participation
Norms, values or culture	(Particularized/specific) trust, reciprocity, loyalty	(Generalized) trust, reciprocity, civic values

and organizations and the social capital of trust and norms? Does the data suggest one syndrome of 'networks, trust and norms' or a split between the 'high generalized trust' social capital owners of political science and the 'strongly integrated' social capital owners of sociology?

After the introduction of the data in section 2, section 3 investigates the relationships between all the indicators in two ways, by principal component analyses (is there such a thing as a social capital dimension, or are there more social capital dimensions?), and by cluster analyses (are there one or more 'high social capital' segments detectable in the population?). In section 4 the analyses are broadened to include additional individual resources and attitudes. This should enable us to judge the relative importance of the internal relationships of social capital indicators. This leads to a brief presentation in section 5 of an alternative conceptualization of the attitudinal side of social capital. Section 6 offers an overall discussion and suggestions for future research.

Data and Indicators

In the fast-growing research literature on social capital a large variety of indicators can be found. These indicators seem to be applied without much discussion—some were used earlier in an exemplary study, others were available as a comparative data set, etc. Survey research is mainly used for the 'norms/values/culture' row in table 1, in particular for the 'public good' cell. With the exception of the illustrious social trust question—'Generally speaking, would you say that people can be trusted or that you can't be too careful in dealing with people?'—there is not yet much consensus about core survey indicators. This is partly so because researchers have different interests, i.e., focus on different cells of table 1, but also because of the vagueness of the concept and the difficulties in isolating social capital from its causes and consequences. For example, for some 'civic engagement' (no matter how it is measured) is social capital, or at least shows that there must be social capital beneath; for others it produces social capital or is a result of social capital (cf. Brehm and Rahn 1997).

As already indicated, in this chapter, I do not want to try to come up with a theoretical selection of social capital indicators. I start from the opposite direction, with a survey that includes a lot of indicators that cover 'networks, trust and norms'. Many of the indicators are similar to the ones that are already used to measure social capital, but the combination is rather unique.[5] In other words: if we do not discover the 'social capital of individuals' with this survey, it will be hard to discover it with any other survey.

The data used are from the Dutch 'Civil Society and Volunteering' survey held in the winter of 1996–97. This survey used a face-to-face questionnaire on general social and political values and opinion, a drop-off list containing questions on volunteering, giving, local involvement and additional norms and values, and a local drop-off list for four locations that were oversampled in the project (De Hart and Dekker 2003). The national sample of 2,320 respondents that is used in this chapter was supposed to be representative for the Dutch-speaking population aged 16 and over.

Table 4.2 shows a list of 20 indicators. All indicators are dichotomies, usually based on a single item.[6] Five groups are distinguished: networks, trust and norms, and additionally social and political participation and civic and political involvement. These additional categories can be considered as working cooperative networks in society ('networks of civic engagement'), and they are current elements in the research of 'praiseworthy' public social capital. The following are the groups and indicators:

- *Networks:* The first indicator is about actual behaviour, the second one is more of a predisposition or attitude, and the other two are perceptions of the existence of supportive networks in one's environment. The four indicators are in fact all directed towards the neighbourhood (NGHVISIT, NGHILL, NGHHELP and NGHPROT). This is not a conceptual choice, but reflects what is available (a more balanced measurement of networks including those in professional life, close friends outside the neighbourhood, etc., would have been better).
- *Participation:* The available questions about belonging to voluntary associations do not distinguish between having face-to-face contacts in the organization or just being on an mailing list. For a list of organizations the question was, 'Are you a member of or a contributor to one or more of the types of organizations listed below', and this explicitly asks respondents even to include non-membership organizations. Because face-to-face contacts are considered to be a condition for generating social capital (see however Wollebæk and Selle 2000), membership

is only taken into account for leisure organizations (LEISURE), for which this kind of contact seems to be the rule. For the other participation indicators we draw on actual activity. As regards religious and philosophical organizations (RELIGION), churchgoing is a criterion. Volunteering is included as regular time investment (VOLUNT), and as at least occasionally doing voluntary work for service organizations (VOLSERV) or political and interest organizations (VOLINTER). Involvement in collective action (COLACT) refers to having made in the last two years 'an active effort together with others for an issue of national importance or for a global problem such as peace and poverty [or] for an issue of local importance or for a specific group in your municipality or neighbourhood').

- *Involvement:* Three indicators for civic and community involvement have been selected: the informal discussion of politics (POLTALK), reading about politics (POLREAD) and reading local news (LOCREAD).

- *Trust:* In addition to 'the question' on social trust (SOCTRUST), disagreement with an item of an anomie scale is used as another measurement of social trust (TRUSTNOW). Although they might be disputed as part of the social capital syndrome (Putnam 1995, Brehm and Rahn 1997, Newton 1999), two more trust indicators are included; one for trust in politicians (POLTRUST) and the other for institutional trust (INSTTRUST).

- *Norms:* Our survey does not offer many possibilities, and, apart from the norm of reciprocity, the literature is not very helpful in identifying relevant norms. Three indicators seem to be acceptable. The first one is a measurement of a positive attitude towards other people (PHILANT), revealed by the selection of one of the two most philanthropic statements ('one should treat other people as brothers and sisters', and 'one should not just live for oneself but also for other people') from a list of seven statements about 'other people'. The best measurement of the norm of reciprocity is found in a series of questions about volunteering: agreement with the statement that everybody should do voluntary work at times (VOLDUTY) (as a measurement of the norm of reciprocity it supposes volunteering as something positive and as a burden). Finally, the readiness to act against injustice (PROTEST) can be considered as a relevant civic norm.

Table 4.2 Social capital indicators: Brief description and percentage positive scores of the Dutch population aged 16 and over [a]

Networks:

NGHVISIT	Has visited or has been visited by neighbours in the last 7 days	39
NGHILL	Would call on their neighbours to do the shopping in the event of illness	64
NGHHELP	Thinks that people in the neighbourhood would definitely help a neighbour without a car to transport nearly purchased furniture	33
NGHPROT	Thinks that people in the neighbourhood would definitely join a protest initiated by some of them to stop local government from realizing a plan that is bad for the neighbourhood	31

Participation:

LEISURE	Is a member or a volunteer of a sports, hobby, cultural or women's organization	45
RELIGION	Is churchgoing, joins religious activities at least once a month or is a volunteer of a church or philosophical organization	28
VOLUNT	Does voluntary work at least one hour a week on an average	29
VOLSERV	Is a volunteer of an organization for children, a school, care or social welfare	20
VOLINTER	Is a volunteer of a union, neighbourhood council, action committee, a political, environmental or idealistic organization	20
COLACT	Has joined a collective action for a local or (inter) national issue in the past 2 years	35

Involvement:

POLTALK	Frequently talks about politics with friends	72
POLREAD	Regularly reads about politics in the country in newspapers	38
LOCREAD	Almost always reads local news in the newspaper	50

Trust:

SOCTRUST	'Do you think that in general most people can be trusted or you cannot be too careful?': most people can be trusted	56
TRUSTNOW	'Nowadays you hardly know who can really be trusted': disagrees	42
POLTRUST	'Members of Parliament pay too much attention to some powerful groups instead of to the general interest': disagree	36

INSTTRUST	'As regards important social and political issues, how reliable are the following institutions as sources of information: churches, scientists, unions, government, parties, business, action groups, television, newspapers?': thinks information of at least 4 institutions is (very) reliable	55
Norms:		
PHILANT	Takes a pro-social position when choosing 1 out of 7 statements about 'other people'	51
VOLDUTY	'Everybody has to do voluntary work at times': agrees	70
PROTEST	'How likely is it you would really try to do something in the event that the Parliament is going to pass an unjust bill?': very/somewhat likely	48

Note: *a*   'Don't know' answers are treated as 0 scores: people who do not know if they participate, do not participate; those who do not know if they trust, do not trust, etc.

Source for table 2 and all following tables: National sample of the 'Civil Society and Volunteering in the Netherlands' survey 1997.

Again, one may dispute almost each and every indicator because of its relevance for social capital—some might be too individualistic, others too formal or too political—or because one might prefer to include them as causes or effects of social capital rather than as part of the construct itself. For several of them one might be able to formulate alternatives. However, compared to what would be possible with other available data sets, this is probably quite a good list to cover the 'networks, trust and norms' aspects of social capital.

Table 4.3 offers a smaller number of indicators for individual resources (education and income) and beliefs and attitudes that indicate ego-security and self-confidence: feeling happy with one's life, optimism about one's future, the belief that one is generally treated fairly, moral security (again disagreement with an anomie item) and a feeling of political efficacy. These indicators will be used in section 4.

Interrelationships: Looking for Dimensions and Groups

The correlations between all 20 indicators are set out in the appendix. The matrix shows that the correlations are weak across the board. To some extent this is no doubt due to the fact that only simple dichotomous indicators have been used, but it also serves as a preliminary warning about making the assumption that there exists

Table 4.3 Indicators for individual resources, ego-security and self-confidence: Brief description and percentage positive scores of the Dutch population aged 16 and over[a]

EDUC	Higher educated: completed at least secondary school education	38
INCOME	Higher income: net family income at least NLG 45, 000 per annum	36
HAPPY	Very content with his or her present life	42
OPTIMISM	Is not worried about his or her own future	60
FAIR	'In general one is treated fairly in our society': agrees	62
MORALSEC	'Change so fast now, that you hardly know what is good and bad': disagrees	46
POLEFFIC	'People like me have no influence on government': disagrees	50

Note: *a* 'Don't know' answers are treated as 0 scores. This also applies to the substantial non-response on the income question (7 per cent 'don't know' and 10 per cent 'don't want to say') after it was checked that this would not change the effects of income.

a strong complex of 'networks, norms and trust'. In this section, we first look for a social capital dimension or for more dimensions if there is no clear evidence for only one, and then for a division in the population between high- and low-level social capital segments in the population. The most persuading finding would be one dimension and two groups.

To get an idea of the dimensionality, some exploratory principal-component analyses are reported in table 4.4.[7] The first unrotated principal component confirms that there is no strong overall social capital dimension. The social trust variables, the participation variables and the political involvement variables do well on this dimension, but the neighbourhood network variables do not. The two-components solution suggests on the one hand a 'civic culture' dimension as it was found by Almond and Verba (1963) long ago, with high loadings for political participation and involvement and trust, and on the other hand a social involvement dimension with high loading for neighbourhood networks and volunteering.[8] The five-components solution reproduces most of the blocks from table 4.2: participation, trust, involvement and networks. The norms do not form one dimension. The fifth dimension looks more like a traditional 'being a good neighbour' dimension.

Table 4.4 Social capital dimensions: Loadings on the first principal component and on 2 and 5 varimax rotated components[a]

	1 component	2 rotated components		5 rotated components				
		1	2	1	2	3	4	5
NGHVISIT	.21	−.10	*.44*	−.06	−.04	.05	*.36*	*.56*
NGHILL	.24	−.12	*.50*	.00	−.04	.02	*.44*	*.52*
NGHHELP	.27	−.10	*.51*	.11	.05	−.03	*.70*	.14
NGHPROT	.18	−.10	.38	.06	.00	.03	*.67*	−.07
LEISURE	*.44*	.32	.30	*.48*	.19	.09	.04	.01
RELIGION	.29	.04	.39	*.44*	−.09	−.08	−.18	*.45*
VOLUNT	*.57*	.32	*.50*	*.72*	.07	.12	.02	.06
VOLSERV	*.46*	.23	*.44*	*.65*	.09	.00	.14	−.06
VOLINTER	*.49*	.26	*.44*	*.50*	−.06	.31	.09	.02
COLACT	*.52*	*.41*	.32	.24	.02	*.61*	.09	.04
POLTALK	*.43*	*.51*	.08	.01	.25	*.55*	−.04	.11
POLREAD	*.45*	*.47*	.14	.04	.14	*.65*	.08	−.03
LOCREAD	.26	.05	.34	.11	−.13	.32	.33	−.01
SOCTRUST	*.46*	*.64*	−.02	.05	*.72*	.14	−.01	.17
TRUSTNOW	*.41*	*.63*	−.10	.03	*.66*	.20	−.09	.05
POLTRUST	.33	*.53*	−.11	.06	*.60*	.11	−.06	−.02
INSTTRUST	.22	.32	−.02	.12	*.53*	−.13	.20	−.16
PHILANT	.36	.23	.28	.17	.17	.08	−.13	*.59*
VOLDUTY	*.41*	.14	*.46*	*.48*	−.01	.05	.03	.29
PROTEST	.37	*.41*	.09	.06	.06	*.60*	−.08	.02
Variance explained	15%	12%	12%	10%	9%	8%	8%	7%

Note: *a* All loadings over .40 are printed in *bold*.

The results of the principal component analyses could be summarized as that there is only a weak overall social capital dimension and some evidence for a pattern of a 'civic culture' and a network dimension.

Our second type of exploratory analysis is the cluster analyses of cases. Different from the 'variable-oriented' component analyses, these analyses offer the data another chance to reveal the social capital connection. By clustering cases we follow a 'diversity-oriented' (Ragin 1987, 2000) approach that, in the case of more than two clusters, may show different configurations of social capital as segments of the population. A number of k-means cluster analyses of all indicators of table 4.2 were carried out in search of a not too unstable segmentation. In this kind of analysis the number of clusters is given and the algorithm tries to find the most homogeneous clusters by minimizing the total sum of squared euclidean distances of cases to their cluster centres (measured in z-scores). As usual, no 'natural' stable partitioning could be found. Except for the two-clusters solution, the five-clusters solution is presented in table 4.5.[9] The table shows for each cluster the percentages with positive scores on the social capital indicators, as well as the percentages of respondents in each cluster in the entire population and in some categories.

Table 4.5 Social capital clusters: Positive scores on the social capital indicators (in per cent) and the proportion of the population in each cluster

	(all)	2 clusters		5 clusters				
		1	2	1	2	3	4	5
NGHVISIT	(40)	33	48	22	28	74	25	50
NGHILL	(64)	58	73	45	64	93	47	78
NGHHELP	(33)	28	40	13	21	68	15	52
NGHPROT	(31)	25	39	17	25	54	19	42
LEISURE	(46)	29	68	18	39	53	46	74
RELIGION	(27)	20	37	20	23	34	14	48
VOLUNT	(29)	10	53	12	13	27	17	75
VOLSERV	(20)	8	36	9	8	22	14	49
VOLINTER	(20)	8	35	5	12	20	8	54
COLACT	(35)	16	59	9	46	23	23	76
POLTALK	(72)	59	90	33	90	61	88	92
POLREAD	(38)	21	59	5	71	13	33	73
LOCREAD	(51)	42	62	22	80	59	32	67
SOCTRUST	(56)	38	79	21	31	39	94	86
TRUSTNOW	(43)	26	64	13	18	19	81	72
POLTRUST	(35)	24	51	16	18	21	62	55
INSTTRUST	(55)	47	66	42	45	45	74	67
PHILANT	(52)	39	70	29	31	66	56	76
VOLDUTY	(70)	57	87	51	68	80	60	92
PROTEST	(48)	32	69	25	66	28	50	75
% of the population		56	44	21	17	19	23	20
% of women		58	42	22	14	23	22	18
% of people aged 45 and over		56	44	19	21	22	14	25
% of the higher educated		45	55	11	16	10	36	27
% of higher income groups		42	58	12	17	15	25	31

The division of the population in two clusters strongly distinguishes on volunteering (VOLUNT: 10 per cent in the 'low on social capital cluster' and 53 per cent in the 'high on social capital cluster'), participation in collective action (16 per cent and 59 per cent), the indicators for political involvement and norms, and, not the least important, on both social trust variables (SOCTRUST 38 per cent and 79 per cent; TRUSTNOW 26 per cent and 64 per cent). The neighbourhood networks measurements appear to be of minor significance. Not unexpectedly, the higher educated and the better-off are over-represented in the 'high on social capital' cluster.

In the five-clusters solution, the first cluster is low on social capital according to all indicators, while the fifth according to the same indicators must have a large amount of social capital. This cluster accommodates the citizens that the allies of civil society and friends of social capital like: well integrated, highly involved, trustful and nevertheless ready to protest.

The citizens in the fourth cluster are at least as trusting as the citizens in the fifth, but they are not very involved in civil society (even volunteering less than the average citizen) and they are less integrated in neighbourhood networks. The second and third clusters show similar levels of trust below the average, but they differ as regards the network and involvement variables. The second cluster is strongly involved in politics and shows above-average levels of readiness to protest and actual participation in collective action (but not in volunteering!); the third cluster is most integrated in the neighbourhood networks, shows average levels of social involvement, but is not very much interested in politics.

The findings as regards trust are interesting. All trust variables vary in the same way. The political and institutional trust variables show more moderate variations, but the differences correspond with the ones of social trust (we do not get something like high horizontal trust clusters with and without vertical trust). The fourth and fifth clusters are high on all trust variables, but in the fourth cluster high trust is combined with passivity, and in the fifth cluster with participation. The second cluster is much lower on trust, but political involvement is not much less. It is probably more often inspired by negative attitudes towards the political system.

Maybe somewhat surprisingly, the higher incomes are most strongly over-represented in the fifth (trusting and active) cluster, and the higher educated most in the (trusting and passive) fourth cluster. People in the 45-plus age group are strongly under-represented in this cluster.

The cluster analyses show segmentation of the population that at first glance confirm the expectations of a social capital syndrome. A division of the population in two groups shows a consistent difference of low versus high scores; a division in five groups shows a greater overall difference between an extremely low scoring group and an extremely high scoring group. The groups that are in-between do not show different levels of social capital, but clearly different patterns: low to average trust with political involvement, low to average trust with strong networks and high trust with low activity. Here the doubts really begin: the network indicators turn out to be rather unimportant in the two-clusters division, and in the five-clusters solution, the cluster with the highest network scores has only moderate scores on social trust and other indicators.

For both ways of searching for social capital complex(es) used in this section, social trust, participation and political involvement appear to be much more important than the network variables. The network variables show low loadings on a common social capital component, and they discriminate weakly in a simple split between a low and a high social capital component. If we construct more dimensions or clusters, the network variables go their own way. The indicators for political and institutional trust and the norms neither show consistently strong relationships with the other social capital indicators. As regards political and institutional trust, this supports earlier findings that this sort of trust should not be seen as an element of social capital (Putnam 1995, Newton 1999). As regards the norms, the problem might well be that the available measurements are too distant from what we should have measured and too close to specific other measurements included (volduty to actual volunteering indicators, protest to actual political activity). The question remains as to whether the relationships between (a selection of) social capital indicators is empirically distinctive enough to speak about the social capital of individuals.

The Explanation of Participation and Trust

In this section we start from another perspective and take two core social capital indicators as dependent variables. How important are the other social capital variables compared to the individual resources and indices of ego-security and self-confidence mentioned in table 4.3? Tables 4.6 and 4.7 give four explanations: by the other social capital indicators (except indicators of the same sort), by the individual resources, by ego-security and self-confidence, and by all three groups together. Presented are adjusted odds-ratios. A coefficient equal to 1 means there is no effect; values above 1 mean positive effects and values below 1 mean negative effects.

Table 4.6 shows the results for volunteering. Together, the 13 social capital indicators do explain volunteering better than resources or personal traits. However, the results are not impressive. Several indicators

Table 4.6 Determinants of volunteering
(VOLUNT); adjusted odds-ratios[a]

	Social capital[b]	Resources	Personal traits	All indicators
NGHVISIT	1.1			1.2
NGHILL	1.3*			1.3*
NGHHELP	1.3*			1.3*
NGHPROT	1.1			1.1
POLTALK	1.2			1.2
POLREAD	1.4***			1.4**
LOCREAD	1.3*			1.3*
SOCTRUST	1.4**			1.3**
TRUSTNOW	1.2			1.1
POLTRUST	1.2*			1.2
INSTTRUST	1.1			1.1
PHILANT	1.6***			1.6***
PROTEST	1.3**			1.3**
EDUC		1.2*		1.0
INCOME		1.4***		1.1
HAPPY			0.9	0.8*
OPTIMISM			1.4***	1.3**
FAIR			1.2	1.0
MORALSEC			1.4**	1.2*
POLEFFIC			1.4***	1.1
Variance explained (Nagelkerke R^2)	9%	1%	3%	10%

Notes: *a* Odds-ratios are adjusted for the effects of the other indicators in the column. A coefficient above 1 means a positive effect of the indicator on volunteering, a coefficient below 1 means a negative effect. Significance: *** p<.001, ** p<0.01 and * p<.05 (one-tailed).

b All indicators except the other participation indicators and VOLDUTY (the norm that everybody should volunteer).

have no significant impact, and several single indicators for individual resources and personal traits do a better job.

The explanations of social trust in table 4.7 tells another story. The two simple indicators for individual resources, education and income are as important as the longer list of social capital indicators. The importance of education is in accordance with a good deal of research (Putnam 1995: 667; Dekker and Van den Broek 1998; Newton 1999).

Table 4.7 Determinants of social trust (SOCTRUST); adjusted odds-ratios[a]

	Social capital[b]	Resources	Personal traits	All indicators
NGHVISIT	0.9			1.1
NGHILL	1.1			1.2*
NGHHELP	1.1			1.1
NGHPROT	0.9			0.9
LEISURE	1.3**			1.1
RELIGION	0.7**			0.8*
VOLUNT	1.4**			1.3*
VOLSERV	1.1			1.1
VOLINTER	1.1			1.0
COLACT	1.3*			1.1
POLTALK	1.9***			1.5***
POLREAD	1.4***			1.1
LOCREAD	0.9			0.9
PHILANT	1.8***			1.7***
VOLDUTY	1.0			1.0
PROTEST	1.1			0.9
EDUC		2.9***		2.0***
INCOME		1.9***		1.4***
HAPPY			1.3**	1.2*
OPTIMISM			1.1	1.2
FAIR			1.8***	1.6***
MORALSEC			2.4***	1.9***
POLEFFIC			2.1***	1.6***
Variance explained (Nagelkerke R^2)	12%	12%	18%	26%

Notes: *a* Odds-ratios are adjusted for the effects of the other indicators in the column. A coefficient above 1 means a positive effect of the indicator on trust, a coefficient below 1 means a negative effect. Significance: *** p<.001, ** p<0.01 and * p<.05 (one-tailed; the effect of 'religion' is contrary to what is expected).

  b All indicators from table 4.2 except the other trust-indicators.

For the time being, however, empirical findings that place associational factors in the shadow of the impact of individual resources do not appear to have much influence on the associational discourse about social capital.

The indicator for optimism does not have much impact,[10] but the other ego-security and self-confidence indicators turn out to be quite important. Together they give the best statistical explanation of social trust. Also, in combination with the other indicators, they and the individual resources clearly outstrip the social capital indicators.

Social Capital or Strong Personalities?

Apart from the rehabilitation of traditional individual resources, table 4.7 suggests an alternative for the social approach of social trust: maybe we should look more at personality indicators than at involvement and network indicators. What have been roughly labelled here as indicators of ego-security and self-confidence may actually best be considered as manifestations of personality strength. The concept of personality strength has roots in the research tradition of opinion leadership. In this tradition, it was recently described by Scheufele and Shah (2000: 109) as 'a feature of individuals, a reflection of their confidence in leadership roles, their aptitude at shaping others' opinions, and their self-perceived impact on social and political outcomes'. The personality-strength scale used by Noelle–Neumann (1999) and Weiman (1994: 255 ff.) includes items such as 'I usually count on being successful in everything I do', 'I'm rarely unsure about how I should behave', 'I like to assume responsibility' and 'I enjoy convincing others of my opinion'. 'High personality-strength people' rate higher on reading books, participating in sports, being with friends (Weiman 1994: 267) and on volunteering (Noelle-Neumann 1999) than 'low personality-strength people'. Scheufele and Shah (2000) measure personality strength with respondents' perceptions of self-confidence and opinion leadership in their community,[11] and they find relatively strong relationships between personality strength, life satisfaction, civic engagement and social trust.

'Personality strength' probably sounds strange to those involved in the progressive social capital discourse about the benefits of horizontal trust and democratic participation. These are evidently words from a completely different discourse about individuals and their inequality, and about personal leadership. Although research in this

104   paul dekker

field could contribute to the adjustment of some naive beliefs in the miracles of civic community that are held within the social capital school, it seems unlikely that a psychology of differences would get a hearty welcome. It is already hard enough to get the attention of this school for simpler persistent differences such as the ones of education, social-economic status or social class.

Conclusion

The results of our explorations strongly support scepticism about the very broadly inclusive definitions of social capital (Newton 1999), at least as observed at the individual level. Correlations between indicators were moderate across-the-board, and in particular the network variables did not fit in very well. Of course, the dichotomous indicators were rough measures and they restricted the possible strength of relationships from the very start. As regards the 'networks', our operationalization in neighbourhood integration was a limited and biased one. However, one may doubt if general surveys can offer much better indicators. If not, the question arises whether it makes much sense to use the concept of social capital in the analysis of this kind of data—or the other way around; whether it makes much sense to use 'uncontextualized' general social survey data to study social capital if that should be more than a 'stand-in for the old political culture variables' (Foley and Edwards 1999: 162).[12] The tendency to upgrade the illustrious social trust question to be representative of real social capital in survey research (Uslaner 2000) is definitely a too-easy escape. The preceding sections suggest that if social trust is important for social capital, it is not because it is social capital, but because *it is typical for the kind of person that might contribute to the formation of social capital in many circumstances*.

The idea attributed to survey-research dependent political scientists, that social capital is 'an individual attribute that constitutes a fully portable resource, the value of which does not fluctuate as the individual moves in and out of numerous social contexts' (Foley and Edwards 1999: 149) not only contradicts the original idea of social capital that 'is not completely fungible but may be specific to certain activities. A given form of social capital that is valuable in facilitating certain actions may be useless or even harmful for others' (Coleman 1988: 98). As the foregoing exercises have shown, the idea as such also has a weak empirical foundation.

Although there is reason to be sceptical about the existence of a social capital syndrome of 'networks, trust and norms', we should not be too quick to skip the idea. Overall relationships might be quite misleading. Neutral aggregates can mask interesting heterogeneous populations (Ragin 2000: 88 ff). As regards socio-political correlations, for instance, we know of well-documented opposite relationships: there are people who are politically active because of trust in others (Almond and Verba 1963), there are people who are politically active because they distrust their neighbours (Crenson 1983), there are people who do nothing if they believe that others are also doing nothing and there are people who do something precisely because no-one is doing anything; for some people involvement in voluntary organizations and voluntary work are stepping stones towards politics (Verba et al. 1995), while for others it offers an opportunity of doing something for the community without getting involved in politics (Eliasoph 1998). If the groups with their opposing logic hold each other in balance, there is no overall statistical relationship between social and political trust and involvement indicators.

Yet these relationships are anything but irrelevant. Because some children of alcoholics later take to drink themselves while others turn teetotal, it does not follow that the alcohol use of the parents evidently had no impact.[13] Strong opposite correlations in sub-populations could underlie the generally weak correlations between indicators for social capital. Strong complexes of 'networks, trust and norms' might exist in specific groups that are not easily discovered by some very simple cluster analyses as presented in section 4. However, even these analyses did reveal segments that combine high levels of social trust with activity and segments that combine the same high levels of trust with passivity. This might suggest a way to continue social capital research with general social surveys. We should probably not try to get any closer to real people in real networks with real assets by loading questionnaires for the general public with a large numbers of questions on concrete networks and interactions. The minor contribution of survey-research should be sought for discovering groups and personality types that are in general more or less inclined to contribute to or to be dependent upon ('praiseworthy') social capital. If it were possible to identify limited numbers of groups or types or of patterns ('mechanisms', 'configurations') in how people tend to relate varieties of social trust and

Appendix Pearson correlation coefficients between the social capital indicators that are statistically significant (p<0.01, one-tailed with in one case a negative relationship)

	NGHVISIT	NGHILL	NGHHELP	NGHPROT	LEISURE	RELIGION	VOLUNT	VOLSERV	VOLINTER	COLACT	POLTALK	POLREAD	LOCREAD	SOCTRUST	TRUSTNOW	POLTRUST	INSTTRUST	PHILANT	VOLDUTY
NGHVISIT																			
NGHILL	.24																		
NGHHELP	.18	.23																	
NGHPROT	.10	.13	.27																
LEISURE	.05	.07	.07																
RELIGION	.06	.07	.06		.12														
VOLUNT	.06	.09	.08	.08	.25	.23													
VOLSERV	.07	.07	.10		.13	.13	.35												
VOLINTER	.06	.08	.10	.06	.17	.11	.35	.20											
COLACT	.09		.08		.16	.06	.28	.20	.25										
POLTALK					.12		.10	.10	.11	.20									
POLREAD			.06		.13		.14	.13	.13	.22	.28								
LOCREAD	.08	.11	.13	.09	.06		.08	.09	.11	.10	.05	.19							
SOCTRUST					.13		.14	.09	.09	.13	.20	.15	.19						
TRUSTNOW					.14		.11	.06	.08	.15	.15	.18		.43					
POLTRUST				-.06	.10			.09	.05	.05	.17	.12		.25	.24				
INSTTRUST			.05		.07			.08			.08	.05		.19	.11	.17			
PHILANT	.09	.07	.06	.06	.11	.17	.14	.11	.11	.11	.10	.07	.10	.16	.11	.05			
VOLDUTY	.08	.14	.10		.15	.18	.24	.18	.20	.11	.07	.09	.10	.08	.11	.05	.08	.14	
PROTEST					.10	.11	.11	.08	.12	.28	.19	.19	.19	.10	.12	.11	.28	.05	.08

social ties to their willingness to contribute to the common good, this would probably be of great help for more contextualized social capital research by other means.

Notes

1. Social and Cultural Planning Office, Government of the Netherlands, The Hague. I want to acknowledge helpful comments of the participants of the social capital workshop in Solstrand (Norway, May 2000) on a preparatory paper, and the hospitality and comments of my temporary colleagues in the Graduate School of Management at the University of Technology of Sydney at Kuring-Gai (Australia, November 2000), where I rewrote the paper.
2. As the topic of this chapter is an empirical and not a theoretical one, I do not want to deal here extensively with conceptual matters. For the differences between Coleman and Putnam, see the introduction to this volume. For a general comparison of their, and other, concepts and uses of social capital, see also Winter (2000) (brief and lucid) and Lin (1999) (rigorous and well-documented with empirical sociological research).
3. One more Putnam (1995: 664–65) quote: 'By "social capital", I mean features of social life—networks, norms, and trust—that enable participants to act together more effectively to pursue shared objectives. Whether or not their shared goals are praiseworthy is, of course, entirely another matter. ... Who benefits from these connections, norms, and trust—the individual, the wider community or some faction within the community—must be determined empirically, not definitionally. Sorting out the multiple effects of different forms of social capital is clearly a crucial task, although not one that I can address here. For present purposes, I am concerned with forms of social capital that, generally speaking, serve civic ends.'
4. Of course, norms are not values (which can be distinguished as being less concrete and less focussed on behaviour, and more related to final goals) and no attitudes (which are less explicit and prescriptive and of more psychological than sociological interest), and a set of norms and values is less than a culture, but in this chapter these words are used interchangeable. Using survey questions, the distinction is highly theoretical anyway.
5. For measurements see the website of the Social Capital Initiative at the World Bank (*http://www.worldbank.org/poverty/scapital/SChowmeas1.htm*) and the references at the end of the chapter, in particular Putnam (1993,

1995, 2000), Johnston and Jowell (1999), Winter (2000), Wollebæk and Selle (2000), and Onyx and Bullen (2001).

6. In general, 'Don't knows' count as a lack of social capital. The inclusion of these 'missing values' keeps the numbers larger, but also introduces noise. On the other hand, in the case of the trust question, excluding the roughly 10 per cent of respondents who avoid choosing between 'most people can be trusted' and 'you can't be too careful' by answering 'don't know' is also problematic.

7. Other analyses have been probed, but had similar results and for that reason the results of the technically simplest and easiest interpretable orthogonal rotations are presented.

8. Here as well as in other analyses, the 'reciprocity measure' as regards voluntary work (VOLDUTY) is loading on the dimension on which actual voluntary work indicators load. It is a pity that a more independent measurement of reciprocity is not available.

9. Several analyses were carried out, but there were no compelling arguments to prefer one number of clusters above the other. The reason to present the two-clusters solution is obvious: it simply draws a line between people with a lot and people with little social capital. The reason to present the five-clusters division is that the two clusters with the highest trust scores were very similar to the highest scoring ones in a four-clusters solution, the cluster with overall the lowest social capital scores were also quite similar. In non-hierarchical clustering, similarity between single clusters of different analyses indicates robustness and supports the idea of their existence in reality. The other two clusters of the five-clusters solution more or less split up the fourth cluster of the four-clusters solution, and show easier interpretable profiles.

10. This result differs from the one of Uslaner (2000), who finds that in America optimism is an important correlate of trust.

11. 'I have more self-confidence than most of my friends', 'I like to be considered a leader', 'I am the kind of person who knows what I want to accomplish in life and how to achieve it' and 'I am influential in my neighbourhood'.

12. The same warning in a policy frame of reference: 'Divorced from its roots in individual interactions and networking, social capital becomes merely another trendy term to employ or deploy in the broad context of improving or building social integration and solidarity.' (Lin 1999: 33).

13. The question then is under what conditions which understandable reaction occurs. The search for general axioms in human behaviour is then replaced by a search for 'mechanisms', as described by Jon Elster (1993, 1998): 'Roughly speaking, mechanisms are frequently occurring and easily recognizable causal patterns that are triggered under generally unknown conditions or with indeterminate consequences. They allow us to explain but not to predict.' (Elster 1998: 45).

References

Almond, G.A., and Verba, S. 1963. *The Civic Culture*. Princeton: Princeton University Press (reprinted by Sage, Newbury Park 1989).

Brehm, J., and Rahn, W. 1997. 'Individual-level evidence for the causes and consequences of social capital'. *American Journal of Political Science* 41, 3: pp. 999–1023.

Coleman, J.S. 1988. 'Social capital and the creation of human capital'. *American Journal of Sociology* 94: pp. 95–120.

Crenson, M.A. 1983. *Neighbourhood Politics*. Cambridge, Massachusetts: Harvard University Press.

De Hart, J., and Dekker, P. 2003. 'A tale of two cities: Local patterns of social capital and political integration and involvement', in M. Hooghe and D. Stolle (eds.), *Generating Social Capital: Civil Society and Institutions in Comparative Perspective*. New York: Palgrave.

Dekker, P. and Van Den Broek, A. 1998. 'Civil society in comparative perspective'. *Voluntas* 9,1: pp. 11–38.

Eliasoph, N. 1998. *Avoiding Politics*. Cambridge, U.K.: Cambridge University Press.

Elster, J. 1993. *Political Psychology*. Cambridge, U.K.: Cambridge University Press.

Elster, J. 1998. 'A plea for mechanisms', in P. Hedstrøm and R. Swedberg (eds.), *Social Mechanisms*. Cambridge, UK: Cambridge University Press.

Foley, M.W., and Edwards, B. 1999. 'Is it time to disinvest in social capital?'. *Journal of Public Policy* 19, 2: pp. 141–73.

Johnston, M., and Jowell, R. 1999. 'Social capital and the social fabric', in R. Jowell et al. (eds.), *British Social Attitudes: The 16th report*. Aldershot: Ashgate.

Lin, N. 1999. 'Building a network theory of social capital'. *Connections* 22, 1: pp. 8–51.

Newton, K. 1999. 'Social capital and democracy in modern Europe', in J.W. Van Deth et al. (eds.), *Social Capital and European Democracy*. London: Routledge, pp. 3–24.

Noelle-Neumann, E. 1999. 'Methoden und Meprobleme', in E. Kistler, H. H. Noll and E. Priller (eds.), *Perspektiven Gesellschaftlichen Zusammenhalts*. Berlin: Edition Sigma, pp. 441–54.

Onyx, J. and Bullen, P. 2001. 'The different faces of Social Capital in NSW Australia', in P. Dekker and E.M. Uslaner (eds.), *Social Capital and Participation in Everyday Life*. London: Routledge.

Putnam, R.D. (with R. Leonardi and R.Y. Nanetti). 1993. *Making Democracy Work*. Princeton: Princeton University Press.

Putnam, R.D. 1995. 'Tuning in, tuning out'. *PS: Political Science and Politics* 28, 4: pp. 664–83.

Putnam, R.D. 2000. *Bowling Alone: The Collapse and Revival of American Community*. New York: Simon & Schuster.

Ragin, C.C. 1987. *The Comparative Method*. Berkeley: University of California Press.

Ragin, C.C. 2000. *Fuzzy-set Social Science*. Chicago: University of Chicago Press.

Scheufele, D.A., and Shah, D.V. 2000. 'Personality Strength and Social Capital'. *Communication Research* 27, 2: pp. 107–31.

Uslaner, E.M. 2002. *The Moral Foundations of Trust*. Cambridge: Cambridge University Press.

Verba, S., Lehman Schlozman, K., and Brady, H.E. 1995. *Voice and Equality*. Cambridge, Massachusett: Harvard University Press.

Weimann, G. 1994. *The Influentials*. Albany: State University of New York Press.

Winter, I. 2000. 'Major Themes and Debates in the Social Capital literature', in I. Winter (ed.), *Social Capital and Public Policy in Australia*. Melbourne: Australian Institute of Family Studies.

Wollebæk, D., and Selle, P. 2000. 'Participation in Voluntary Associations and the Formation of Social Capital'. Paper presented at the ARNOVA (The Association for Research on Nonprofit Organizations and Voluntary Action) Conference, New Orleans, 16–18 November 2000.

II
Empirical Approaches

5

Social Capital and Institutional Legitimacy:
The Corleone Connection

Bo Rothstein[1]

'I Believe in America'

In the year 2000 the National Society of Film Critics, consisting of 57 leading film critics from the United States, issued a list of what they considered to be the most important movies produced during the 20th century. As number one on their list they placed Francis Ford Coppola's *The Godfather* (above landmarks such as *Citizen Kane*, *Casablanca, Schindler's List* and *Gone with the Wind*). Among the many reasons for their choice, one must surely be that *The Godfather* illustrates something very important about our civilization. It shows, maybe, what human existence has been like during the past century; it examines family relations, immigration and multiculturalism, patriarchy, and the eternal questions about good and evil. There are countless ways in which *The Godfather* can be analyzed. But for me, *The Godfather* is above all a story about trust and distrust.

Trust, says Piotr Sztompka, can be defined as 'a bet on the future contingent actions of others' (Sztompka 1998: 20). When we put our trust in an individual or an institution, we are not completely convinced about what will happen (that would be 'blind faith', which is different from trust). Even if we do not calculate the risks every time we decide whether or not to trust, absolute certainty would make a concept such as trust unnecessary. The first scene in *The Godfather* is about such a bet on the future and, moreover, one that has failed miserably. The very first sentence uttered in this movie (in halting English, the voice breaking) is the following: 'I believe in America'. The person who says this is Mr Bonasera, an undertaker of Italian descent. And the person who he says this to is Mr Corleone, also known as Don Corleone—The Godfather. The scene takes place in the latter's study on the day of his daughter's wedding. The story Bonasera relates is truly heartbreaking. His own beloved daughter has been attacked by two 'all-American' boys who 'tried to take advantage of her'. When she, according to her father, in desperation 'defended her honor,' the two young men beat her up 'like an animal', and so she has ended up in the hospital with serious wounds. Her wounds are so bad that she, the light of her poor father's life, 'will never be beautiful again'.

As a true believer in America, Bonasera tells the Don, he had gone to the police. And the police apparently did their job, because the two thugs were produced before the Court. But here, things started to go awry. Probably because the two WASP boys' families were 'well-connected', the judge decided to give them only a suspended sentence. To Bonasera's astonishment 'they go free the very same day'. The result is that Bonasera's trust in the US legal system instantly breaks down as the two perpetrators leave the Court smiling and laughing at him. Not only is his sense of justice violated, he also loses face before the two people who ruined his daughter's (and, by extension, his own) life. And so he now sits before the Don (whose wife happens to be the victim's real Godmother) and asks for *justice*. Just as back in the 'old country', the government institutions and the legal system of America could not be trusted to act according to the basic principles of justice in a situation like this. Instead, in order to obtain some sort of justice, Bonasera is compelled to turn to 'private protection' in the form of his old friend, the local Mafia boss.

Hearing the story, the Don becomes irritated. First, he is annoyed because his old friend Bonasera has for a long time avoided his friendship. Apparently this is for good reason; Bonasera wanted to stay out of trouble. In the new country, his family and his business seemed to have no need for the type of service the Don could provide. Second, he mocks Bonasera's faith in the police and the courts that were supposed to protect him. How on earth could he believe that the courts and the police would act impartially in a case between an Italian immigrant girl and two boys from old WASP families? As, to a large extent, his criminal organization is based on bribing judges, police officers and politicians, Corleone finds Bonasera's trust in these institutions ridiculously naive. The Godfather seems to argue that because Bonasera decided to place his bet on the wrong horse(s), he now has to pay the price.

But the two men are, after all, old friends, and so Corleone asks what Bonasera wants him to do. To his surprise, Bonasera wants him to kill the boys who harmed his daughter, and says he is prepared to pay whatever the Don asks for such a service. It is at this moment in the scene that one can really feel the tension rise. The Don, hearing this in front of his son and his *consiligieri*, is truly offended by Bonasera's request. In no way is he, in his own eyes, a man who can be paid to kill, as though he were simply a hired gun. Moreover, as he tells Bonasera, that would not be justice; his daughter is alive. 'Then make them suffer,' begs the poor undertaker. This, according to the Don, is a more reasonable request; but still he feels insulted. He does not want any money from Bonasera for punishing the two young perpetrators; he wants something else, namely, loyalty, respect and, most of all, subservience. If, he says, Bonasera had shown him friendship and respect earlier, the two thugs would already have been punished. But, he says, Bonasera hasn't treated him with respect, hasn't shown friendship and even forgets to call him 'Don'. At this point, Bonasera suddenly seems to remember the customs from the old country—the tone of his voice changes, he kisses the Don's hand and asks him to be his friend. And so, the scene ends with The Godfather assuring Bonasera that he will take care of the problem in a suitable manner and that Bonasera should forget about the money and instead think of this service as an act of friendship. And then he adds the central words— 'and one day, and that day might never come, I may come asking you for a favour'.

This famous scene illustrates the relationship between social capital, trust and the legitimacy of political institutions. Poor Mr Bonasera had tried to adjust his life to what he thought would be the rules of the game in the United States as compared to those in southern Italy. He had, moreover, tried to move out from the community of 'unsocial capital' that characterized the social relations in the old country by removing himself from the circles of the Corleone family. However, according to his sense of justice, the political institutions in the new country let him down despite what had been implicitly promised. Even if it is not directly stated in the scene, it seems reasonable to believe that the most obvious betrayal of trust has been the broken promise of *impartiality in the principle of rule of law*. Obviously, Bonasera thought that the fact that he and his daughter were Southern-European Catholic immigrants and that the defendants were from an old white Anglo-Saxon Protestant community would be of no importance to the court. He falsely presumed that the principle of equality before the law, as stated in the constitution, would be implemented. But, as is well known, public policies can take one form on paper, and then can look quite different once they are put into practice. The scene also illustrates the demand and supply sides of trust. If the judicial system fails to deliver, the demand for some trustworthy protective institution will not just disappear. Instead, Bonasera turns to a 'private institution' in his search for a trustworthy supply of justice.

'What,' one may ask, 'does this Hollywood image of the relationship between social capital and the political institutions in the world of organized crime in the 1950s have to do with our contemporary problems'? 'A lot,' is my answer, and I will illustrate this with a more recent, real-life event from my homecity of Göteborg, Sweden. In November 1998, 63 young people died (and at least as many were seriously wounded) in a fire at a discotheque. This was one of the worst human catastrophes in Sweden since World War II, and it made headlines all over the world. The victims of this horrible tragedy were mostly, though not all, young people from immigrant families living in the northern parts of Göteborg. During the past 15 years, many public housing areas in the larger cities in Sweden have become heavily dominated by non-European immigrants.

One of the main reasons why so many died was because of the fire's explosive nature. Very soon, the police and the media suspected that the fire was not accidental but was instead a case of arson. Speculations about who was guilty were rampant, and the city was soon full of strange rumors. Many suspected that the fire had been started by anti-immigrant groups or individuals. After about a year of police investigations, four young men from immigrant backgrounds were arrested and, in May 2000, were convicted of arson. The reason these young men gave for setting the place on fire was that their friends, who had organized the disco, had demanded that they pay the entrance fee; this, in their eyes, was a sign of disrespect.

What is interesting in this case, from our perspective, is that media reports of the trial indicated that a sizeable group of young people living in the immigrant areas—who had been to the disco and had lost many of their friends in the fire—knew who the guilty persons were, but had refrained from telling the police. Thus, the situation was very special: even though a lot of their friends had died or been seriously hurt in the fire, and even though they knew who had caused the fire, these young people felt that going to the police was not an option. The victims who had survived and the families of those who had perished in the flames were suffering from not knowing what or who had caused the fire. But only after the police had issued a sizeable reward did one young person come forward with the information that made it possible for the police to solve the case. The question is, what can explain such apparently irrational behaviour among those who were withholding the necessary information?

One clue appears in an op-ed article that was published in a leading Göteborg newspaper about three weeks before the arrest of the four young men. A former social worker with extensive experience from Göteborg's northern suburbs described the situation in an interesting way. She argued that the situation had deteriorated into one in which young people in these neighborhoods were convinced that during the fire, 'the police were standing by laughing while their friends were dying around them'. Anyone who had seen the media coverage of the fire (and who knows anything about the Swedish police) will know that this could not be true. However, the social worker stated that, as a consequence of this deep mistrust of public institutions, 'the rule of law is in a bad situation in Sweden's so-called "exposed neighbourhoods". The alternative of the rule of law, to report to the police, to testify before the court about what you have seen, heard or been part of, and to let the court take care of administrating justice, is gradually becoming a less realistic alternative.' Instead, one does nothing, or one chooses to 'take the matter into one's own hands, to make one's own justice'.

However, this option is open only to those who have enough angry and well-armed brothers or cousins or uncles to take on the task. According to this well-informed source, young people in these areas are absolutely convinced that they are being discriminated against because of their immigrant background and, therefore, the idea of going to the authorities is not a relevant option in their minds. (Helena Gustafsson, *Göteborgsposten*, 18 January 2000).

Obviously, genuine distrust in the impartiality and fairness of government institutions such as the police and the courts is not confined to the third world, nor to the former communist countries or to the Hollywood image of the Italian Mafia in 1950s New York. It happens also in 'high trust' and 'high social capital' contemporary Sweden (Stolle this volume; Rothstein 2001). As many have argued, we need to understand the causal mechanisms between interpersonal trust, collective action, civil society and trust in government institutions (Levi 1998; Rothstein 2000). Several questions are of importance in this discussion. For example, what different types of interpersonal trust exist? How do different types of interpersonal trust relate to different types of political institutions? Can political institutions be arranged so as to increase their legitimacy? As Ronald Inglehart has argued, 'it seems likely that democratic institutions are conducive to interpersonal social trust, as well as trust being conducive to democracy' (Inglehart 1999: 104). The difficulty in this discussion is, according to Inglehart, how to specify the causal connection(s) between these variables.

The logic presented in the scene from The Godfather and in the real-life situation of the Göteborg tragedy exemplifies what Russell Hardin has explained as the coordination problem (Hardin 1995). Universal norms, such as the impartiality of the legal system, and principles such as equality before the law and the rule of law, are always weak. This is because, from a self-interested rationalistic perspective, there is no special interest that has any immediate reason to defend them. This political weakness of universal norms and institutions is simple: they are by definition not intended to serve any special interest, but instead 'the common' or 'the public' interest. Thus, organizing a defense of such a common or public interest is a genuine collective action problem, and many can be expected to adopt a 'free-riding' strategy. Universal norms are therefore constantly under pressure from groups arguing that they are not really universal, either in their very construction or, more likely, in the way they are being implemented. Instead, the ruling class, the patriarchal network, the dominant religious and/or ethnic group, etc., mask what is only their raw self-interest behind the shining principles of universalism and impartiality.

According to Hardin, political entrepreneurs are likely to exploit such a situation by coordinating the prescribed disadvantaged group behind an attack on such universal norms and institutions. The potential members of such a group usually have only a limited understanding of the actual workings of the universal political norms and institutions, especially of the implementation process. Therefore, Hardin argues, coordination to attack and destroy universal political institutions is much easier to accomplish than the standard 'problem of collective action' literature tells us. The political entrepreneurs can easily create a 'one for all' logic, touting the benefits from the future 'particularistic' institutions, which will attend to the special needs of the sometimes 'imagined' group(s), and which will be much greater than what may come from defending existing universal institutions. The lack of accurate information readily available to disadvantaged groups, the difficulty of organizing a defense of universal norms and the existence of highly publicized cases in which the authorities have broken universal norms can combine to create a much larger following than the standard theory of collective action suggests. In recent work in political philosophy, this goes under the name of 'the politics of difference', where it is argued that, in practice, universalism and impartiality are impossible ideals that can never be accomplished in practice (Young 1990). Instead, each group should be governed under its own special norms and institutions.[2] Other political philosophers, Brian Barry for example argue that justice and impartiality go hand in hand (Barry 1995). Hardin, who has stated the problem so eloquently, is silent on the empirical question of whether impartiality is possible in cases such as the ones described above.

But is Trust in Government Institutions a Good Thing?

It is often taken for granted, not least in the Scandinavian context, that trust in government institutions is normatively a good thing, necessary for a healthy and well-functioning democracy. Against this starting point, Russell Hardin has argued that liberal democracy is, to a large extent, constructed on the basis that governments should not be trusted, nor can they be. The whole set of liberal constitutional ideas such as 'checks and balances', judicial review, Bills of Rights, etc., rest on the idea that we ought not to trust governments, even if they are democratically elected. A liberal constitution rests to a large extent on the assumption that unchecked political power will lead to abuse of that power. Moreover, Hardin argues that it is in fact impossible to trust an entity such as a government, because those governed cannot have enough information to monitor such a large organization. We can only trust persons we know reasonably well, because only then can we have collected the necessary amount of information to (en)trust them with something important.

Hardin comes to this conclusion working from a rational choice theory of human behaviour. He argues that we trust a person because we have reason to expect that this person has an interest in acting in our own interest on the specific matter on which we decide to trust him/her. 'To say that I trust you means I have reason to expect you to act, for your own reasons, as my agent' (Hardin 1999: 26, emphasis in original). Hardin calls this 'encapsulated trust' and it is by definition a person-to-person relationship. For example, I trust my doctor because I know that he or she has an interest in providing the right type of treatment or else risks losing his/her license to practice. But even in such a case, Hardin is suspicious of the idea that we could institutionalize trust by the way we organize the government. In principle, he says, it would be possible to have trust in government institutions if the incentive structure were such that officials would have an interest in acting as our agents. In this case, we need not have any personal knowledge of the individual judge, public hospital doctor or public school teacher, because we trust the incentive structure (and, implicitly I guess, the persons administrating the incentive structure, and then the ones who manage those who administer the incentive structure ...). But according to Hardin this is not a likely scenario, because ordinary citizens cannot have accurate information about such a complicated structure. 'Hence, as a matter of actual practice, it is utterly implausible that trust underlies most citizens' views and expectations of government' (Hardin 1999: 35). Thus, according to Hardin's definition of trust and his analysis of trust in government institutions, Mr Bonasera was indeed misguided to even think that he could 'believe in America'. His personal knowledge of Mr Corleone's competence and trustworthiness on matters such as these should instead have made his choice of protective agency obvious.

I think that Hardin's analysis of the problem of trust is a very healthy reminder in the ongoing discussion that not all trust in government institutions is a good thing, and that the issue of providing citizens with enough information about government activities is of great importance. His argument—that liberal democracy rests to a large extent on the assumption that governments should not be unconditionally trusted—is important. Furthermore, his point that increased distrust in government institutions often reported from survey research may be well-founded, is well taken (Holmberg 1993; Newton and Norris 1999). It is not unheard of, not even in Sweden, for governments to act in ways that give citizens good reason not to trust them.

Yet, I think Hardin's understanding of 'trust in government' is not completely accurate. The reason we trust a government institution (in a liberal democracy) is not because we always think it will act in our interest 'as our agent' on a specific matter. The problem in this discussion is that many different types of government institutions are collapsed under one label. There are certainly government institutions that we may see as our 'agents'—for example, a city government run by the party I support. In such a case, I'm likely to trust the government—as long as it keeps its promises. But, of course, people who oppose the ruling party are more likely to distrust that very same government, especially if the ruling party does what it has promised to do. Political majorities are not expected to be impartial; instead they are supposed to implement policies according to their specific ideologies or interests.

However, in the two cases discussed above, the situation is very different. For the legal branches of the state, and also for many government organizations responsible for implementing public policies, universalism and impartiality are the ideals. In these cases, a government institution that simply acts in my interest as my agent, no matter what, is one that I have bribed (or one that is run by my cousin). And if I can bribe a judge, so can someone else, including my adversaries. Obviously, when we decide whether or not to trust a government institution of this type, what we expect is something very different from what we expect of the people around us whom we trust. In a decision to entrust my child's education to a private or public school, it is not the type of 'encapsulated' trust that Hardin describes which is important; nor is it when I decide whether to entrust my medical treatment to a private or to a public hospital, or, as in the case of Mr Bonasera, to decide whether to 'believe in America' or to believe in Corleone's Mafia. What we expect from government organizations in these cases is that they be competent, fair, and, most of all, impartial (Levi 1998; Rothstein 1998).

Being fair and impartial is very different from—in fact the opposite of—acting as an agent of someone or acting on behalf of someone. My argument is that if we have reason to believe that government institutions responsible for implementing laws and policies behave according to the principles of fairness and impartiality, we may trust them with our demands for education, social insurance, health care and other essentially private goods. We may even, as in the case of Mr Bonasera, entrust them with our demands for protection and justice. According to Hardin's argument, we are unwise to delegate tasks to the government when it is not necessary, that is, when they can be provided by private organizations. According to Hardin, therefore, governments should be limited to keeping social order and to managing the economy, because these are essentially public goods that cannot be provided by private organizations. In Hardin's view, the reason for distrusting governments is that they are in a position to harm us, or they can fail to take care of our interests. But in many countries, for example the welfare states, people have delegated to government institutions many tasks that are vital to their well-being, notably health care, basic education, and social insurance such as pension systems. Of course, it could be argued that the citizens in these countries are looking at the world through rose-coloured glasses, or that they are acting out of some kind of false conscious-ness towards their governments. But, as I have argued elsewhere, it can also be the case that their political institutions, especially those that implement social policy, have been designed in a more univer-sal way (Rothstein 1998).

I will not deal further with the importance of competence in whether or not to trust government institutions (Sztompka 1998). My argument is simply that there is no reason to believe that gov-ernment organizations are less competent than private organiza-tions. They may be less innovative, but that is a different matter. Mr. Bonasera did not stop 'believing in America' because he thought that the judicial system was incompetent in punishing the two young men who had attacked his daughter. Instead, the system failed him on the two other grounds: fairness and impartiality. The decision to give the two young men a suspended sentence was not, in his mind, fair in comparison to their crime against his daughter. The most important reason for distrusting this government institution was that he thought the judge's decision was based on discrimination because of his background; that is, he believed that the principle of impartiality had been violated. Bonasera probably did not expect the judge to act as his agent. In his mind, he thought that the right punishment for the two young men would be death. But he could not reasonably have expected the judge to sentence them to the electric chair, and if this was Bonasera's hope for the outcome, his 'belief in America' was doomed from the start. Instead, it is more reasonable to believe that what he had hoped for was a fair and impartial trial, what Tom Tyler and others have called 'procedural justice' (Tyler 1990). As Tyler has shown, most people have two different ideas of what is justice, and they think it is important that the system comply with both. One concerns the outcome or substance (what you get), the other concerns the process (how you are treated). Procedural justice demands that government officials are perceived as unbiased and neutral and that they treat people with respect. According to Tyler, unfavourable outcomes can be accepted as long as people think the process that led to the outcome was fair. Imagine a soccer match in which the referee acts as an agent of both the teams. The teams will not trust him; in fact, it would ruin the whole game. The teams trust the referee because he is supposed to be impartial (and competent). They may accept a loss only on the condition that the referee has been impartial.

In two recent articles, four prominent economists have analyzed this 'quality of government' factor which the political economists cited above argue is crucial for economic growth. In an empirically impressive analysis, with data from between 60 and 209 countries, they have tried to find out what determines the 'quality of government' factor. They use several measures to determine each country's 'quality of government', such as 'the rule of law', protection of property rights, business regulations that support standard market transactions, the degree of corruption, bureaucratic delays and political freedom. They also add the production of 'public goods' such as low levels of infant mortality and high ambitions in basic education. First, while good economic performance yields better government institutions, there is much in their analysis that confirms that the causal logic works the other way around—that the historically established 'quality of government' factor determines economic growth (La Porta, Lopez-de-Silanes et al. 1997; La Porta, Lopez-de-Silanes et al. 1999).

Their second conclusion is more surprising—contrary to most economists, who argue that 'small' governments with low taxation rates are better positioned to achieve economic growth, this article concludes with the statement: 'Finally, we have consistently found that the better performing governments are larger and collect higher taxes. Poorly performing governments, in contrast, are smaller and collect fewer taxes' (La Porta, Lopez-de-Silanes et al. 1999: 42). The reason may be that creating 'high quality' government institutions are costly. But, the authors would not be true economists if they did not immediately follow the above sentence with the following. 'This result does not of course imply that it is often, or ever, socially desirable to expand a government of a given quality, but it tells us that identifying big government with bad government can be highly misleading' (La Porta, Lopez-de-Silanes et al. 1999: 42). This result does not fit very well with Russell Hardin's argument that we should be very restrictive in entrusting the government with tasks other than maintaining social order and managing the economy (see above). His argument may, however, be rescued if 'social order' and 'managing the economy' are given wide interpretations.

Trust, Social Capital and Political Institutions— The Causal Mechanism

In his famous *Asian Drama*, published in 1968, Nobel Laureate Gunnar Myrdal had already stated the problem that Douglass North and Mancur Olson have more recently brought to our attention. Myrdal's concept for inefficient government institutions was 'the Soft State'. Without using its formal techniques, Myrdal also captured the essence of the importance of game theory in this discussion; namely, the idea of agents as strategic actors using information from 'history of play' when making their decision whether to cooperate or to defect. Agents in 'soft states' decided to defect, according to Myrdal, because they reasoned in the following way: 'Well, if everybody seems corrupt, why shouldn't I be corrupt' (Myrdal 1968: 409).

How should we understand the causal mechanism (Hedström and Swedberg 1998) between social capital, trust and the quality of political institutions in a society? Social capital can be defined in many ways, but to simplify things, I will assume that a society in which most people think that most other people can be trusted has a high level of social capital. This type of 'generalized trust' is, as Eric Uslaner has convincingly shown, different from 'particularized trust', in which a person only trusts close relatives and friends, and thinks that people outside his close circle cannot be trusted (Uslaner 2002). For people to have this type of 'generalized trust', they are likely to think that not only will most other people play by the rules in 'person-to-person' contacts, they will also 'play by the rules' in their contacts with government institutions. That is, they will generally not try to bribe, threaten or in other ways corrupt the officials working in these institutions.

The reason they will refrain from such 'non-cooperative' actions may of course be that they are guided by a particular moral orientation. But, it may also be the case that individuals refrain from such 'non-cooperative' behaviour because it is generally known in society that government officials usually do not expect to be bribed or in other ways be corrupted. They will do what they are supposed to do without asking for bribes or being forced by Mafia-type threats. But if Person A starts thinking that Person B is corrupting the impartiality of government institutions and getting away with it, Person A's trust in government institutions and civil servants will of course go down, but so will his trust in his fellow citizens. If the same person starts thinking that such corrupt exchanges are the norm in his society rather than the exception, both his 'generalized trust' and his trust in government institutions will go down. Thus, the causal mechanism (that is, the rationality at the micro-level) between trust in government institutions responsible for the implementation of laws and policies, and generalized trust, has three dimensions.

1. If public officials are known to be corrupt, A will infer that even individuals given the responsibility to guard the public interest are not to be trusted, and if they cannot be trusted, then nor can 'most people' be trusted.
2. A will infer that most people cannot be trusted because they are engaged in direct or indirect corruption of these government institutions.
3. In order to 'survive' under such a system, A will find himself forced to engage in corruption, even if it is against his moral orientation. But because A cannot trust himself to behave according to the rules, he is likely to infer that nor are 'other people' likely to play by the rules, and thus they cannot be trusted.

The causal mechanism I want to specify here is that 'generalized trust' runs from trust in the impartiality of government institutions to trust in 'most people.' It makes no sense to trust 'most people' if they are generally known to bribe, threaten or in other ways corrupt the impartiality of government institutions in order to extract special favours. One reason 'most other people' may be trusted is that they are generally known to refrain from such forms of behaviour. Mr Bonasera did not only lose his trust in the judicial system, he probably also lost his trust in those of his fellow American citizens who belonged to the white Anglo–Saxon protestant community. And if his demand for justice could only be handled by a criminal organization, the same goes for 'most other people'.

My argument is certainly not that all forms of 'generalized trust' are caused by trust in the impartiality and honesty of government institutions. There are probably other important sources that are creating such social capital. Instead, I am trying to make sense of how the causal mechanism between trust in political institutions and 'generalized trust' may work. One could argue, of course, that the causal mechanism runs the other way—that people known to be trustworthy would not try to corrupt government officials (Inglehart 1999). I do not deny that such altruistic individuals may exist, but I would dare to argue that they are the exception. To refer to Gunnar Myrdal again, most individuals would reason as follows: 'If everybody seems corrupt, why shouldn't I be corrupt?'. That is, they are willing and interested in 'doing the right thing' provided that they believe that most other people are also 'doing the right thing'. But if they are convinced that most people are 'doing the wrong thing', it makes no sense to be the only one who 'does the right thing', i.e., to be what in game theory is known as 'a sucker'. As Margaret Levi has argued, we should expect most people to have this kind of 'dual' utility function (Levi 1991). An uncorrupted civil service can thus be understood as a 'common pool resource', meaning that it will only exist if (almost) all agents agree not to break its basic rules about impartiality, etc. (Ostrom 1990). In other words, it is certainly heroic but rather pointless to be the only one to defend your country, sort your garbage or, as in this case, refrain from bribing or threatening government officials.

This is also what comes out from empirical studies about corruption—that many individuals clearly see that they are in a 'social dilemma', that is, they use bribes in order to get what they want from government officials because they know that 'everyone else' is doing the same. Still, they know that they are in an 'inefficient equilibrium', meaning that it would be much better if everyone refrained from such uncooperative behaviour (Della Porta and Vannucci 1999). Thus, in such 'inefficient equilibria', it seems reasonable to argue that most other people in principle could be trusted, given that government officials were honest and impartial. But, because bribes, threats, dishonesty and other forms of corruption are 'the rule', neither 'most other people' nor government institutions can be trusted in the actual situation.

The Causal Mechanism—Some Empirical Illustrations

In this empirical section, I will use data from Swedish surveys to illustrate this causal mechanism. One could argue that data from a country that has historically been rich in social capital is of special interest, provided that there is some variation in the reported trust in government institutions. The interesting thing with such variation is that this could tell us something about what types of government institutions are beneficial for the creation of social capital and 'generalized trust'. The assumption above is that corrupt government institutions would be detrimental to the creation of trust. However, uncorrupted government institutions and policies come in many forms, and there is no reason to expect that all of them would be beneficial for the creation of social capital.

The first data-set is from the yearly SOM survey that has been carried out at Göteborg University since 1986 (SOM stands for Society, Opinion, Media). Swedish citizens between the ages of 16 and 80 have been asked whether they have very high, high, middle, low or very low trust/confidence ('förtroende') in different political and societal institutions such as the banks, Parliament, the unions, the police, the courts, etc. One important result is that there is great variation in trust both over time and between different institutions. While public trust/confidence in, for example, the public health care system, the courts and the public school system remains high, trust in the central political institutions have gone down dramatically.

There are of course many reasons for this change, which I will not go into here (cf. Holmberg 1999; Norén 2000). The interesting thing from a social capital perspective is that this big drop in trust in the central and party-dominated political institutions is not paralleled by any similar change in 'generalized trust' in Sweden. On the contrary, as measured in both the Swedish section of the World Values study and in the SOM surveys, generalized trust remains high and stable in Sweden.

Figure 5.1 Trust in political institutions: 1986, 1991 and 1996

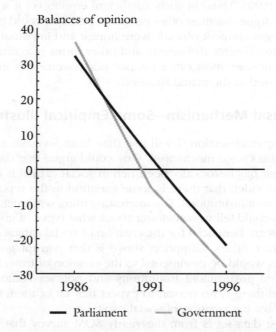

Source: Holmberg, Sören and Weibull, Lennart. 1997. *Trends in Swedish Opinion.* Göteborg: Göteborg University, the SOM Institute. Balance of opinion is calculated by subtracting the number of 'distrust' responses from the 'trust' responses.

Thus, on this aggregate level, it seems that we should not expect there to be a relation between 'generalized trust' and trust in party-dominated political institutions. This is also what Eric Uslaner argues from his extensive analysis of survey data from the US (Uslaner 2002). The problem with Uslaner's otherwise convincing argument is that he does not give enough attention to the possibility that different political institutions may have different effects on 'generalized trust'. Another problem is that Uslaner also argues that trusting people are more supportive of the legal system, and that 'laws and values only sustain a cooperative community if they are universal' (Uslaner 2002). If this is so, the design of laws and the political institutions responsible for the implementation of laws and public

Figure 5.2 Opinions about trust in other people: 1981 to 1997

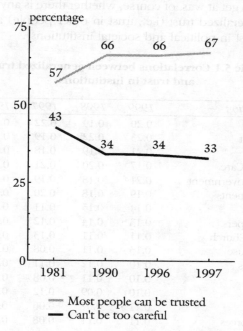

Sources: Data for 1981 and 1990 are taken from the Swedish section of the *World Values Survey* (n=876 and 994). In 1996, two different surveys were conducted in Sweden with this question, the third *World Values Survey* (n=957) and one made for this report by the SOM Institute at Göteborg University (n=1,707). The figures shown are the means from these two studies. The data for 1997 is from an FSI (*Forskningsgruppen för Samhälls-och Informationsstudier*) survey (n=1,640).

policies should be important for, if not the creation, then at least the reproduction of, 'generalized trust'.

Since 1996, the yearly SOM surveys have included the same question about 'generalized trust' as in the World Values study. However, we have also asked the respondents to place themselves on a ten-point scale on this question in order to get more variation in this variable. Below is a table with simple correlations (Pearson's r) between this ten-scale question about 'trust in most people' and five-scale questions about trust in different social and political institutions. The question we wanted to get at was, of course, whether there is any correlation between generalized trust (i.e., trust in other people) and vertical trust (i.e., trust in political and societal institutions).

**Table 5.1 Correlations between generalized trust
and trust in institutions**

Type of institution	1999	1998	1997	1996	Mean
The Courts	0.20	0.19	0.22	0.18	0.20
The Parliament	0.23	0.22	0.19	0.15	0.20
The Police	0.21	0.19	0.18	0.18	0.19
Public Health Care	0.17	0.20	0.21	0.16	0.18
The Central Government	0.21	0.18	0.19	0.12	0.17
Local Governments	0.19	0.18	0.20	0.13	0.15
Public Schools	0.14	0.15	0.11	0.10	0.12
Daily Newspapers	0.13	0.14	0.12	0.07	0.11
The Swedish Church	0.11	0.11	0.13	0.10	0.11
The Royal House	0.13	0.11	0.08	0.10	0.10
Big Companies	0.10	0.12	0.11	0.08	0.10
Radio/TV	0.10	0.11	0.08	0.10	0.10
Unions	0.10	0.09	0.12	0.08	0.10
Banks	0.11	0.07	0.06	0.05	0.09
The Armed Forces	0.11	0.11	0.08	0.08	0.07
The European Parliament	0.10				
The European Commission	0.10				

Source: The National SOM surveys 1996, 1997, 1998 and 1999. N varies between 1,707 for 1996 and 2,586 for 1999. For further information about the sampling techniques, etc., visit *www.gu.som.se.*

A number of conclusions and interpretations can be drawn from these data. First, even though all of these correlations are weak (which should be expected given the type of scale questions they are based on), they all point in the same positive direction. Thus, the more people trust other people, the more they tend to have confidence in societal and political institutions. But again, the difficulty is to understand in what direction the causal link goes. A second interesting conclusion is the relative stability in the results. Despite the sharp decline in trust in, for example, the government and parliament, the correlations with 'generalized trust' stay almost the same. Third, and most important for the argument I am trying to make, is that two of the strongest correlations are between generalized trust and trust in the institutions of law and order, that is, the courts and the police.

One possible way to interpret this is that the causal link runs in the following way: the more you trust the institutions that are supposed to keep law and order, the more reason you have to trust other people. In a civilized society, institutions of law and order have one particularly important task compared to other political institutions; namely, to detect and punish people who are 'traitors', that is, those who break contracts, steal, murder and do other such non-cooperative things and who should therefore not be trusted. Thus, if you think that these particular institutions do what they are supposed to do in a fair, impartial, uncorrupted and effective manner, then you also have reason to believe that the chance people have of getting away with such treacherous behavior[3] is small. If so, you will believe that people will have good reason to refrain from acting in a treacherous manner, and you will therefore believe that 'most people can be trusted'. Add to this that you will probably also think that most people can be trusted not to try to corrupt, threaten and/or bribe the officials operating these institutions. If so, you will be among those who 'believe in America.'

Working with the SOM survey data, Staffan Kumlin has found support for the existence of such a causal mechanism. His analyses show that experience with selective client-based public authorities (such as means-tested social assistance) has a sizeable and significant negative effect on generalized trust, controlling for membership in voluntary associations, satisfaction with the way the Swedish democracy works, political interest, social class, income, life satisfaction and trust in politicians (Kumlin 2000).

A third set of data comes from the a recent SIFO or *Sifo Opinion OCH Samhale* (*www.sifo.se*) survey study which asked Swedes about their views about the existence of misuse of power. The percentage of respondents answering that they thought 'serious misuse of power exists' is reported below.

Once again, it stands clear that even in a society with a comparatively high level of interpersonal trust, government institutions in general are not thought to be trustworthy. Almost 70 per cent of those surveyed indicated they believe that politicians in local governments seriously misuse the power vested in their hands. This result should be seen in the light of a development in which local governments in Sweden have been given increased responsibility for many of

Table 5.2 Attitudes towards serious misuse of power

Category	Percentage
Local Politicians	69
Civil servants in the EU	64
Civil servants in the national administration	43
CEOs in large companies	41
Civil servants in the local administration	40
Union leaders	39
The Cabinet	38
Members of Parliament	36
Journalists	30
The Police	22
Defense lawyers	18
Judges and public prosecutors	14

Source: SIFO samhällsbarometer 2000 (n = 946). *Svenska Dagbladet*, 17 July 2000. Percentage answering yes to the question, 'Do you believe that serious misuse of power exists?'

the central parts of the social welfare system, such as old-age care and education. Moreover, there is considerable variation in public opinion about the ethical standards of different institutions. And again, it is the legal system that fares best. According to this survey, it is five times more likely that a respondent will think that power is seriously misused by a local politician than by a judge or a public prosecutor.

The question is of course if trust in, for example, the courts and the police, would have an independent effect on generalized trust compared to other variables which are usually thought to be of importance, such as education, income, optimism and activity in voluntary associations. Below are the results from a step-wise multiple regression model based on the 1998 SOM survey.

From this table we can conclude the following. Trust in the police and the courts have independent and significant effects on generalized trust, controlling for other usual suspects such as education, income, interest in politics, activity in voluntary associations, optimism and xenophobia. The effect from trust in the police is almost as strong as is the effect from the (index of) activity in voluntary associations. It should also be noted that the overall effect of all these variables is pretty modest.

Table 5.3 Step-wise multiple regression models[4]
(Generalized trust dependent variable)

	Model 1 $R^2=0.048$			Model 2 $R^2=0.100$			Model 3 $R^2=0.131$		
	B	ß	sign.	B	ß	sign.	B	ß	sign.
Intercept	0.506		0.000	0.251		0.000	0.268		0.000
Education	0.052	0.092	0.000	0.028	0.049	0.007	0.017	0.031	0.084
Income	0.026	0.004	0.000	0.019	0.090	0.000	0.019	0.092	0.000
Interest in politics	0.103	0.017	0.000	0.049	0.017	0.000	0.054	0.057	0.001
Association index[5]				0.170	0.203	0.000	0.156	0.095	0.000
Satisfied with life				0.156	0.132	0.000	0.130	0.110	0.000
Take less refugees into Sweden				0.130	0.167	0.000	0.117	0.151	0.000
How much trust do you have in the way the police is conducting their work?							0.133	0.128	0.000
How much trust do you have in the way the courts are working?							0.082	0.088	0.000

Source: SOM national survey 1998. Education is coded a three-scale index, income a four-scale index, all other independent variables are five-scale questions. *Comments:* B is unstandardized b-value, that in a sense has been standardized as all scales are transformed to 0 to 1 scales. *ß* is standardized beta (based on the standard deviation) and sign. is the column where to find the values respective significance.

Conclusion

The discussion about the connection between 'generalized trust' and 'trust in government' has suffered from a conceptual problem in that the latter variable has been under-specified. Government institutions come in many forms, and there is no reason to believe that all of them influence interpersonal trust in the same way or even in the same direction. As should be clear from the data presented above, people have very different opinions about the trustworthiness and ethical standards of different types of government institutions. In a democracy, some government institutions, for example a city government, are expected to act in a partisan way. That is, after all, what they are elected for. So far as I can see, there is no reason why such government institutions should influence inter-personal trust at all. If 'my party' runs the city, why should my trust in other people be affected? The democratic system has two sides, one for input and one for output. My argument is that it is the quality of the 'output' institutions that may be crucial for the development of 'generalized trust'. The implementation side of the political system is what most citizens come into direct contact with, much more often than with the 'input' side. Contacts with politicians and voting are rather rare events for most citizens compared to contacts with government institutions responsible for the implementation of public policies.

I think one can make sense of how the causal mechanism between government institutions responsible for implementing laws and policies and 'generalized trust' may work. In a society where it is 'common knowledge' that the impartiality of government officials can be corrupted, most people who have the necessary resources to do so will try to take advantage of this possibility. The 'common knowledge' will be that not only government officials, but also 'most people', cannot be trusted to play by the rules. But it may also be the case that individuals refrain from such 'non-cooperative' behaviour because it is generally known in that society that government officials usually do not expect to be bribed or in other ways corrupted. But if Person A starts thinking that Person B is corrupting the impartiality of government institutions and getting away with it, his trust in government institutions will of course go down, but so will his trust in his fellow citizens. If the same person starts thinking that such corrupt exchanges are the norm in his society rather than the exception, both his 'generalized trust' and his trust in government institutions will go down. The causal mechanism I want to specify here is that 'generalized' trust runs from trust in the universalism of government institutions to trust in 'most people'. It makes no sense to trust 'most people' if they are generally known to bribe, threaten or in other ways corrupt the impartiality of government institutions in order to extract special favours. Again, one reason 'most other people' may be trusted is that they are generally known to refrain from such forms of behaviour. Simply put, the more universal the government institutions responsible for the implementation of laws and policies are, the more social capital you will get.

Notes

1. Department of Political Science, Göteborg University, Sweden.
2. The problem is, of course, who is to decide what is a relevant group, and who is to decide who should be counted as a member of such a group. If we combine sex, race, religion, ethnicity, region, social class and disabilities, we get 512 possible combinations. The implementation problems would be rather difficult.
3. Game theorists usually use the term 'opportunistic behaviour', which I think is much too nice a term to describe what this is all about.
4. Thanks to Ylva Norén for constructing the association index and for help with computing the statistics.
5. Association engagements 1998 is based on question no. 88 in the questionnaire: 'which types of associations are the respondents members of?'. The answers can be: (*a*) Sports or outdoor life, (*b*) Environmental organization, (*c*) Union organization, (*d*) Rental-/houseowner-/neigbourhood organization, (*e*) Culture, music, dance etc., (*f*) Organization for retired persons, or (*g*) Other organizations. Alternative (*h*), Political party, is not included here. The respondents were also asked to mark their activity in each organizational (type), 1=Not a member, 2=Member but have not attended meetings the last year, 3=Member and has visited meetings during the last year, and 4=Member with a position. For each respondent, a value of association activity is calculated, where each 1 ticked gives 0 points, for each 2 ticked 1 point is received, for each 3 a 2 point and for each 4 a 3 point is given. 31 per cent of the respondents received 0–1 points in total (*low*), 35 per cent received 2–3 points (*medium*), and another 34 per cent received 4–17 points (*high*).

References

Barry, B. 1995. *Justice as Impartiality*. Oxford: Oxford University Press.

Della Porta, D. and Vannucci, A. 1999. *Corrupt exchanges: actors, resources, and mechanisms of political corruption*. New York: Aldine de Gruyter.

Hardin, R. 1995. *One for All: The Logic of Group Conflict*. Princeton: Princeton University Press.

Hardin, R. 1999. 'Do we want trust in government', in M. E. Warren (ed.), *Democracy and Trust*. New York: Cambridge University Press, pp. 22–41.

Hedström, P. and Swedberg, R. 1998. 'Social Mechanisms: An Introductory Essay', in P. Hedström and R. Swedberg (eds.), *Social Mechanisms: An*

Analytical Approach to Social Theory. New York: Cambridge University Press, pp. 1–31.

Holmberg, C. 1993. *Det Kallas Kärlek*. Göteborg: Anamma Facklitteratur.

Holmberg, S. 1999. 'Down and Down We Go: Political Trust in Sweden', in P. Norris (ed.), *Critical Citizens*. Oxford: Oxford University Press.

Inglehart, R. 1999. 'Trust, Well-being and Democracy', in M. E. Warren (ed.), *Democracy and Trust*. New York: Cambridge University Press, pp. 88–120.

Kumlin, S. 2000. 'Welfare State Institutions and Generalized Trust'. Göteborg: Department of Political Science, Göteborg University.

La Porta, R. Lopez-de-Silanes, F. et al. 1999. 'The Quality of Government.' *Journal of Law, Economics and Organization*, 15(1): pp. 222–79.

La Porta, R. Lopez-de-Silanes, F. et al. 1997. 'Trust in Large Organizations.' *American Economic Review* 87(2): pp. 333–38.

Levi, M. 1991. 'Are There Limits to Rationality.' *Achives Européennes de Sociologie* 32(1): pp. 130–41.

Levi, M. 1998. *Consent, Dissent, and Patriotism*. New York: Cambridge University Press.

Levi, M. 1998. 'A State of Trust', in V. Braithwaite and M. Levi (eds.), *Trust and Governance*. New York: Russell Sage Foundation: pp. 77–101.

Myrdal, G. 1968. *Asian Drama: An Enquiry into the Poverty of Nations*. New York: Twentieth Century Fund.

Newton, K. and Norris, P. 1999. 'Confidence in Public Institutions'. Atlanta: Annual Meeting of the American Political Science Assocation.

Norén, Y. 2000. 'Explaining Variation in Political Trust in Sweden'. Copenhagen: European Consortium for Political Research Joint Session of Workshops.

Ostrom, E. 1990. *Governing the Commons: The Evolution of Institutions for Collective Action*. New York: Cambridge University Press.

Rothstein, B. 1998. *Just Institutions Matter: The Moral and Political Logic of the Universal Welfare State*. Cambridge: Cambridge University Press.

_____. 2000. 'Trust, Social Dilemmas and Collective Memories.' *Journal of Theoretical Politics* 14(4).

_____. 2001. 'Social Capital in the Social Democratic State. The Swedish Model and Civil Society.' *Politics and Society* 29(2).

Stolle, D. 2000. 'Communities, Citizens and Local Government: Generalized Trust and the Impact of Regional Settings (this volume).

Sztompka, P. 1998. 'Trust, Distrust and Two Paradoxes of Democracy.' *European Journal of Social Theory* 1(1): pp. 19–32.

Tyler, T. R. 1990. Justice, Self-Interest, and the Legitimacy of Legal and Political Authority', in J. J. Mansbridge (ed.), *Beyond Self-Interest*. Chicago and London, The University of Chicago Press: pp. 171–79.

Uslaner, E. M. 2002. *The Moral Foundations of Trust*. Cambridge: Cambridge University Press.

Young, I. M. 1990. *Justice and the Politics of Difference*. Princeton: Princeton University Press.

6

How Associations Matter:
An Empirical Assessment of the Social Capital-Trust-Voluntary Action Link

Mario Diani[1]

Introduction

In literature on social capital, the relationship between social networks, trust (in particular generalized trust) and collective goods is notoriously ambiguous (Newton 1997; Portes 1998; Foley and Edwards 1999). It is unclear whether trust and social networks, in particular those based on membership of associations, should both be treated analytically as social capital, or whether we are dealing with a simple correlation—no matter how strong—between independent social processes. This complicates the analysis of the relationship between participation in associations and institutional legitimacy, to which social capital scholars have nonetheless devoted important reflections (Portes 1998: 18–21). Does the mere fact of participating in associations, regardless of their specific traits, facilitate social integration and conflict mediation? Or is this function performed by some forms of associational participation only, with others operating in the opposite direction? Finally, when dealing with the associations-trust link, should we focus on generic sentiments towards 'others' or towards 'institutions' or instead on trust in specific actors and/or institutions (e.g., parliament: Newton 1999)?

Although routinely acknowledged in theoretical discussions, the multiple uses of the social capital idea are rarely addressed systematically in empirical research (see, however, Putnam 2000). In this chapter I use survey data collected on active members of voluntary associations in Lombardy in 1993 to discuss the relation between social capital and a specific type of trust; namely, trust in a broad range of political and social institutions. Here—although not in general—by social capital I mean exclusively the social ties which accrue to individuals by virtue of their involvement in associations. By showing how ties which originate in different associational milieu affect trust in various types of institutions in different ways, I intend to propose a *context-dependent* version of social capital (Foley and Edwards 1999; Edwards, Foley, and Diani 2001). So far, the social capital debate has largely focussed on which social ties may foster generalized trust, and should therefore be treated as social capital, and which fail to do so.[2] In contrast, I argue that the same ties may or may not operate as social capital and generate that distinctive good called 'trust' in separate contexts, i.e., in relation to different institutional actors.

Social Capital, Social Ties and Trust: A Context-Dependent View

Some analysts regard social capital mainly as civic values and generalized trust (Fukuyama 1995; Inglehart 1997), others as social relations (Bourdieu 1986; Boissevain 1974; Burt 1998); most, however, conceive of it as consisting of both linkages and cooperative civic values and predispositions (among them Coleman 1990; Putnam 1995a, 2000; Van Deth 2000). Yet, too strict an integration between a view of social capital as networks and a view of social capital as a set of civic values and mutual obligations risks making the whole argument opaque. It remains unclear as to which extent should social capital be regarded as a globally positive phenomenon, inextricably associated with collective goods, generalized trust, etc. (as some versions of Putnam's argument—e.g., 1995a: 67—seem to suggest), rather than as a social property, which may facilitate action within specific social groups while generating more dubious, or even clearly negative, outcomes from the point of view of the general good (Coleman 1990; Greeley 1997; Burt 1998; Stolle and Rochon

1998; Portes 1998: 17–18; Woolcock 1998; but also Putnam 1995b and 2000: 350–63).[3]

Any time a society is fragmented along specific lines (whether ethnic, religious, national, class, etc.)—any time *bonding* social capital, to put it in Putnam's words, prevails over *bridging* social capital—dense intra-group networks should not be expected to entail generalized trust, but rather to be in a zero-sum relation to it (Stolle 1997; Stolle and Rochon 1998; Foley and Edwards 1999). Moreover, in societies where institutions are discredited and often hated, like in the formerly socialist countries, social capital is not an instrument of integration but rather an opportunity for people to generate autonomously the goods and services the state cannot provide, and often also a means for people to defend themselves from the state (Rose, Mishler, and Haerpfer 1997; Rose 1998).

The relation between networks and institutional trust is probably the most problematic. While participation in voluntary associations has been found to be correlated with interpersonal trust, both in the U.S. (Brehm and Rahn 1997) and in other countries (albeit more weakly, and with a number of exceptions: Newton 1999), there seems to be little evidence of a correlation between voluntary associations and trust in political institutions (Newton 1999). The direction of the causal relation between interpersonal trust and associational life is also questionable: re-examining survey data on the U.S., some have argued that the former determine the latter, rather than vice versa (Uslaner 2000). Moreover, people may participate—and therefore be embedded in dense social networks—either out of generalized trust or deep distrust in other people's will to mobilize on behalf of collective goods (Oliver 1984). The question is therefore what type of social capital is generating what type of trust (Stolle and Rochon 1998)?

Many studies have focussed on the relationship between social capital and interpersonal trust (Putnam 1993, 2000: 137; Uslaner 2002). In this chapter I focus instead on the link between associations and institutional trust. By institutional trust, I mean trust in a broad range of actors whose role in Italian public life tends to be taken for granted, although not necessarily with positive connotations: the Catholic Church, business organizations, the media, trade unions and political parties, alongside local and national institutions proper. I expect trust in these actors to be affected by variations in the social capital individuals may draw upon, more specifically in the social ties originating from their present and past involvement with different kinds of associations.

This *individualist* and *associational* view of social capital requires clarification. Treating social capital as individual property, and in our case as the aggregate of an individual's associational experiences, might well conceal its relational nature. If opportunities arise for individuals from their embeddedness in specific social milieus, then we cannot assume individuals to rely on them once the social context in which such opportunities have developed changes (Bourdieu 1986; Foley and Edwards 1999; Edwards et al. 2001). For example, the resources made available to an individual in the 1970s through her membership of a radical feminist group can in no way be automatically attributed to her 20 years later in the same way as the cognitive resources originating from her professional and educational development could be. Even though ties developed in the 1970s' movements have been preserved, their function might well be totally different in the two contexts. Relations developed in a given context will not necessarily operate as social capital at later stages and/or in different contexts.

Moreover, focussing on associational social capital does not mean ignoring the fact that involvement in any kind of social network (in particular, private networks: Putnam 2000: 80–115) may well generate social capital. At the same time, though, too inclusive a notion of social capital can lead to ambiguity in the definition of outcomes and the specification of causal mechanisms, making the whole social capital–trust argument tautological (Portes 1998). The question then becomes whether, in relation to my specific research questions, it is legitimate to treat social capital as an individual property and limit the analysis to linkages originating from associational membership. A reply requires recognizing the context-dependent nature of social capital. Social relations as such neither facilitate nor discourage individual or collective outcomes; on the contrary, different types of ties may prove more or less conducive to the achievement of specific results, i.e., their capacity to operate as social capital varies considerably across situations. Following Coleman (1990), social capital comprises all those features of social structure which facilitate the pursuit of individual and collective goals. A context-dependent view of social capital rules out the possibility of identifying its constitutive elements in the abstract, i.e., of clarifying once and for all which social relations represent social capital, and which do not. There is no social capital *per se*, only social ties, which, in relation to certain purposes, may operate *as* social capital.

In our specific case, the 'profit' generated by social capital consists of the growth of trust in various institutional actors. In turn, this may positively affect the civic role of the individual as well as, indirectly, the overall democratic performance of the polity. In relation to this specific outcome, we may legitimately regard participation in associations as a form of social capital and treat it cumulatively, i.e., consider the overall amount of individuals' experiences in associations as an indicator of their social capital. Associations offer opportunities for regular interaction between individual who share goals, interests or values. They facilitate the exchange of ideas, experiences, skills and information, as well as, in the long term, the emergence and consolidation of specific identities. If social capital as a rule allows individuals to maximize their opportunities through their social contacts, one should expect associational participation to maximize opportunities for interest representation, identification processes and collective action.[4]

One should in particular ask to which extent the linkages developed within specific organizations or associational milieus may generate trust in other types of actors; in other words, to which extent bonding social capital may also create trust in actors who are external to, and often explicitly distant from, the group where social capital is generated. It is worth considering the possibility of a more diversified relation between different types of social capital and different types of trust.

Looking at social capital as individual property also seems legitimate in our specific context. Although participation in associations affects individuals differently when in progress and when it has become a fact of the past, the resulting social relations maintain some vitality even when the context in which they originally developed is no longer present. Such relations increase people's capacity to act collectively and shape their long-term orientations (McAdam 1989; McAdam and Paulsen 1993; Della Porta and Diani 1999: ch. 5). In this particular sense they may be regarded as a form of transferable social capital which individuals carry through different periods of their lives.

The Study

While most studies of social capital are based on national samples (Listhaug and Wiberg 1995; Inglehart 1997; Norris 1999), this study uses data collected among members of voluntary associations in Lombardy (see also Stolle and Rochon 1998). Focussing on those who are positively active in a specific territorial context, rather than on the general population, allows us to explore the impact of different types of participation and frees us from having to concentrate on the crudest differences between the inactive majority and the tiny, active minority. It also reduces the risk of distortion that differences in social and political structure across regions might generate, were we to analyse a national sample.

Evidence for my analysis comes from 1,091 questionnaires returned (at a rate of 55 per cent) by members of voluntary organizations in five Lombardy provinces (Bergamo, Como, Cremona, Milan and Varese) in 1993. The respondents belonged to 164 associations (either independent groups, or local branches of national organizations), selected on the basis of a stratified sample by domain of activity (sports and leisure, cultural, welfare, and political advocacy-human rights/ environment) and size of the urban setting (Biorcio and Diani 1993). Although the last few years have seen significant changes in Italian politics, especially in citizens' voting choices and partisan loyalties, available data does not suggest radical changes in the overall profile of the Italian voluntary sector (Iref 1998: 71, 157).

Dependent Variables

Trust in political and institutional actors was measured on a 0 to 10 point scale. Factor analysis identified five different types of actors (see table 6.1) who were similarly trusted by Lombardy volunteers: political actors (including both political parties and different types of political institutions: government, parliament, regional and city councils), unions (both 'official'—CGIL (Italian General Labour Confederation), CISL (Italian Confederation of Workers' Unions), UIL (Italian Labour Union)—and 'autonomous' unions), Catholic institutions (both the church in general and local parishes), business (including business associations and banks) and the media, and law and order agencies (the police, the military, the judiciary).[5]

Any notion of general trust seems disputable given the strong differences in trust in different institutions and actors (see table 6.2).

Only Catholic institutions and law and order agencies were trusted to an acceptable level, while trust in other actors was clearly low. One can note both analogies and differences to orientations recorded in the Italian population during the same period. The poor levels of trust in political actors and unions, and the trust in the Catholic Church, the police and the judiciary, have long been emphasized in comparative perspectives (Cartocci 1994: 20–28; Ricolfi 1993: 113–16; Listhaug and Wiberg 1995; Dalton 1999; McAllister 1999; Miller and Listhaug 1999). However, in the early 1990s, members of Lombard voluntary associations were far less trustful of business actors than the Italian (and even the Lombard: Bernardi and Diamanti 1991) general population. That this distrust in political actors and unions was in line with what ordinary citizens felt is also striking. Given the significant background and even current involvement of many of our respondents in those milieus, one would have expected a more trustful attitude despite all the criticism.[6]

Table 6.1 Trust in political and social institutions
(principal components; varimax rotation)

Factors	Political Actors	Social Control	Catholic Church	Business and Media	Trade Unions
Political Parties	0.67				0.42
Government	0.74				
Parliament	0.84				
Town Council	0.81				
Regional Council	0.79				
Military		0.67		0.45	
Carabinieri		0.84			
Judiciary		0.81			
The Church			0.85		
Local Parish			0.86		
Business Association				0.66	
Banks				0.73	
Mass Media				0.53	
Mainstream Unions (CGIL–CISL–UIL)					0.73
Other Unions					0.82
Eigenvalue	6.23	2.35	1.54	1.29	1.11
Explained Variance	32.80	12.40	8.10	6.80	5.80

Table 6.2 Dependent and independent variables:
Descriptive statistics

	Mean	Standard Deviation
Trust (1–10)		
Political Actors	4.25	1.76
Trade Unions	4.01	1.91
Business and Media	4.41	1.65
Catholic Church	6.12	2.69
Social Control Agencies	5.99	1.96
Social Capital		
Active After 1991 (0/1)	0.24	0.12
Radical Break with Past (0/1)	0.32	0.47
Time Devoted to Collective Action (1–4)	2.01	0.91
Representative Roles (0/1)	0.31	0.46
Range of Experiences (1–7)	2.42	1.19
Parties and Unions	0.35	0.48
Altruistic Associations	0.47	0.49
'New' Social Movements	0.27	0.44
Environmentalism	0.22	0.41
Cultural Associations	0.48	0.50
Catholic Associations	0.41	0.49
Sport and Leisure	0.45	0.50
Socio-Demographic Profile		
Milan Resident (0/1)	0.46	0.50
Gender (Female=1)	0.39	0.49
Age	39.57	14.32
University Education (0/1)	0.69	0.46
Self-Employed (0/1)	0.05	0.23
Student (0/1)	0.14	0.35
Values and Beliefs		
Regular Mass Attendance (0/1)	0.51	0.50
Left-Right (L=0;R=10)	3.93	2.15
Post-materialism (0–2)	0.96	0.68

Independent Variables

Social capital Three different dimensions of participation are expected to shape individuals' social capital. First, *levels of commitment* are measured by three indicators: time spent in collective action (four-point scale from 'a few days every year' to 'a few hours every day'), membership of central bodies of one's organization (if existing at all) and length of participation.[7] Second, differences in the *associational milieus* in which social capital is generated are assessed with reference to seven major associational domains: conventional politics (including unions and political parties), environmental groups, welfare organizations, cultural associations, sport and leisure, Catholic associations, and new social movements (women, students and peace). Third, the *differentiation of associational linkages* is measured here as the range of different types of groups in which respondents were active at any stage of their lives. However, we have also to allow for the possibility of traumatic breaks in respondents' experiences which would nullify the cumulative impact of past participation.[8]

Socio-Demographic Properties Available evidence suggests some impact of socio-demographic traits over levels of trust, even though this changes across institutions and depends on the level of measurement. For example, the 1991 World Values Survey shows a relationship between levels of education and trust when data are aggregated at the national level, but no significant relation at the individual level (Listhaug and Wiberg 1995; Newton 1999: 183). Here I use the following variables: *gender, age, university education, profession* and *residence in the Milan area*. Given the persistent decline of interest of women in political affairs (Topf 1995: 63–64), being a woman may decrease trust in political institutions, and increase trust in private and social institutions. People in high-status professions should be broadly more trustful in political and economic institutions, less so in those with a strong solidarity-oriented culture like the church (Uslaner 2000).[9] As for age, European Values Survey data suggest overall higher levels of trust among elderly people, but for political actors and unions.[10] Analyses of the relation between education and political participation (Dalton 1988) suggests a positive link between university instruction and political trust. Finally, living in a metropolitan area like Milan rather than in a provincial town might affect one's levels of trust in two ways: on the one hand, metropolitan dwellers might be more trustful towards a broader range of actors by virtue of being exposed to a more varied set of social ties, on the other, the stronger social relations one experiences in small towns might prove more conducive to the development of trust.

Values and attitudes Trust might also be affected by a respondent's values, measured here by three variables: *left-right scale* (10 points), *postmaterialism* (based on Inglehart's four basic items) and *regular* *mass attendance.* People on the right, and/or subscribing to materialist values, should be more trustful in the church, in law and order agencies, and in business. Religious practice (which I equate here, surely inadequately, with the Catholic religion) should generate greater trust across the board (Greeley 1997); however, given the historical role of religion in Italy and the resulting state/church tensions, one might well expect practicing Catholics to be less trustful in political institutions than others.

Results

I will look first at the relation between social capital and trust, then control results by introducing socio-demographic traits and value orientations in the models. I will start with the least trusted actors (political institutions, unions, and the business and media: table 6.3), and then move to the most trusted ones (the Catholic Church and social-control agents: table 6.4).

Trust in political actors The base model (table 6.3, column 1a) shows trust in political actors to be correlated with several indicators of social capital. Possibly the most interesting finding relates to the forms of participation, and therefore to the process which generates social capital. People who invest less time in their associations are more trustful than those who are more heavily committed. Highly committed citizens seem to be driven by very low expectations regarding institutional performance, rather than by the hope to find opportunities for dialogue and collaboration with institutions. Strong ties to one's association do not seem to extend to relations with institutions; bonding social capital apparently does not convert into 'bridging trust'.

However, trust is higher among people who occupy representative roles in the regional or national bodies of their organizations (when these exist at all). The opportunities for regular contact with institutions that such positions usually entail may positively encourage trust. By contrast, ordinary rank-and-file members would have a more vague image and understanding of institutions, and this might lead to greater distrust. Overall, intense commitment *per se* seems unlikely to increase institutional trust; rather, what matters is the role played within voluntary associations.

Looking at the impact of embeddedness in different associational milieus, we find once again some not-so-obvious relations. We might have expected higher levels of political trust among those with present and/or past experiences in institutionalized political organizations such as parties and unions. Likewise, we might have expected some relationship between this specific type of trust and the social capital developed in environmental associations and other social movement organizations. Those who subscribe to an anti-institutional view of movements would expect in particular a negative relationship; however, the reverse is more realistic if we follow the argument that even radical, unconventional political participation and collective action is driven by some positive expectations of favourable systemic response (Dalton 1988; Tarrow 1989; Della Porta and Diani 1999: ch. 8). Neither argument is borne by the data: a background in explicit political collective action does not affect political-institutional trust at all. In contrast, this kind of trust is facilitated by linkages to cultural and Catholic associations.

This is actually the only case when all the social capital variables remain significant even when control variables are brought into the equation—with the partial exception of participation in Catholic associations (table 6.3, model 1b). Among control variables, only regular mass attendance and being a student seem to have a (positive) impact over trust, while being self-employed has a small and scarcely significant negative effect. When we bring religious practice into the model, the independent effect of social capital in Catholic associations disappears, suggesting that value orientation still prevails over relational practices; none the less, the Catholic tradition in Italy is confirmed as a powerful factor of integration in Italian society, at least within the voluntary sector.

This will turn out to be the only case in which the model performance improves marginally, and not significantly, after control variables are introduced. Altogether, trust in political institutions seems the one most explicitly dependent on social capital; in particular, on a social capital developed in non-political associations (Putnam 1993).

Trust in unions   Both the basic model (which includes social capital variables only) and the expanded model account for trust in unions only to a limited extent. The basic model (table 6.3, column 2a) explains only 2 per cent of the variance. People who only recently joined the voluntary sector, and those with links to cultural and Catholic associations, are more inclined to trust unions. Recent members of associations actually tend to be more trustful across the board; I shall comment on this finding later. It is also striking that links to political and union organizations do not increase trust in unions, and nor does social capital developed in social movements. There is in other words a gap between what people do or have done and the broader feelings they have towards organizations they should in principle be close to. The crisis experienced by Italian trade unions in the 1990s is dramatically reflected in this evidence.

When we introduce control variables (table 6.3, column 2b), social capital developed in Catholic associations turns out to have no significant impact, but—interestingly, and contrary to what will emerge as a regular pattern—neither does religious practice. In contrast, and unsurprisingly, self-placement on the left-right axis matters, and so does area of residence, self-employment and levels of education. People who do not live in Milan, are self-employed and lack a university education, are significantly more distrustful than highly educated Milanese residents with professional profiles. It is unclear to what extent such a profile, which is close to stereotypical representations of Northern League Sympathizers, actually corresponds to an area of potential sympathy within the Lombard voluntary sector for the northern Italian secessionist discourse. While only a tiny minority of the sample voted for the Northern League (Biorcio and Diani 1993), people with a social profile closer to that of the stereotypical Northern League supporter (Diamanti 1993) seemed more sympathetic to some of the League's core themes.

Trust in business and media Members of Lombard voluntary associations were hardly predisposed to trust business and media actors. Those who emphasize the emancipatory and critical potential of the third sector (Ranci 1992) will hardly find this surprising. It is more interesting, however, to look at the best predictors of this attitude. None of the specific forms of social capital included in the basic model seems to affect trust in business. When a significant relation can be found, this is negative: personal experiences in political organizations, 'old' (parties and unions) and 'new' (environmentalists and other movements), predict distrust in economic actors. If one might expect negative attitudes from activists in the new politics sector, the same is not necessarily true for people from traditional political organizations: the respondents' political profiles were mostly moderate and highly heterogeneous, if skewed towards the left (see table 6.2). The persistent distance between the voluntary sector and the business world at the beginning of the 1990s was therefore

Table 6.3 Regressions on trust in political actors, trade unions, and business and media (only beta-coefficients significant at .10 level or above)

Model	Political Actors		Trade Unions		Business and Media	
	1a	1b	2a	2b	3a	3b
Social Capital						
Active After 1991	-.10*	-.07*	.13***	.09*		.08*
Time Devoted to Collective Action	.10**	.09**			.06	
Representative Roles						
Range of Experiences						
Parties and Unions					-.17***	-.11**
Altruistic Associations						
Social Movements					-.14***	-.07
Environmentalism					-.14***	-.07
Cultural Associations	.10*	.11*				
Catholic Associations	.16***	.08	.16***	.11*		.08
Sport and Leisure						
Socio-Demographic						
Profile						
Milan Resident						
Age			.13***			.07*
University Education	-.06			-.07*		.17***
Self-Employed	.12**			-.10**		
Student				.07		.14***
Values and Beliefs						
Regular Mass						
Attendance	.15***		.07			.12**
Left-Right (L=0;R=10)			-.17***			.22***
Post-materialism						-.10**
Adjusted R2	.1***	.11***	.02***	.08***	.07***	.18***
F	9987	2569	4281	7115	9237	9547
N	878	942	840	937	839	939

Note: *: $p < .05$; **: $p < .01$; ***: $p < .001$

confirmed by this evidence. It would be, however, be interesting to test the same model on more recent data given the spread of collaboration between associations and business in areas like anti-poverty initiatives and environmental protection (Donati 2000).

When we introduce control variables, the explanatory capacity of the model increases substantially (table 6.3, column 3b). Among variables measuring social capital, ties to political parties and unions have a significant impact on (dis)trust in business. Overall, however, this seems mostly dependent on the volunteers' personal orientations: those with moderate political beliefs, those with materialist values, and churchgoers, are the most trustful. That Catholic practice turns out to be influential here is particularly relevant; recurrent claims from Italian political commentators that Catholic culture is full of anti-industrial and anti-profit attitudes finds no support in the Lombard case.

Older people and students are more likely to trust business than other volunteers, and the same holds true for Milan residents. The high density of small firms one finds in the Lombard provinces does not seem conducive to trust in business as an abstract category. It is also worth noting that, once we introduce control for other variables, one social capital indicator is found significant which was not in the basic model. Having recently got involved in associational activities seems to increase trust (Stolle 1997).

Trust in Catholic institutions Our models account for a considerable share of the variance in trust in Catholic institutions. When we focus on social capital variables only (table 6.4, column 1a), we note a strong polarization: while ties to Catholic associations affect trust positively, linkages to virtually any other associational milieu, from political parties and unions to environmentalists and new social movements, to sport and leisure-time associations, reduce trust. In the early 1990s the Catholic church seemed still to be one of the reference points—if not *the* reference point—for the whole voluntary and associational sector, an important source of identity and internal polarization.

Trust in Catholic institutions was also higher among those with lower time commitments to their associations, and with a more differentiated social capital. However, the impact of both factors disappeared once control variables were introduced (table 6.4, column 4b). Some of the relationships that emerged from the data were in line with our expectations: older people were more trustful in the church, while the self-employed were less so. In the latter case, however, the relationship was only modestly significant, nor could one find any relation to education or gender. The most important variables were by far those measuring beliefs and attitudes, in particular regular mass attendance (as one would expect) and politically moderate orientations. When one controlled for these variables, social capital developed in political organizations and unions was no longer significant. In contrast, we could still identify tensions between forms of social capital that developed in the Catholic milieu, and forms which grew out of environmentalism and other social movements. The persistent significance of ties to Catholic

Table 6.4 Regressions on trust in the catholic church and social control agencies (only beta-coefficients significant at .10 level or above)

Model	Catholic Church		Social Control Agencies	
	4a	4b	5a	5b
Social Capital				
Active After 1991		.08*		.10**
Time Devoted to Collective Action	−.08**		−.07*	
Representative Roles				
Range of Experiences	.18**	0.10	0.13	
Parties and Unions	−.13***		−.09	
Altruistic Associations				−.07
Social Movements	−.27***	−.10**	−.28***	−.16***
Environmentalism	−.17***	−.06*	−.12***	
Cultural Associations				−.09*
Catholic Associations	.31***	.10**		
Sport and Leisure	−.09**			
Socio-Demographic Profile				
Milan Resident				.07**
Age		.19***		.25***
University Education				
Self-Employed		−.05		
Student				.07*
Values and Beliefs				
Regular Mass Attendance		.52***		.08*
Left-Right (L=0; R=10)		.17***		.24***
Post-materialism				−.07*
Adjusted R2	0.26***	0.52***	0.07***	0.22***
F	29408	43915	7083	11982
N	973	865	964	858

Note: *: p <.05; ** p<.01; *** p<.001

associations is a meaningful finding. It suggests that trust is not a mere product of broad belief systems; rather, associational linkages maintain a specific impact on its levels.

Trust in social control agencies Members of Lombard associations generally trusted agencies of social control (the police, the army, and the judiciary) less than the Italian population (Cartocci 1994: 20–28), but their trust in them was still relatively high. It was not increased, however, by linkages to any specific social milieu; where significant, the relation of trust to specific measures of social capital was negative (table 6.4, column 5a). Roots in the environmental and social movement sectors reduced trust in the judiciary and the armed forces. The same held for cultural associations (the only time these specific linkages had a negative effect on trust, and for traditional political activism too), albeit with modest levels of significance. Devoting a lot of time to voluntary action proved once again a predictor of lower rather than higher levels of trust.

Introducing control variables dramatically improved the overall explanatory capacity of the model (table 6.4, column 5b). Among social capital variables, only ties to social movements kept a significant negative impact on this type of trust. Moreover, those who had got recently involved in associations turned out to be more trustful than those with longer experiences of collective action. Similarly to the case of business actors, residence in Milan, older age, and student status facilitated the development of trust. The same held for mass attendance and centre-right political orientations, while post-materialism worked according to expectations to reduce trust. Altogether, introducing control variables reduced the impact of associational milieus with a highly differentiated internal composition like cultural associations or environmentalism.

The overall profile is sufficiently clear. Variables that account for levels of trust in the police, the army and the judiciary reflect different dynamics operating within the voluntary sector. Our data reinforce the traditional image of people with moderate (although not right wing) political orientations and of a more advanced age as being more prone to trust law and order actors.

Does Social Capital Explain Trust?

Altogether, beliefs and socio-demographic traits (especially the former) seem to account for variation in levels of trust better than associational social capital. Among variables measuring beliefs, post-materialism operates as expected, increasing distrust in business and social control actors. It is, however, the other two variables that play the biggest explanatory role. Regular mass attendance consistently predicts higher levels of trust in any institutional actor. Apart from the obvious case of Catholic institutions, its impact is highest on trust in political actors. In Italy (and not only in Italy: Greeley 1997) religion remains a powerful—perhaps the most powerful—source of social integration and trust. The left-right axis also significantly accounts for trust in any institution, with the exception of political ones. While volunteers with left-wing orientations are more inclined to trust unions, those with a centre-right profile are usually most trustful (or least distrustful). Ideological orientations do not seem to matter only for trust in political actors, a finding consistent with available evidence on the Italian population (Newton 1999).

Different socio-demographic traits affect trust in different types of actors. Living in metropolitan Milan has no impact on trust in Catholic and political institutions, but facilitates trust in business and social control agents. This finding does not support the neo-communitarian rhetoric on the easier social integration in small localities, and the weakening of the social fabric in metropolitan areas: despite exposure to above average levels of criminal behaviour and faster social change, Milan residents are more trustful than other Lombard volunteers. Living in provincial towns may possibly facilitate interpersonal trust, but not institutional trust.

Age also matters, as older people tend to trust more actors who do not perform explicit political roles—business actors, law and order agencies, the church. The same applies to students, who however do not trust the church particularly highly, and who instead show higher trust in unions. Interestingly, being a student affects trust in exactly the opposite way to being self-employed, even though coefficients in the latter case are only weakly significant. Neither gender—despite stereotypes about women's modest political involvement in Italy—nor education affect trust to any extent. Evidence about gender matches Newton's (1999) data about the Italian population. Given the extremely high proportion of people either holding or studying for university degrees among Lombard volunteers (about 70 per cent), education does not substantially affect their trust in institutions.

Is there any relation between social capital (at least associational capital) and institutional trust, having controlled for other factors?

Although it's impact decreases, it remains statistically significant and substantively meaningful. However, this is a complex relation. First, although one might have expected people with a broad range of experiences to be more trustful, given the greater richness of their networks and their political socialization (Stolle and Rochon 1998), this does not seem to be the case. However, we need more sophisticated measures of individuals' structural positions within complex networks (e.g., Burt 1998) before denying any relevance to these variables.

The intensity of commitment to collective action also matters very little, but when it does, its impact is counterintuitive; the most engaged among the volunteers seem to be the most distrustful, not the most trustful. There are analogies here to those accounts of collective action which see it as the consequence of lack of trust in other people's conduct (Oliver 1984): working hard in voluntary associations may well reflect institutional distrust rather than trust.[11]

At the same time, however, the incumbents of senior roles in the regional or national bodies of their associations tend to be more trustful in institutions, in particular, in political institutional. Direct contacts to institutions seem to facilitate the development of a trusting relationship.[12] To sum up, while devoting substantial amounts of time in collective action is hardly conducive to trust in institutions, taking up qualified roles within associations is.

Among general properties of social capital, the length of the period spent in voluntary associations of some sort seems to be most influential on trust: newcomers to collective action tend to be more trustful than people with long-term commitments. As experiences accumulate, the original enthusiasm seems to give way to a more disenchanted and pessimistic view (Stolle 1997). Doubts are cast over the necessarily positive impact of associational membership over trust; if anything, associational social capital, created over a longer time span, seems to discourage the formation of trust.

Social capital operates differently, depending on the associational context in which it has been created. Despite the introduction of many control variables, two types of social capital seem to consistently affect trust. On the one hand, ties to cultural associations reinforce trust in political and business actors. On the other hand, links with social movements correspond to particularly low levels of trust in all actors but political actors and unions—for which no relationship is found. The opposition between cultural associations, conducive to trust, and social movements as sources of distrust are in line with Putnam's (1995a) doubts that social movements may generate social capital and trust. At the same time, however, the point is only partially borne, as sport clubs do not seem to affect trust at all.

Linkages to other associational milieus have a more occasional, but still meaningful, impact: environmentalists are particularly distrustful of two institutions both associated with 'anthropocentric', if very different, worldviews—the church and business; ties to parties and unions predict lower trust in business. Finally, one is struck by the absence of any relation between ties to welfare, sport, leisure-time associations and trust. One might attribute this finding to the nature of collective action in the two sectors, the scope of which may easily fall outside the boundaries of public and civic action (or may at least be perceived as such by these groups' adherents). For very different reasons, sport and solidarity action may actually be seen as opportunities to engage collectively without having to relate explicitly to the political and public sphere. Therefore, they may attract individuals with a very differentiated range of attitudes towards the latter. However, these remarks only apply partially to welfare associations, where explicitly political orientations are also present (Ranci 1992), and they might also apply to cultural associations, which have proved to be important sources of institutional trust. The issue clearly requires further investigation.

Conclusions

The social capital literature is not short of attempts to disentangle concepts such as trust, social capital and participation in associations. In most cases, participation in associations is regarded as a potential predictor of social capital, which tends to be identified with trust (Stolle 1998; Newton 1999). Here I have taken a different approach, and proposed an explicitly relational view of social capital. Focussing on participation in associations as a source of specific ties has not entailed reducing social capital to this specific set of practices once for all. I have adopted an inclusive view—à la Coleman—of social capital as any social structure able to facilitate the achievement of certain goals. Emphasizing the context-dependent nature of social capital has then allowed me to show that while any social relation may in principle operate as social capital, it may not do so under all circumstances and in relation to all outcomes. Whether or not a social tie operates as social capital is ultimately dependent on its appropriateness in relation to specific goals (Foley and Edwards 1999). Ties originating from associational involvement were regarded as capable of operating as social capital in relation to the specific outcomes this study is interested in, namely, levels of institutional trust.

Differentiating between forms of associational social capital and outcomes has generated a richer portrait of the relationship between associational life and trust than is usually offered by surveys among the general population. The small percentage of people who are actually active in associations usually prevents us from distinguishing between associational types. This may account for the modest relation usually found between participation in associations and institutional trust. Focussing on active members of associations allows us to differentiate more accurately between forms of associational life and forms of trust. The findings presented here, it seems to me, validate this strategy.

There is no constant relation between social capital and trust. Not only that: both are internally differentiated. Factor analysis identified sub-sets of actors who commanded very uneven levels of trust, and regression analysis illustrated how trust in different actors could be explained at least partially by different types of associational experiences. Consistent with findings from general surveys (Newton 1999), socio-demographic traits and values are the best predictors of institutional trust. However, by comparison to these analyses, participation in associations and the resulting social capital have a significant impact which persists even after the introduction of control variables. This evidence speaks to a view of social capital as context-dependent: being active in associations does not automatically generate institutional trust across the board, but being, or having been, active in specific types of associations may affect (though not necessarily increase!) levels of trust in specific institutions. While people tend to join associations with compatible values and beliefs, the linkages that originate in associational life do play an independent role in shaping levels of institutional trust. Associations do matter, but *how* they matter is the more important question, and one that I have attempted to focus on here.

Notes

1. Professor of Sociology and Social Research, University of Trento, Italy. This chapter originates from a project funded by the Lombardy Regional Council in 1992–1993 (Biorcio and Diani 1993). I am grateful to Roberto Biorcio, Bepi Tomai and Nicoletta Cerrani for their collaboration. Bob Edwards and Mike Foley gave me many useful insights into the social capital debate. Drafts of this chapter were discussed at meetings at the Universities of Strathclyde and Trento; a previous version appeared as '*Capitale Sociale, Fiducia Istituzionale, e Azione Volontaria*' in *Rivista Italiana di Scienza Politica*, vol. 30, 2000, pp. 475–511.

2. I am thinking, for instance, of criticisms of Robert D. Putnam's earlier work for its neglect of non-associational ties such as private and informal ones, which have been addressed in his later publications (Putnam 1993, 2000; Newton 1997).

3. Not to consider positions like Bourdieu's (1986), who regards social capital mainly as a powerful mechanism of social closure.

4. One should obviously keep in mind that associational participation is also driven by instrumental motivations, and as such does not automatically contribute to the creation of collective goods (Uslaner 2000). However, the actual impact of selective incentives over decisions to participate in collective action of any kind has been severely questioned (Opp 1989).

5. Instead of factor scores, I use as dependent variables the means of the trust scores in the actors who load heavily on a specific factor (e.g., trust in unions is measured as the average trust in official and independent unions).

6. An expectation also supported by the findings collected in Norris (1999).

7. Some recent analysis of the social capital-participation link actually suggest that a long-term commitment does not necessarily reflect greater trust; to the contrary, this may be stronger among those with a more recent involvement in associations (Stolle 1997).

8. I included answers to the question 'Did your joining your current association imply a radical break with your previous experiences in other associations?' in the regression models as control variable (not shown in the actual tables).

9. Profession is measured as a series of dichotomous variables: professionals, self-employed, workers, clerks, teachers, housewives, students and retired people. In fact, only being a student or a self-employed person has proved occasionally significant, which is why they are the only variables of this group actually included in the tables.

10. See Listaugh and Wiberg (1995, pp. 318–19). However, results from their analysis should be taken with care, as they are based on the aggregation of data from several European states. This procedure exposes all the problems which have been identified by critics of an undifferentiated view of social capital, as they ignore the possibility of skewed distributions across social groups (Foley and Edwards 1999; Dekker, this volume; Foley et al. 2001). What is the substantive meaning of a variable such as 'trust in the press', given the enormous cross-country differences in European media (Schmitt-Beck 1998)?

11. However, the causal direction is still unclear: is it high commitment— and the level of identification and bonding social capital associated with it—that generates trust? Could not lower levels of trust encourage more intense commitment to one's group or association? For recent discussions of this point see Stolle (1998) and Uslaner (2000).

12. For example, 44 per cent of those who occupied central roles in their associations claimed to provide at least occasional advice and consultancy to some public agency, but only 14 per cent of those who were not playing any major role did.

References

Bernardi, L., and Diamanti, I. 1991. *Opinioni dei cittadini nei confronti delle istituzioni pubbliche in Lombardia. Indagine di scenario*. Milan: Regione Lombardia.

Biorcio, R., and Diani, M. 1993. *Primo rapporto sull'associazionismo in Lombardia*. Milan: Regione Lombardia.

Boissevain, J. 1974. *Friends of Friends*. Oxford: Blackwell.

Bourdieu, P. 1986. 'The Forms of Capital', in J. Richardson (ed.), *Handbook of Theory and Research for the Sociology of Education*. New York: Greenwood Press, pp. 241–58.

Brehm, J., and Rahn, W. 1997. 'Individual-Level Evidence for the Causes and Consequences of Social Capital'. *American Journal of Political Science* 41: pp. 999–1023.

Burt, R.S. 1998. The Network Structure of Social Capital.' Paper for the Conference 'Social Networks and Social Capital'. Durham, NC: Duke University.

Cartocci, R. 1994. *Tra Lega e Chiesa*. Bologna: il Mulino.

Coleman, J. 1990. *Foundations of Social Theory*. Cambridge, Massachusetts: Belknap.

Dalton, R. 1988. *Citizen Politics in Western Democracies*. Chatham, NJ: Chatham House.

Dalton, R. 1999. 'Political Support in Advanced Industrial Democracies', in P. Norris (ed.), *Critical Citizens*. Oxford: Oxford University Press, pp. 57–77.

Della Porta, D., and Diani, M. 1999. *Social Movements*. Oxford/Cambridge, Massachusetts: Blackwell.

Diamanti, I. 1993. *La Lega Lombarda*. Rome: Donzelli.

Donati, P. 2000. *The Industrial Class in Post-Industrial Age: Corporate Political Strategies in the Environmental Issue*. Fiesole: European University Institute, doctoral dissertation.

Edwards, B., Foley, M., and Diani, M. 2001. 'Social Capital Reconsidered', in B. Edwards, M. Foley, and M. Diani (eds.), *Beyond Tocqueville: Social Capital, Civil Society, and Political Process in Comparative Perspective*. Hanover: University Press of New England.

Foley, M., and Edwards, B. 1999. 'Is It Time to Disinvest in Social Capital?', *Journal of Public Policy* 41: pp. 141–73.

Fukuyama, F. 1995. *Trust*. New York: Free Press.

Greeley, A. 1997. 'Coleman Revisited: Religious Structures as a Source of Social Capital'. *American Behavioural Scientist* 40: pp. 587–94.

Hall, P. 1999, 'Social Capital in Britain'. *British Journal of Political Science* 29: pp. 417–61.

Inglehart, R. 1977. *The Silent Revolution: Changing Values and Political Styles Among Western Publics*. Princeton, NJ: Princeton University Press.

Inglehart, R. 1997. *Modernization and Postmodernization*. Princeton: Princeton University Press.

IREF (Institute for Education and Training Research). 1998. *La società civile in Italia*. Rome: Edizioni Lavoro.

Listhaug, O., and Wiberg, M. 1995. 'Confidence in Political and Private Institutions', in H. D. Klingemann and D. Fuchs (eds.), *Citizens and the State*. Oxford: Oxford University Press, pp. 298–322.

McAdam, D. 1989. 'The Biographical Consequences of Activism'. *American Sociological Review* 54: pp. 744–60.

McAdam, D., and Paulsen, R. 1993. 'Specifying the Relationship between Social Ties and Activism'. *American Journal of Sociology* 99: pp. 640–67.

McAllister, I. 1999. 'The Economic Performance of Governments', in P. Norris (ed.), *Critical Citizens*. Oxford: Oxford University Press, pp.188–203.

Miller, A., and Listhaug, O. 1999. 'Political Performance and Institutional Trust', in P. Norris (ed.), *Critical Citizens*. Oxford: Oxford University Press, pp. 204–16.

Newton, K. 1997. '*Social Capital and Democracy*'. *American Behavioural Scientist* 40: pp. 575–86.

Newton, K. 1999. 'Social and Political Trust in Established Democracies', in P. Norris (ed.), *Critical Citizens*. Oxford: Oxford University Press, pp. 169–87.

Norris, P. (ed.) 1999. *Critical Citizens*. Oxford: Oxford University Press.

Oliver, P. 1984. 'If You Don't Do It, Nobody Else Will: Active and Token Contributors To Local Collective Action'. *American Sociological Review* 49: pp. 601–10.

Opp, K. D. 1989. *The Rationality of Political Protest*. Boulder, CO: Westview Press.

Portes, A. 1998. 'Social Capital: Its Origins and Applications in Modern Sociology'. *Annual Review of Sociology* 24: pp. 1–24.

Putnam, R. D. 1993. *Making Democracy Work: Civic Traditions in Modern Italy*. Princeton: Princeton University Press.

————. 1995a. 'Bowling Alone: America's Declining Social Capital'. *Journal of Democracy* 6: pp. 65–78.

————. 1995b. 'Tuning In, Tuning Out. The Strange Disappearance of Social Capital in America'. *PS: Political Science and Politics* 28: pp. 664–83.

————. 2000. *Bowling Alone*. New York: Simon & Schuster.

Ranci, C. 1992. 'La mobilitazione dell'altruismo. Condizioni e processi di diffusione dell'azione volontaria in Italia'. *Polis* 6: pp. 467–505.

Ricolfi, L. 1993. 'Associazionismo e partecipazione politica', in A. Cavalli and A. De Lillo (eds.), *Giovani Anni 90*. Bologna: il Mulino, pp. 103–26.

Rose, R. 1998. '*Getting Things Done in an Anti-Modern Society: Social Capital Networks in Russia*', Studies in Public Policy Papers n. 304. Glasgow: University of Strathclyde.

Rose, R., Mishler, W., and Haerpfer, C. 1997. 'Social Capital in Civic and Stressful Societies'. *Studies in Comparative International Development* 32: pp. 85–111.

Schmitt-Beck, R. 1998. 'Of Readers, Viewers, and Cat-dogs', in J. Van Deth (ed.), *Comparative Politics*. London: Routledge, pp. 222–46.

Stolle, D. 1997. '*In a League of Their Own? Towards a Micro-Theory of Social Capital.*' American Political Science Association (APSA) Annual Meeting, Washington D.C.

————. 1998. 'Bowling Alone, Bowling Together: Group Characteristics, Membership and Social Capital'. *Political Psychology* 19: pp. 497–525.

Stolle, D., and Rochon, T.R. 1998. 'Are All Associations Alike? Member Diversity, Associational Type, and the Creation of Social Capital'. *American Behavioural Scientist* 42: pp. 47–65.

Tarrow, S. 1989. *Democracy and Disorder*. Oxford: Clarendon Press.

Topf, R. 1995. 'Beyond Electoral Participation', in H. D. Klingemann and D. Fuchs (eds.), *Citizens and the State*. Oxford: Oxford University Press, pp. 52–91.

Uslaner, E. M. 2002. *The Moral Foundations of Trust*. Cambridge: Cambridge Unviersity Press.

Van Deth, J. 1998. 'Equivalence in Comparative Political Research', in J. Van Deth (ed.), *Comparative Politics*. London: Routledge, pp. 1–19.

Van Deth, J. 2000. 'Interesting but Irrelevant: Social Capital and the Saliency of Politics In Western Europe'. *European Journal of Political Research* 37: pp. 115–47.

Woolcock, M. 1998. 'Social Capital and Economic Development: Toward a Theoretical Synthesis and Policy Framework'. *Theory and Society* 27: pp. 151–208.

7

Organizational Memberships and Crosscutting Ties:
Bonding or Bridging Social Capital?

D. Douglas Caulkins[1]

Introduction

Among the list of recent theorists who have created neo-Durkheimian interpretations of civic culture and social capital is cross-cultural researcher Raoul Naroll (1983), now deceased, who promoted the idea of 'moralnets', or value-homogeneous social support networks. According to Naroll, these moralnet support systems are important in helping individuals avoid mental illness, alcoholism and inter-personal violence.[2] While Naroll used a different vocabulary than the current social capital theorists, his concept of moralnets certainly fits Coleman's (1990: 302) definition of social capital as 'some aspect of social structure that facilitate certain actions of individuals who are within the structure'. By creating strong moralnets, Naroll maintained, a society could decrease the incidence of mental illness, alcoholism, suicide, child abuse and youth crime (1983). His passionate advocacy for developing support networks of kin, colleagues, friends and fellow organization members matches Putnam's crusade for reversing the apparent decline of social capital in the U.S. For Putnam, of course, the apparent decline in participation in voluntary organizations in the U.S. signals a decline in the kinds of 'structures of cooperation', trust, solidarity, tolerance and civic engagement essential for the continuity of civil society (Putnam 1993, 1995a, 2000).

Like Putnam, Naroll produced a great deal of quantitative evidence to support his contentions. Unlike Putnam, however, his strategy was to search for evidence of the importance of homogenous support groups in ethnographic data from a worldwide sample of more than 100 tribal and peasant societies. At a key point, however, Naroll's argument was flawed by a lack of attention to the mechanisms for the production of moralnets, just as social capital theorists are often not clear about the mechanisms by which voluntary organizations produce the generalized trust required for civil society.

As part of his project, Naroll searched national statistics for exemplary nation states. He contended that Norway represented a near ideal society since it had a low rate of the social ills mentioned above. Sweden and the Netherlands were nearly as successful in his view. The logic of his argument forced Naroll to assume that Norway (as well as Sweden and the Netherlands) had strong value-homogeneous support networks, yet he produced no convincing evidence for this assumption. He claimed, rather weakly, that Norway seemed a well-run society with strong family values. While he argued that voluntary organizations were important for creating moralnets in complex societies, he seemed unaware that Norway could be characterized as an 'organizational society' having a high density of voluntary organizations and high rates of membership and participation (Selle 1996). Thus, Naroll's research agenda and that of many current social capital theorists appear to converge.

The goal of this paper is to use a case study of organizational life in a Norwegian community to provide the missing evidence to reflect on Naroll's speculations about levels of social capital in Norway, and to question the assumption by Putnam and others that high density of voluntary organizations necessarily generates social capital. I will argue that a high density of organizations can concentrate or reinforce value-homogeneity within social networks composed mainly of persons who hold similar views. Hierarchical cluster analysis of organizational membership data in this case study reveals a set of ideologically focused organizational clusters, rather than the kind of interconnected social network assumed by most current social capital theorists.[3] Finally, using materials from current ethnographic

field work, I will suggest a different locus for social capital formation—in the relations between organizations, local government and
local business—and not, as Putnam has argued, in face-to-face interaction within organizations.

Social Capital and Crosscutting Ties of Membership

In Naroll's formulation, social capital in homogeneous moralnets
has dual benefits, both individual and collective, but primarily individual. The individual may avoid dysfunctions with the aid of his or
her value-homogeneous support network. In aggregate, society also
avoids the social costs of suicide, alcoholism and interpersonal violence. For Putnam, however, the main benefits of social capital are
collective: the creation or maintenance of a civil society; although in
his recent work he has placed relatively greater emphasis on the benefits of social capital for individual health and welfare (Putnam 2000).

Putnam's contention that voluntary organizations act as generators
of social capital must rely, at least partly, on one or both of the
following assumptions:

(1) Trust is generated in face-to-face group experiences and then is
generalized to the wider society outside those groups, and
(2) Generalized trust is increased by high organizational densities that
facilitate crosscutting ties of membership between different organizations.

Let us consider each of these assumptions in turn.

First, if people develop trust and solidarity with the fellow members of an organization to which they belong, they will generalize
that trust and solidarity to non-members, or to members of other
organizations. Stolle and Rochon (1998: 48) call the first kind of
trust, that developed in face-to-face interaction within the group,
'private civicness' or private social capital, while the trust that gen-
eralizes beyond the group they label 'public civicness' or public
social capital. However, the universality of this tendency to develop
public civicness out of private civicness is doubtful, and, as Stolle
and Rochon (1998) note, some types of organizations may be more
conducive to this development than others. Drawing on Putnam
(1995b: 665), they hypothesize that organizations whose members
'bridge major social categories will be more effective in fostering
generalized social trust and other components of social capital than
will associations whose membership is socially constricted' (Stolle

and Rochon 1998: 57). Putnam (2000: 23) distinguishes between bridging and bonding social capital, the latter being the more common form. While acknowledging that bonding social capital may have negative effects by creating 'out-group antagonisms' as well as creating in-group solidarity, bridging social capital seems to be entirely beneficial, creating wider identities by linking solidarity groups (Putnam 2000: 23). He notes that 'bonding and bridging are not "either-or" categories into which social networks can be neatly divided, but "more or less" dimensions along which we can compare different forms of social capital' (Putnam 2000: 23). However, as we will see, bridging social capital can be less well-distributed than Putnam implies, and is not always facilitated by the mechanisms that he indicates.

Second, a high organizational density suggests that many individuals will belong to multiple organizations. These organizations, then, will have an 'overlapping membership'. Individual members will be exposed to a wider network of individuals than just those who are fellow members of a single association. As a consequence, they will develop generalized trust of other organizations because they are apt to know at least a few people from those other organizations. In short, as a member of organization A, I may know a fellow member who is also a member of organization B. This provides an opportunity for the generalization of social capital beyond organization A to organization B because, in Putnam's view, social capital develops primarily through face-to-face contacts. In short, this argument linking organizational density and the development of trust assumes the existence of *crosscutting ties of membership between organizations in order to develop public civicness*.[4] This is the bridging form of social capital that Putnam finds most important for civic culture (Putnam 2000: 362–63).

Another way of conceptualizing the importance of crosscutting ties is to note that high organizational densities facilitate the development of 'bridging individuals' who link different organizations. In Granovetter's phrase, these bridging persons create the 'weak ties' that have been shown to be important in status attainment (Lin 1999, Granovetter 1973). Other social capital theorists also emphasize the importance of crosscutting ties or the relative openness or closure of social networks. In his formulation of the social capital concept, Bourdieu assumes closed class divisions, while Coleman and Putnam consider dense, connected networks as a distinct advantage

(Lin 1999a: 33–34). Clearly, the existence and nature of crosscutting ties among unlike or heterogeneous groups is an important empirical and theoretical question for social capital formation. As Putnam argues, 'To build bridging social capital requires that we transcend our social and political and professional identities to connect with people unlike ourselves' (Putnam 2000: 411).

Organizations and Social Capital in a Fjord Community

The evidence for this analysis of crosscutting ties in voluntary organizations comes from an ethnographic study of organizational life in two Norwegian municipalities from 1967 to 1969 (Caulkins 1980, 1994) and a current restudy of one community. The original study took place during a time of transition in organizational life in Norway, from the older organizations based on the social movements of the 19th century to the newer, more specialized and professionalized organizations (Selle 1996: 17). In the 1960s most voluntary organizations were democratically constituted, locally based, participatory, usually self-funded and hierarchically organized, with district and national offices.

For purposes of illustration, we will concentrate on Volda, a coastal municipality with a population of approximately 7,200 in 1968. The town itself had approximately 4,373 inhabitants, with the rest situated in small neighbourhoods along both sides of a fjord. My census of organizations in 1968 identified 160 groups including sports, music, health, religious, temperance, youth, cultural, hobby, missionary, service and economic organizations. All of these organizations met locally, in face-to-face activities, sometimes as often as every other week for some neighbourhood women's groups. More than 2,693 persons held 5,444 local organizational memberships. Of the adult residents in the municipality, 54.3 per cent of the women and 45.7 per cent of the men were members of at least one local organization. Nearly 29 per cent of the women and 20 per cent of the men belonged to more than one local organization. In different communities and neighbourhoods, the average density of memberships per household ranged from a high of 2 to a low of 0.5 memberships in neighbourhoods with a high proportion of the elderly.

This organizational membership density *appears* to represent a great deal of social capital. However, as Edwards and Foley (1998: 130) contend, 'To assume that we can simply aggregate social capital to produce some measure of resources available to society or the polity … is to make the same mistake that economists make in using the gross national product (GNP) per capita as a valid indicator of the national economic development'. To make the leap from the density of organizations or memberships to a generalized level of trust is inappropriate on several counts. First, it assumes, rather than demonstrates, a connection between the two variables. Second, Putnam's survey strategy transforms social capital into 'a characteristic of individuals acquired through social networks'. (Edwards and Foley 1998: 131) and reveals little about group-level measures of the production of social capital or trust.

In contrast, the strategy that I propose is more taxing than simply counting organizations and memberships, but it gives a better sense of the potential mechanisms for generating social capital through cross-cutting ties among organizations. This formulation makes social capital a characteristic of network relations rather than of individuals. The analysis requires the mapping of social networks of organizations. Sampling techniques I used are classified by Lin (1999a: 38) as the 'saturation survey' method that provides for a total mapping of the network. In this case, I obtained membership and participation information from each of the 160 local organizations.

Taking organizations as the unit of analysis in an organizational network, we consider two organizations to be connected if they share members.[5] The more members they have in common, the more connected they are. We can imagine an organizational field of 160 voluntary associations, all of which are interconnected, directly or indirectly, in a single closed network. In this case, crosscutting ties link all of the organizations. To consider a different result, we can also imagine cleavages in the network, so that there are several clusters of overlapping organizations that are not connected to each other. Conceptually, the analysis of this kind of network is simple and straightforward, requiring a hierarchical cluster analysis of a matrix of 160 organizations by 5,444 memberships. Memberships were first aggregated by household. By using the household rather than the individual as the membership unit, we avoid generating misleading cleavages such as men's versus women's organizations or youth versus adult organizations. This would be especially misleading in cases such as the one cited, in which the men's, women's and youth organizations have the same ideological focus.

Organizations that have a large percentage of their members in common will cluster, while those that have no members in common with other organizations will be isolates. Isolates obviously provide no crosscutting ties, but clusters of organizations are potential sites for such ties depending on the ideological focus of the constituent organizations. Clustered organizations either reinforce each others' ideology, or crosscut it (as would be the case if two members of opposing political parties were also members of the same service organization). Ties among ideologically *homogeneous* organizations are unlikely to produce generalized trust: this may be one of the limits of bonding social capital (Putnam 2000: 178, 358). Crosscutting ties or bridging social capital among ideologically *differentiated* organizations, on the other hand, might well produce such trust. Again, the distinction is between bonding social capital and bridging social capital. Thus, we are addressing two questions:

(1) Do organizations cluster in terms of overlapping membership?
(2) If so, are the clustered organizations diverse or homogeneous in values and ideology? Diversity produces bridging social capital; homogeneity produces bonding social capital.

Organizational Clusters: Ideologically Homogeneous or Heterogeneous?

In the 1960s, voluntary organizations in Volda had explicit values and ideologies, reflecting their historic development out of social movements of the 19th century. Whole sets of organizations were focused on the peasant movement, the labour movement, the lay religious movement, the temperance movement and the New Norwegian language (*Nynorsk*) movement. These organizations are the institutionalized carriers of ideologies (Selle 1996: 191). Up through the 1960s, individual identity was often associated with organizational membership, which frequently passed from father to son and mother to daughter. Taking the household as the unit of analysis, a typical husband, wife, and children each belonged to one to three organizations. In this way, family households were tied into larger social networks that included neighbours, other relatives, friends, and possibly work colleagues.

As Stolle and Rochon (1998) suggest, not all organizations are alike, and some have more capacity for generating social capital than others; therefore we must be attentive to the purpose or ideology of each organization. Stolle and Rochon (1998: 47) show that 'homogeneous associations are less likely to inculcate high levels of generalized trust and community reciprocity among their members.'[6] Our argument is similar: homogenous *clusters* of organizations are less likely to inculcate generalized levels of trust.

Consider the concrete example of Fjordend, one of the smallest communities within Volda municipality, an isolated seashore neighbourhood of 89 households and 213 residents. These residents are members of 18 different voluntary organizations, six of which are purely local and have overlapping memberships. The remaining 12 draw on a wider operating territory. Half of them have overlapping memberships with local organizations.

As table 7.1 indicates, the 12 organizations with overlapping membership (6 local and 6 non-local) form a single cluster. This cluster, if ideologically homogeneous, would constitute the core network sector for the community. Among the organizations in the cluster, 8 are ideologically affiliated; all are Christian groups along with the Men's Quartet, which is devoted to religious music. The remaining 4 organizations in the cluster are ideologically compatible with the others even if they have no explicit religious focus. The Public Health Association, Farmer's Association, New Norwegian Language Association and Folk Arts Association all are associated with the

Table 7.1 Clustered organizations in Fjordend

Organization	Number of Fjordend Members
1. Fjordend Women's Seamen's Mission Society	19
2. Fjordend Public Health Association	27
3. Fjordend Missionary Association	18
4. Volda Christian Temperance Association	16
5. Middalen Mission for Seamen Abroad	1
6. Volda Folk Arts Association	1
7. Volda *Nynorsk* Language Association	2
8. Fjordend Christian Youth Association	9
9. Volda Christian People's Party	5
10. Fjordend Men's Quartet	5
11. Fjordend Farmer's Association	12
12. Volda Christian People's Party Women's Group	1
Total	116

kind of rural-oriented revitalization movement that accompanied
the religious revivals of the last century. The variety of Christian
organizations present in the cluster reinforces the pietistic focus of
this community in a variety of contexts. Thus the cluster is ideologically homogeneous, but institutionally multifaceted and mutually
reinforcing. Institutional diversity should not be confused with ideological diversity. This ideological homophily in network sectors or
clusters is more problematic for Putnam's version of social capital
production than for Naroll's. For Naroll homophily is essential; for
Putnam it is less productive because bonding social capital needs to
be balanced with bridging social capital (Putnam 2000: 362–63).

Several of the non-clustered organizations (see table 7.2) are ideologically incompatible with the clustered organizations. The Centre
Party, Socialist People's Party and Labour Party are secular competitors with the Christian People's Party. These organizations have no
neighbourhood branches and do not meet in Fjordend. From the
perspective of the core Fjordend community, the members of the
non-clustered organizations are marginal. These members participate
in organizational clusters that are centred on other neighbourhoods
or communities; they have built their networks outward to other
communities rather than within their own communities. Thus it is
not the case that the community itself is culturally homogeneous,
because there are residents who choose ideologies other than pietistic Christianity. However, those people who choose the non-
dominant ideology participate in social networks located outside of
Fjordend. This makes for self-reinforcing homogeneous social networks and sharpens the distinction between the core residents of
the community and the marginal ones. If the members of the Socialist

**Table 7.2 Fjordend residents' memberships in organizations
outside their community**

Organizations	Number of Fjordend Members
1. Volda Rifle Club	2
2. Volda Liberal Party	2
3. Volda Arts League	1
4. Volda Centre Party	1
5. Volda Socialist People's Party	1
6. Volda Labour Party	2
Total	9

People's Party or the Labour Party were also members of the Fjordend Public Health Association, there would be crosscutting ties among the Christian core locals and the marginal locals. However, such voluntaristic crosscutting ties tend not to occur in any of the small communities in the municipality.

The core populations in the small communities, as indicated by their organizational clusters, were ideologically homogeneous. This created a kind of 'private social capital', to use the terminology of Stolle and Rochon (1998), which pertains not just to solidarity in a single organization but also to solidarity with the hegemonic ideology of an organizational cluster. This promotes a kind of bonding social capital that does not generalize beyond the cluster of organizations out of which it is generated. An incident from my fieldwork will illustrate the point. Introducing myself to the female leader of one of the Christian associations, I noted that I was interviewing leaders of all of the organizations in the municipality. As I enumerate the types of organizations that I was contacting, she looked especially horrified when I mentioned the Liberal Youth Association (*Frilynt Ungdomslag*). 'How can you talk to those people?' she remarked—it wasn't really a question. Growing even more suspicious of me, she then inquired sharply, 'Are you a personal Christian—have you been saved? If not, I don't think I want to talk with you'. So much for generalized trust. As Putnam notes, evangelical Christianity may be less prone to produce bridging capital than mainline Christianity (Putnam 2000: 78).

The ideological focus of the small communities was not always on pietistic Christianity. In other communities the core population focused on the Centre Party plus the Public Health Association and some other secular organizations, with the fundamentalist Christians in a marginal position. The marginal individuals attended organizational meetings in other communities where the ideological focus matched their interests. None of the small communities had genuine crosscutting ties between organizations with contrasting ideological foci. For core members of these small communities, the evidence fits Naroll's moralnet version of social capital theory, with its emphasis on the individual benefits of moralnets. It also fits the conceptions of Bourdieu and Coleman but casts doubts on the civic benefits of such homogeneous networks.

One possible benefit of the homogeneous networks for civil society could be that the *diversity* of the society is masked or hidden, so that citizens assume that others have the same interests.[7] The ideological focus of organizational life in these small communities reinforces the Norwegian cultural theme of *likhet*, the 'sameness' or homogeneity of a people (Gullestad 1985). This notion of 'sameness' is reinforced in small communities since one ideological perspective becomes hegemonic and individuals who subscribe to a different or minority perspective join compatible organizations in other communities.

In larger and more central communities in the municipality with populations of over 300, two or more distinct non-overlapping organizational clusters emerged. In these cases, for example, a community might support both a cluster of Christian organizations and a cluster of rural cultural organizations. But, again, these clusters were ideologically homogeneous, contrary to the expectation of social capital theory.

The town centre of Volda, with a population of approximately 4,373, had a more complex set of 12 organizational clusters (see table 7.3). As in the smaller communities, however, the organizational clusters are ideologically reinforced rather than crosscutting, with only trivial exceptions. Note that two cultural organizations, the Volda Folk Arts Association and the Volda *Nynorsk* Language Association, are clustered with the Liberal Party (cluster 2). Since the 19th century, the Liberal Party has had an important role in supporting the development of an 'authentic' Norwegian rural culture. However, in Fjordend (table 7.1), the Folk Arts Association and the *Nynorsk* Language Association were clustered with the Christian People's Party and other Christian organizations. This might seem to be a genuine case of crosscutting ties between members of two political parties mediated by common membership in cultural organizations. In fact, the case is trivial because only three members from the Fjordend Christian cluster are involved in the *Nynorsk* and Folk Arts associations out of a total membership of 146 in both cultural organizations.

In summary, 41 organizations within the town centre overlap to form 12 distinct clusters, with a total of 2,146 members (see appendix A for a complete listing of the organizations in each cluster). Note that four out of the five largest clusters incorporate different political parties. This suggests that the clusters are contending or ideologically competitive sectors in the field of voluntary associations. The largest cluster centres on the kinds of cultural issues that

Table 7.3 Organizational clusters in Central Volda, by decreasing size

Type or focus of organizations in cluster	Organizations in cluster	Members in cluster
1. Liberal Party, culture, *Nynorsk*, homemakers	9	1,084
2. Christian Peoples Party, missionary, temperance	6	303
3. Hunting and fishing	2	182
4. Conservative Party, business	3	153
5. Center Party, farm associations	4	97
6. Foreign mission, service	4	75
7. Public health, household	2	62
8. Teachers' professional association	2	57
9. Christian missions, youth	3	32
10. Mission and religious music	2	28
11. Socialist Party, track club	2	8
12. Youth mission	2	7
Total	41	2,146

have been historically important locally in the Liberal Party and associated movements from the 19th century.[8] The second largest cluster focuses on the Christian People's Party and associated religious organizations. Note that there are also smaller clusters of religious organizations that are not attached to this major cluster (see clusters 6, 9,10,12). This fragmentation into several clusters for the Christian organizations is not unexpected since it reflects the factionalism between the pietistic and more liberal wings of the movement. The third largest cluster represents a major interest group, hunting and fishing, which does not draw significantly from the major political/ideological groups. Next in size is the Conservative Party and business organizations (cluster 4), followed by the Centre or Agrarian Party and its associated organizations (cluster 5). The remaining clusters not yet mentioned are a secular women's organization cluster (cluster 7) and a strange but minor alliance between the Socialist People's Party and the Track Club (cluster 11).

Table 7.4 Comparison between clustered and non-clustered organizations in Volda centre

Clustered Organizations			Isolated Organizations	
Organizations	Clusters	Members	Organizations	Members
41	12	2,146	35	701

As table 7.4 shows, the non-clustered or isolated organizations in the town centre are numerous but generally small and specialized, accounting for a total of 701 memberships in contrast to 2,146 memberships in clustered organizations. This comparison gives a sense of the dominance of the organizational clusters and their ideological foci in the organizational life of the community. Crosscutting ties between ideologically different organizational clusters seem empirically unrepresentative. Our search for bridging social capital in crosscutting ties, then, ends in disappointment.

Social Capital Formation: Relations Between Organizations and the State

Rather than analyzing further the face-to-face socialization potential of voluntary organizations in Norway, I suggest refocusing our attention on what may be a more important site for the development of 'structures of cooperation': relations *between* organizations and government or private business. My survey of organizations in Volda in 1968 revealed that 26 organizations (12 women's groups 5 men's groups, and 9 mixed groups) had been consulted by local government, some of them routinely, concerning actions and public funding under consideration. This gave me the sense that voluntary organizations are increasingly partnering with the government in providing the civic services that are needed. In the past 30 years this relationship has been extended and formalized, so that local government committees and offices routinely deal with voluntary organizations and contract with them for the provision of services (Selle 1996, 1998).

The degree of change over the past 30 years can be illustrated with one simple example. In 1968 when local government wanted to put on a leadership programme for organizations, they came to me to get a complete census of the organizations. In 1998 when I returned to Volda for fieldwork, I went to the Cultural Affairs Director who by then had a complete listing of all 300 organizations in the municipality (which she updated constantly). Many of the new organizations are support organizations for individuals with special needs. Others are devoted to recreational and hobby activities that were not widespread 30 years ago. Organizational life has become more professionalized, specialized, and connected with state functions (Selle 1996). However, many familiar organizations from the earlier period continue to appear on the register kept by the Cultural Affairs Director.

During this recent fieldwork with the Cultural Affairs government committee[9] in Volda, I thought that I saw the issues of social capital formation more sharply. The committee members were responding in person to issues raised by representatives of different organizations. This seemed to be the kind of face-to-face experience where social capital was generated. The interaction between the organization representatives and council committee members was collaborative rather than adversarial. I noted one exception, when a member from a peripheral community asked whether his district was the only one whose cultural heritage was not worth being supported.[10] This is a common rhetorical strategy in local politics, and assurances were offered that, of course, there would be support; the only question was how to make it most efficient. The cultural committee clearly was concerned about the heritage of this peripheral place: they had to travel half-an-hour by bus, 20 minutes by a small fishing boat and 15 minutes by foot to see and admire the cultural artifact in question. The collaborative tone returned to the interaction. This is a locus for social capital formation: in face-to-face discussions the *organizational representative* learns that *local government representatives* are sympathetic to his situation, appreciate his efforts, and will try to reach a rational and effective solution to the problem according to criteria widely accepted in business and government. Voluntary organizations, in routine interaction with public officials, are important vehicles for social capital formation. They are not simply training grounds for learning trust that will be generalized to other arenas.

The consequences of this kind of formation of 'structures of co-operation' came to me when I was sitting in the Volda town hall in 1998, going over stacks of funding applications from organizations directed toward the Cultural Affairs Committee over the past several years. Each application had a coversheet that listed the organization's name, the amount of funding they were requesting, the amount they had received the previous year and the recommendation of the Cultural Affairs Director. Most applications were for relatively modest amounts of money, ranging from around 50 to 150 dollars, for small projects like improving facilities at a community center, developing educational exhibitions or preserving artifacts of local historical importance. The majority of the 300 organizations found some project that required funding, and virtually all received at least a minimal amount. In this annual quest for a bit of funding, only very large or very controversial applications were turned down. The applications were meticulously completed, year after year, and the requisite small sums were dispensed year after year. I also examined and recorded a collection of several years of applications for funding from the local bank. The forms were slightly different from the government forms, but much of the same information was required whether public or private funding was being sought.

As I attended organizational meetings I gained the understanding that first, organizations routinely looked to the government and the private sector as important parts of their environment. Second, I found that organizations had become much more project-driven than in the past. This joint public/private funding of local organizational projects has further diminished the barriers between the three sectors in society. Organizations were under pressure to make these projects 'saleable', not just to their own members, but also to the government and corporate committees who would scrutinize their funding applications. For example, several of the old organizations that grew out of the 19th century social movements have now shifted their activities toward local heritage projects. Projects for archiving, collecting or restoring local material and intellectual culture of the past have become a more active part of the mission of these organizations.

Project and goal-oriented organizational activities, of course, can be measured for success or progress in the same terms used by business and governmental administration. Applications from organizations often detailed the estimates of the number of hours of labour and costs of materials that would be required for different parts of a project in a kind of rational administrative budgeting approach, accompanied by appropriate accounts from the previous year's activities. The anticipated amount of volunteer labour was often specified in the application.

Because I was handling all of these original application documents, I began to see a pattern: unless the organization asked for an unusual amount of funding, the application was undisturbed. That is to say, it was clear from the impressions and indentations of the paper clips that most of the applications had not been examined after they were originally assembled: the paper clips themselves had not been moved.[11] The exceptions were those very few applications that had been controversial. The Director of Cultural Affairs had, of course, checked all of the applications beforehand for completeness and compliance with the regulations. The applications had subsequently been made available to the committee members prior to and at the meetings where they made funding decisions. But they were not inspected. This suggests a routinization of trust and cooperation between the organizational representatives and the members of the government committee: reasonable and legitimate requests will be honored.

The annual applications are not just for funding, I would argue, but also for *legitimacy*. From the narrow perspective of time efficiency, many of the applications cost more in labour for preparation than they netted in funding. The application process is an annual renewal of legitimacy, a kind of contract between the organization and funding agency without which the organization would cease to exist as a proper organization. And, of course, to present an application to the government committee is an acknowledgment of the legitimacy of that committee. The annual applications are indicative of a new kind of organizational culture, radically changed since the 1960s, in which the routine activities of organizations are project-driven and integrated with the goals of the state and private sectors.

This kind of undramatic, everyday practice of *performing civil society* leads to the development of *habitus*, to use Bourdieu's (1990) terminology, or a cognitive schema or cultural model (Strauss and Quinn 1997) that is important for the development and maintenance of civil society. A cultural model is a highly schematized, skeletal representation of some cultural domain and includes the elements, structure, associations and processes within that domain. A cultural model is constructive, in that it defines the elements that constitute the domain. It also conveys how those elements relate to one another and how the domain 'works'. These models are templates for behaviour that constitute a set of expectations about the way that civil society operates. This kind of routinization of practice on the part of organizations and their members leads to routine expectations of fair, rational and co-operative treatment from the public and private sectors, the essence of civil society.

This case of the undisturbed paper clips, in my view, has much to tell us about the mystery of social capital formation in Norway. Both in the literal sense of the English term—paper clip—and of the Norwegian term—*binder*—organizations, business and local government are clipped or bound together in a system of contractual paperwork transactions. Furthermore, I suspect that while participation in organizations is useful in fostering social capital, it would also seem that passive membership is enough to keep the cultural model in practice. As long as a member is able to learn the outcome of dealings between his organization and the public and private sectors, the practice can continue and the cultural model of civil society, with all its expectations, remains intact. Once we have arrived at that understanding of this aspect of contemporary organizational society in Norway, we are no longer as concerned with whether or not organizational memberships are structured to generate trust among heterogeneous populations, among people who are not like each other.

Conclusion

As Stolle and Rochon (1998: 49) have observed,

> Many claims made about the effects of associational memberships on social capital rely on the formative experience of interaction with other members. If those interactions bring one into contact with a broad sampling of members of society then the formative experience is likely to be more pronounced than if the association itself is a narrowly constituted segment of society.

But we can go even further: the data from Volda shows that cross-cutting ties of membership among different organizations do not necessarily produce contact with 'a broad sampling of members of society', but may, instead, reinforce the ideological hegemony of a cluster of organizations and their members. This leaves us with a sense that Naroll may have been right about the importance of homogeneous social networks (moralnets) for the mental and physical health of populations, and that Norway may, indeed, have been fortunate to have such moralnets in recent history. The findings also leave us with a sense of the incompleteness of Putnam's earlier formulation of the mechanisms of social capital. Bonding social capital does not *necessarily* produce bridging social capital. To see the creation of the bridging type of social capital, I suggest we need to look at a wider social field, one that encompasses the interactions of local government with organizations. I contend that the empirical evidence provided in this case study forces us to revise the simple equation of 'the greater the organizational density, the greater the social capital and generalized trust'.

When, in a brief conversation with Robert Putnam in 1998 I reported the findings outlined above, he professed surprise. The occasion of the conversation was Putnam's visit to Iowa (a state in the upper midwest of the U.S., and not to be confused with Idaho or Indiana) for a conference. In his lecture, Putnam explained that the upper midwest, populated mainly by people of Scandinavian, Dutch, German and British ancestry, is the 'capitol of social capital'.[12] The rest of the U.S. was in a state at decline, at least a decline of social capital.[13] What perhaps surprised Putnam most (in my interpretation) was my observation that Volda has apparently not suffered the decline in organizational life that Putnam has documented for America. With approximately the same population size as it had in 1968, the municipality now has more than double the number of voluntary organizations. Active participation seems to have declined, according to some leaders, and it is difficult to get people to take up leadership roles (but these are complaints that I heard 30 years ago as well).

If there is indeed a serious decline in active participation in Volda and other places in Norway, this may one day threaten the kind of moralnet-related individual benefits that Naroll assumed for Norwegian society. On the other hand, contrary to Putnam's argument, a decline in active participation is not fatal to social capital. If the argument in this paper is correct, socialization through participation in meetings is not the key to the formation of social capital. What is important, I am persuaded, is continued membership in local organizations and the continued capacity of such organizations to represent the interests and beliefs of a wide range of people in society. Membership in these organizations now implies a contractual, project-based relationship with private and public sector organizations, not just for funding but also for legitimacy. If the leaders of these organizations, who in Norway are increasingly paid professionals, can demonstrate that their members' interests, concerns and identities are continually acknowledged and legitimized in interactions with the state and the private sector, then the necessary structures of cooperation will be formed and maintained. We need to look for evidence of this process, not only in Norway but perhaps elsewhere as well, in a different mechanism than that which Putnam has suggested. We need to look for undisturbed paper clips.

Appendix A Inventory of Organizations in Town Centre Clusters

Type or focus of organizations in cluster	Members in organization	Members in cluster
1. Liberal Party	82	1,084
Liberal Party Women's Group	30	
Folk Arts Association	75	
Nynorsk Language Association	71	
Art League	140	
Garden Club	86	
Association for the Handicapped	140	
Homemakers' Association	122	
2. Christian Peoples Party	89	303
Christian Peoples Party Women's Group	48	
White Band Temperance Association	77	
Israel Mission	18	
Volda Temperance Association	77	
Women's Norwegian Mission Society	42	
3. Volda Hunting and Fishing Association	75	182
Volda Rifle Club	107	
4. Conservative Party	2	153
Conservative Party Women's Club	31	
Business Association	50	
5. Centre Party	16	97
Centre Party Women's Group	11	
Farm Women's Association	29	
Farmers' Association	41	
6. International Order of Good Templars	12	75
Red Cross Hospital Visitors	15	
Mission for Seamen Abroad	29	
Santal Mission	19	
7. Public Health Association	33	62
Neighbourhood Women's Association	29	
8. Volda Teachers' Association	39	57
Volda Practice Teachers Association	18	
9. Men's Mission Union	12	32
Young Christians	15	
Men's Mission Association	5	
10. Mission Union	14	28
Mission Choir	24	
11. Socialist People's Party	3	8
Track Club	5	
12. Junior Mission for Seamen Abroad	1	7
Good Templar Youth	6	–
Total	2,146	2,146

Notes

1. Harold D. Strong Professor of Social Science, Grinnel College, Iowa, USA. I am grateful to Per Selle for hospitality at The LOS Centre, Bergen, Norway, during a research visit in the spring of 1998. Jørgen and Ragnhild Amdam made my return to Volda productive and pleasant. My thanks also to the staff at Møre Forsking and to Volda College. The Grinnell College Grant Board, chaired by Dean James Swartz, provided financial support for this research.

2. I have examined this argument in greater detail in Caulkins 1995.

3. Lin (1999,1999a) is an exception since he claims that high-density social networks are not necessary to generate social capital.

4. Borgatti, Jones and Everett (1998) discuss a variety of network measures for different conceptions of social capital. For Putnam's conception, which they label 'internal measures for collective actors', two of the measures positively associated with social capital are 'density', the number of members of a group who are tied in a positive relationship, and 'centralization' or 'the extent to which the network is NOT divided into cliques that have few connections *between* groups' (table 7.5). A third measure, homophily, or the extent that group members are tied to persons like themselves, is negative in terms of bridging social capital. Another way of phrasing these measures is to suggest, as I have done, that crosscutting ties between homogeneous groups (cliques) are positive for the creation of social capital in Putnam's conception. Crosscutting ties counteract homophily.

5. Hierarchical, agglomerative cluster analysis with the average-linkage method was used in this research. Jaccard's coefficient was used to calculate the similarity of each pair of organizations. This coefficient is calculated by dividing the set-theoretic intersection of the membership of two organizations by their set-theoretic union. If the two organizations have no members in common, the coefficient is zero; if they share all their members the coefficient is one.

6. Stolle and Rochon's (1998) data allows only an indirect test of this hypothesis since they are only able to assess the diversity of persons belonging to particular types of associations, and not the diversity within particular associations. The results reported here give us greater confidence in this hypothesis since the data pertains to the composition of particular organizations and clusters of organizations rather than to aggregated data.

7. Anderson's (1983) notion of the 'imagined community' is, of course, partly dependent on this assumption of common interests and background. Given the ubiquity of media coverage of cultural differences, even within a relatively homogeneous society such as Norway, it is

increasingly difficult to 'imagine' any community in as simple a fashion as implied by '*likhet*'. But therein lies the challenge of multiculturalism.

8. Hodne (1995: 112–15) correctly argues for the important role of voluntary organizations in the formation of Norwegian national culture.

9. As Selle contends (1998: 170), 'culture' is no longer high culture, but a more anthropological version of the concept implying everyday ways of life.

10. This tension between the centre and periphery is an old one in local as well as national politics, and is becoming less and less important as communication improvements continue to erase the distinction between centre and periphery. National policy, in comparison with many other countries, such as Sweden, has been extremely responsive to the needs of infrastructural developments in the periphery.

11. As an anthropologist I embrace methodological heterogeneity and 'triangulation' through assembling of evidence from many sources to provide a context. The undisturbed paper clips can be considered an 'unobtrusive measure' of behavioural traces not consciously created.

12. Rice and Feldman (1997: 1,143) have shown that the civic culture of Americans of European ancestry bears a 'strong resemblance to the civic attitudes of the contemporary citizens of the European nations with whom they share common ancestors'.

13. Putnam also said in his lecture that he was unconvinced that e-mail exchanges were conducive to the development of social capital since they did not involve face-to-face relations. For a contrary view, see Lin 1999a.

References

Anderson, B. 1983. *Imagined Communities: Reflections on the Origin and Spread of Nationalism*. London: Verso.

Bourdieu, P. 1990. *The Logic of Practice*. Palo Alto: Stanford University Press.

Borgatti, S., Jones, C. and Everett, M. 1998. 'Network measures of social capital', *Connections* 21; pp. 2–36.

Breiger, R.L. 1974. 'The duality of persons and groups,' *Social Forces* 53: pp. 181–90.

Caulkins, D.D. 1980. 'Community, sub-culture, and organizational networks in western Norway'. *Journal of Voluntary Action Research*, vol. 9 no. 1–4: pp. 35–44.

Caulkins, D.D. 1994. 'Norwegians: cooperative individualists', in M. Ember, C. Ember, and D. Levinson (eds.), *Portraits of Culture: Ethnographic Originals, Vol III*. Upper Saddle River, N.J.: Prentice Hall, pp. 1–30.

Caulkins, D.D. 1995. 'Are Norwegian voluntary associations homogeneous moralnets? Reflections on Naroll's selection of Norway as a model society'. *Cross-Cultural Research*, vol 29 no. 1: pp. 43–57.

Caulkins, D.D. 1999. 'Social capital'. *Anthropology Newsletter*, Society for the Anthropology of Europe, March, p. 53.

Coleman, J.S. 1990. *Foundations of Social Theory*. Cambridge, Massachusetts: Harvard University Press.

Edwards, B., and Foley, M.W. 1998. 'Civil society and social capital beyond Putnam'. *American Behavioural Scientists*, 42, 1: pp. 124–39.

Granovetter, M. 1973. 'The Strength of Weak Ties'. *American Journal of Sociology* 78; pp. 1360–380.

Gullestad, M. 1985. *Livsstil og Likhet*. Oslo, Norway: Universitetsforlaget.

Hodne, B. 1995. *Norsk Nasjonalkulture: En Kulturpolitisk Oversikt*. Oslo, Norway: Universitetsforlaget.

Lin, N. 1999. 'Social networks and status attainment'. *Annual Review of Sociology* 25: pp. 467–87.

Lin, N. 1999a. 'Building a network theory of social capital', *Connections* 22, 1: pp. 28–51.

Naroll, R. 1983. *The Moral Order: An Introduction to the Human Situation*. Beverly Hills, CA: Sage.

Putnam, R.D. 1993. *Making Democracy Work: Civic Traditions in Modern Italy*. Princeton, N.J.: Princeton University Press.

————. 1995a. 'Bowling Alone: America's Declining Social Capital'. *Journal of Democracy* 6: pp. 55–78.

————. 1995b. Tuning In, Tuning Out: The Strange Disappearance of Social Capital in America'. *Political Science and Politics* 28: pp. 664–83.

————. 1998. 'Personal Communication.'

————. 2000. *Bowling Alone: The Collapse and Revival of American Community*. New York: Simon & Schuster.

Rice, T., and Feldman, J. 1997. 'Civic Culture and Democracy from Europe to America'. *The Journal of Politics* 59, 4: pp. 1143–72.

Selle, P. 1996. *Frivillige Organisasjonar i Nye Omgjevnader*. Bergen, Norway: Alma Mater.

Selle, P. 1998. 'Organisasjonssamfunnet–Ein Statsreiskap?', in T. Grønlie and P. Selle (eds.), *Ein Stat? Fristillingas Fire Ansikt*. Oslo: Samlaget, pp. 141–78.

Stolle, D. and Rochon, T.R. 1998. 'Are All Associations Alike? Member Diversity, Associational Type, and the Creation of Social Capital'. *American Behavioural Scientist* 42(1): pp. 47–65.

Strauss, C., and Quinn, N. 1997. *A Cognitive Theory of Cultural Meaning*. Cambridge: Cambridge University Press.

8

Communities, Social Capital and Local Government:
Generalized Trust in Regional Settings

Dietlind Stolle[1]

Introduction

How are the norms of reciprocity and trust generalized and institutionalized, and what is different about groups, regions and nations where this is not the case? This is the most under-researched area in social capital studies, providing only a few hypotheses, all of which need more development and testing. The social capital literature is divided on this question (Hooghe and Stolle 2003). Society-based accounts suggest that local, regional or national patterns of social capital are fixed and shaped by historical factors that occurred centuries ago (see Putnam 1993; Fukuyama 1995; and earlier accounts of similar arguments in Banfield 1958). At the most, governments, and particularly oppressive regimes, can damage and destroy social capital, as the examples of the Norman kingdom in Southern Italy or several authoritarian and totalitarian regimes in Southern and Eastern Europe indicate, but they might not be able to facilitate or foster the generation of social capital. The implications of this observation have left many social scientists and policy makers dissatisfied. State-based accounts of social capital theory respond that for social capital to flourish it needs to be embedded in and linked to formal state institutions (Berman 1997; Levi 1998; Rothstein and Stolle 2003; Skocpol 1996; Tarrow 1996). According to this group of scholars, social capital does not exist independently in the realm of civil society; instead, governments and political institutions channel and influence social capital to a degree that it becomes either a beneficial or a detrimental resource for democracy. In an attempt to bridge these camps, Putnam has recently argued that in the U.S. context, it needs the combined effort of all the employers, the mass media, voluntary associations, individual citizens and government to restore levels of social capital in the country (2000: 402 ff.). The debate about whether social capital can be intentionally developed, and if so how, lies ultimately at the heart of the matter for low social capital areas in their attempt to struggle to restore or facilitate this resource (Petro 2001).

This chapter will shed more light on the sources of one important aspect of social capital, i.e., generalized trust. The findings of this chapter are twofold. First, the examination of three Swedish regions reveals that the character of both local government and local institutions, as well as their effects on political trust, emerges as the most important factor in explaining variation in generalized trust. This result is confirmed even when other prominent causes of generalized trust, such as regional membership in associations, socio-economic differences and parental child rearing practices are taken into account. Second, the study finds that *contemporary* political and institutional arrangements at the regional level are important determinants of social capital. It might also be true that generalized trust has been shaped by historical forces from the middle ages, but present-day local and regional (as well as national) governments and institutions also make an impact on generalized trust. This chapter thus informs the controversy about the various sources of social capital.

Regional Sources of Generalized Trust

How can we explain regional differences in generalized trust? In this section, the main theoretical and empirical ideas with regard to societal and governmental sources of generalized trust will be introduced. Most commonly, differences in contemporary forms and levels of social capital have been traced to historical societal experiences. In Putnam's account of the differences between Italian regions, the new regime in the South, founded by Norman mercenaries, and the experiences of self-government in the North both left their mark and led to the development of cultures of trust and of mistrust in the North and South respectively, both of which lasted over centuries as they became generalized and institutionalized (see Putnam 1993: 122 ff.). In other words, both vicious and virtuous circles started centuries ago and left their imprint on institutions and society, and they have now come to influence the performance of regional governments that look identical on paper. The message of Putnam's historical excursion is that today's levels of social capital were developed over long periods of time, and therefore cannot be changed easily. In fact the differences in today's patterns of cooperation are reflected in the varying regional density of horizontal networks of associations. The claim is that in areas with strong, dense, horizontal and extensive crosscutting networks, there is a spillover from membership in organizations to the development of cooperative values and norms among citizens.[2] In areas where networks with such characteristics do not develop, there are fewer opportunities to learn civic virtue and democratic attitudes, resulting in a lack of trust (Putnam 1993: 122 ff.; de Tocqueville 1835).

Yet if institutions foster trust and cooperation among citizens, how are these institutions structured? If the Norman kingdom in the South, on the one hand, and the self-governed communities in the North, on the other, had such an enormous impact on shaping social capital centuries ago, what parallels do we find in today's state structures that should or should not be replicated? What is the role of other institutions such as voluntary associations in the development of generalized values and attitudes *vis-à-vis* governmental factors? These questions need to inform any analyses of the sources of social capital, and this chapter will set out to answer some of them.

However, what do we know about the role of governments and institutions in fostering, maintaining or destroying social capital? Contemporary governmental aspects have rarely been the focus of the search for the sources of social capital (Petro 2001; Tarrow 1996).Two kinds of governmental influences on trust have been suggested to explain why some democracies have more trusting people than others. On the one hand, differences in low levels of generalized trust have been explained by high inequalities that prevail within society (Boix and Posner 1998). For example, the rise of income inequality in the United States has led to diminishing levels of generalized trust (see Uslaner 2002). Also, cross-nationally, income inequality and trust are strongly correlated. Citizens who see their fellow citizens as equals and as 'one of their own' can more easily make a leap of faith and give a trust credit to others who are not necessarily known. The second argument, one that I will advance in this chapter, relates generalized trust between citizens to political and institutional trust. Levi argues that governments generate trust only if citizens consider the state itself to be trustworthy (Levi 1998: 86). States, for example, enable the establishment of contracts in that they provide information and monitor laws; they enforce rights and rules that sanction lawbreakers and protect minorities (Levi 1998: 85 ff.). In his analysis of the Swedish case, Rothstein writes: 'If people believe that the institutions that are responsible for handling "treacherous" behaviour act in a fair, just and effective manner, and if they also believe that other people think the same of these institutions, then they will also trust other people' (2000). These differences in government and state capacity to monitor free-riding and to punish defection, as well as their varied levels of fairness and justice, have not been examined thoroughly in an empirical and comparative way. However, they provide a plausible explanation for national and regional differences in social capital levels, and also for differences between various types of democracies.

Most problematic in this discussion about the relationship between state institutions and social attitudes is the issue of the causal flow. Mixed interpretations have been developed in light of the strong correlation between political factors or political trust on the one hand, and generalized trust on the other hand. Whereas some authors claim that this correlation is based on the causal relationship from social to political forms of trust (Lipset and Schneider 1983; Newton and Norris 1999; Putnam 1993), others conclude exactly the opposite (Brehm and Rahn 1997; Rothstein 1999; Sides 1999). Although social scientists attempt to determine the causal flow of the relationship between governance and generalized trust, the main problem is that the causal mechanism in both claims remains unclear. In this chapter, the argument is advanced that the quality of local (or national) service delivery, a healthy politician–citizen relationship and fair political and social institutions can cause differences in political and institutional trust which in turn influence generalized trust. The reason, as I argue below, is that citizens who are disappointed with their politicians and who have experienced the effects of institutional unfairness, as well as politicians' dishonesty, unresponsiveness and lack of respect, transfer these experiences and views to people in general. In sum, social capital has been seen mostly as a societal resource that is fairly immune to contemporary governmental influence. This chapter challenges this view. The main argument advanced here is that social capital is not just a societal trait that develops purely in the realm of civil society; rather, the institutionalization of generalized values such as trust and reciprocity also depend on the character of government.

The Argument

Which aspects that relate to the character and experiences of local government matter for citizens' generalized trust? Citizens mostly experience local government in two main ways: they consume local services that are provided by the local government, and they experience local politicians in an indirect (media, neighbours) or direct (personal contact) way.[3] If citizens feel that they are not treated fairly and respectfully by their local politicians, they will extend these experiences to their dealings with strangers or other people who are not known (although not to people they know personally). If even government is not fair, then why should the rest of society be? If even politicians cannot act honestly, why should the rest of society be different? If citizens perceive that their opinions are not heard and that their thoughts do not matter for political decisions, then why should they be willing and open to engage with people not known to them? Alternatively, citizens who feel that politicians take them seriously and listen to and respect them, may also develop a belief in other people or people in general. If they perceive politicians to act fairly, honestly and responsively, they feel more secure and encouraged to trust others. In other words, I suggest that there is a relationship between political and generalized trust, and although the relationship is surely reciprocal, I also suggest that the main flow of causality goes from state performance (services and perceived actions and the behaviour of local politicians) to political trust to generalized trust.

So how can governmental and societal factors be identified and examined in a comparison between three Swedish regions? The three regions were chosen based on the prior knowledge about their level of social capital, particularly generalized trust. Despite the fact that social capital differences among Swedish regions are less pronounced than those in the Italian context, it was possible to choose a region with low (remote Kiruna), low to medium (central Kiruna) and relatively high (Gnosjö) levels of social capital. The selection of cases by variance in the dependent variable for small N case studies in comparative politics gives the researcher a lot of openness and flexibility to find and choose suitable explanatory variables, once certain similarities of the regions have been established (King, Keohane, and Verba 1995).

If the argument is correct, then we should expect to see the aggregate regional differences in satisfaction with political and service performance, as well as political trust, match the same regional differences found in generalized trust. In other words, these three variables should change in unison across the three regions. In addition, the relationship should hold at the individual level. However, besides citizens' perceptions, it is important to understand how political realities differ from one region to the other. Furthermore, if the societal hypothesis is correct, then the associational tradition should have a long-term diffused effect on regional generalized trust, and we should be able to observe regions with high levels of associational life and high levels of generalized trust, as well as regions with low levels of associational life and low trust. Most importantly, the study needs to consider other potential regional influences that could be responsible for the trust differences. Such factors include the family (Erikson 1963: 249 ff.; Uslaner 2002; Wuthnow 1997), and socio-economic resources such as education (Brehm and Rahn 1997), income, employment level and status (Smith 1997). All of these factors might not just be individual influences, but they can vary systematically between the regions, and should therefore be considered at the regional level as well. The remainder of this chapter presents a qualitative and quantitative examination of these regional differences in citizens' perceptions of local politicians and government services, as well as political trust in differing local political realities, which are the main independent variables.

Data

For the regional comparison, I distributed almost 700 questionnaires in three Swedish regions located in two different municipalities, one in the north of Sweden, Kiruna (two regions), and one in the south, in Gnosjö (one region). In each region, two groups of the population were examined; first, schoolchildren's parents and second, blue-collar, and also a small group of white-collar, workers. The questionnaires sought information about the respondents' generalized trust, other forms of trust, and civic engagement in their communities and in their children's schools. In half of the questionnaires information about the respondents' views of political issues and political trust in their communities was obtained. Most questionnaires also included data on the respondents' participation in local and national voluntary associations.[4] I also interviewed citizens, local leaders and politicians in more depth, obtained materials from the local governments and conducted research in local archives.

Results

The remainder of this chapter is divided into three main parts. The first section examines the regional variations in generalized trust as an important aspect of social capital and as the main dependent variable. The second section moves to the regional examination of potential local governmental influences on generalized trust that might be transmitted through citizens' perceptions of political realities as well as political trust. These citizen-local government relations are influenced by local service delivery, and by the contact citizens have with their local politicians. The importance here is to demonstrate the regional link between political realities and political trust, as well as the regional symmetry between political trust and generalized trust. Third, the effects of local government are compared and evaluated by considering additional hypotheses in a quantitative model.

Generalized Trust in Three Swedish Regions

Anyone familiar with Swedish regional cultures has heard about Gnosjö, and the famous 'Gnosjöandan', with its elaborate networks of free churches, local associations, a strong entrepreneurial spirit and its openness to newly arrived immigrants. Without drawing an overly rosy picture, the relatively small community of Gnosjö seems to exhibit high levels of social capital. The municipality of Kiruna is located in northern Sweden, and is much larger. For the purposes of the study I divide the municipality into two regions; namely, central Kiruna and eastern Kiruna. Kiruna is also known to be a friendly community with a rich associational life, yet people seem a bit less open toward strangers, and in eastern Kiruna in particular, one can observe signs of a disturbed dynamic of collective action and tensions among the citizens. In interviews I learned that in one of the villages there, for example, citizens were not even willing to give up a piece of their property in order to build a sidewalk, which would have helped prevent accidents in the community. The sidewalk problem that has remained unresolved for months and even years is a classic example of a collective action dilemma. In addition, it has been difficult in eastern Kiruna to start one's own business, as citizens intentionally avoid shopping in local stores, mainly because they seem jealous of the success of their neighbours. Even though the motivations for this behaviour can be various, the consequence is damage to the larger public good in the region (in this case economic development of the area). This attitude is described in Sweden by the term 'jantelagen', and has been observed in smaller communities before. How can these differences be described as variations in the levels of generalized trust?

Table 8.1 Generalized trust and regional difference

Dependent Variable: Generalized Trust

Variables	Standardized Coefficient T value	Standardized Coefficient T value
Age	−.02	−.00
	(.1)	(−.09)
Education	.12***	.12***
	(2.9)	(2.9)
Gender	−.06	−.06
	(−1.4)	(−1.4)
Region: Kiruna (central)	−.18****	
	(−3.7)	
Region: Kiruna (remote)	−.27****	−.11**
	(−6.1)	(−2.5)
Region: Gnosjö		.16****
		(3.6)
Number of cases	633	633
R Square (adjusted)	.08	.07

Note: Statistical significance tests: *p<.10; **p<.05; ***p<.01; ****p<.001.

The regional differences in generalized trust can be observed in a basic regression model, in which dummy variables distinguish the regions, and other important predictors of generalized trust control for age, education and gender.[5] Column 1 in table 8.1 indicates that education influences generalized trust positively. Higher levels of education contribute to a more trusting attitude toward people who are not personally known. Gender is not significantly related to generalized trust. Age does not have a clear influence on trust in this sample, something which might be attributed to the fairly narrow age variance in the sample (in contrast to findings in Brehm and Rahn 1997; and Putnam 2000). 75 per cent of the respondents were between the ages of 35 and 50.

Even after controlling for these personal variables, there exist highly significant differences in generalized trust between the three regions. These differences are particularly pronounced between Kiruna and Gnosjö, yet they also exist between the two northern regions, which is confirmed by an additional regression analysis (see column 2 of table 8.1) in which different regional dummy variables were included. These quantitative findings regarding differences in generalized trust clearly correspond to the brief descriptive differences presented above. Gnosjö exhibits the highest levels of generalized trust, whereas the two northern regions in Kiruna have lower levels, particularly in the remote areas at Kiruna-Östra.[6]

It is the task of the remaining analytical part of this chapter to explain what aspect is responsible for the significant regional differences. A close examination of local political and social life revealed that there are aspects of local politics that are important for citizens' development of political and generalized trust.

The Role of Local Government

We know that generalized trust is at least in part influenced by education, and we also know that there are intra-regional differences. Now we need to take the next step and try to understand what exactly it is about regional life that contributes to different developments of generalized trust. What is different in the southern region as compared to the two regions in the North? What is the difference between the two northern regions? To what extent is generalized trust influenced by the character of local government as hypothesized earlier?

In the following section, a systematic examination of regional differences in citizens' perceptions of political realities and political trust will be presented. Citizens experience local services and build an opinion about its quality, and about politicians' responsiveness and fairness. They also have direct or indirect contact with politicians. The regional differences in this relationship between citizens and local politics will be examined.

Citizens' Perceptions of Local Politics

Local Services

In a regional comparison in the same national welfare system, we can expect regional differences in service provisions to cause differences in citizens' evaluations.[7] However, it is important to compare citizens' evaluations against objective service realities, as the main causal argument here is that service satisfaction is a result of the actual service performance and delivery. In the analysis we may distinguish between overall and specific service evaluations, where the former is measured by one survey item and the latter by a battery of specific service-satisfaction questions (health care, schools, daycare, etc.). Interestingly, the overall and the specific service evaluations present some of the starkest differences between the three regions. The overall service evaluation is significantly different between the three regions (p < .001),[8] with citizens in the South (Gnosjö) evaluating it most positively and those in the North (Kiruna) more negatively—particularly so in the remote areas.

One important reason why citizens of the remote northern region are less satisfied with services is because of their remote location and an insufficient availability of services. This is confirmed by analyzing the item that asks about whether local services are offered in a fair way. In Gnosjö 69 per cent of respondents believed that this was the case, the figure was 73 per cent in central Kiruna, and only six per cent in the remote area. Around 80 per cent in the remote areas believed that the central town was offered too much by way of services in comparison to themselves. The remote area is disconnected from the rest of the municipality and people who live there, for example, have to make long and inconvenient bus rides into town. Most importantly, they experience higher unemployment rates than the other two regions and are therefore more dependent on official labour market measures that are nationally and locally provided. It is clear why they must be more dissatisfied with the services than citizens in the other regions. In sum, even though both citizens in central Kiruna and Gnosjö found the local service provisions somewhat fair, the satisfaction with local governmental services varied significantly between the three regions and, most importantly, the regional differences in satisfaction moved in tandem with those of generalized trust. In the remote areas in particular, we find a syndrome of low generalized trust, low satisfaction with services and extremely high perceptions of unfair service provisions.

Satisfaction with Contact with Local Politicians

What did the data indicate about citizens' experience with local politicians? The interviews and observations revealed that especially active citizens in both the Kiruna regions were rather disappointed. In Gnosjö, by contrast, most active citizens spoke positively about their direct experiences with politicians. A similar picture unfolds when looking at the survey responses, which included a question on whether citizens felt their activities in contact with local politicians, such as writing a letter or scheduling a meeting, had made a difference or not. Here again, we can see a regional difference along the lines that have been shown before. In Gnosjö more than 60 per cent of the respondents who tried to influence a political decision experienced some or a great deal of influence. On the other hand, in central Kiruna the number was less than 50 per cent, and in the remote areas it was only around 35 per cent (outcomes between Gnosjö and the remote areas are statistically significantly different at the $p < .02$ level, unlike the differences between central Kiruna and Gnosjö). This result shows that citizens perceive their contacts with local politicians differently in the three regions. Are these differences in service evaluations and contacts also reflected in the views citizens have of their local politicians, and in the levels of political trust they have developed in their politicians?

Political Trust

We have seen so far that the evaluation of local services as well as citizens' contacts in their attempts to influence political decisions varied in the three regions in a pattern similar to that of generalized trust. These evaluations of services and contacts are, of course, strongly connected to developments of political trust and views of local politicians (Nye, Zelikow, and King, 1997). It should therefore be no surprise that in terms of political trust as well, we find similar differences among the regions. Indeed, one of the strongest differences between the regions (besides service evaluation) appeared in the answer to the question as to whether citizens thought that local politicians did their best to improve the situation in the locality. In Gnosjö, by far the majority of people—more than 60 per cent of the respondents—thought local politicians tried their best, whereas in central Kiruna only 35 per cent and in the remote northern area only 22 per cent of the respondents thought local politicians tried their best. A similar difference, though to a lesser degree, was observed in responses to questions about whether local politicians listened to people or not, and whether there was a lot of corruption among local officials. These responses are shown in figure 8.1. All of these regional differences are significant at the $p < .001$ level between Kiruna and Gnosjö.

Interestingly, the questions about corruption and about politicians' ability to listen to their citizens were not significantly different

Figure 8.1 Experience with local politics

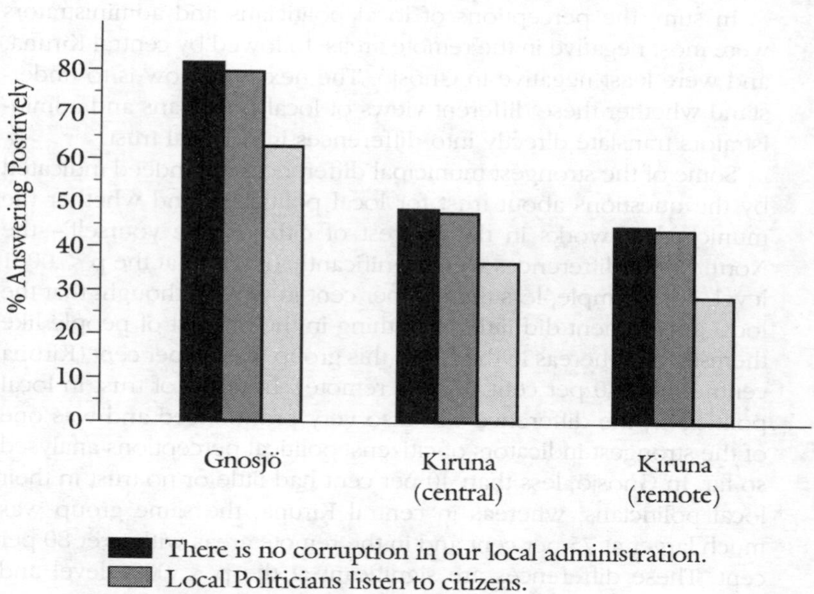

■ There is no corruption in our local administration.
▨ Local Politicians listen to citizens.
□ Local Politicians try their best.

between the two northern regions. This supports the expectation that citizens within the same municipality experience the same corruption and the same abilities of politicians to listen—as the politicians in both cases are the same group of people. It is a 'reality' check that citizens in the remote areas are not just 'more negative' in their views and judgments. However, turning to typically regional experiences, citizens in the remote areas felt that it was much harder to find a local official when there was a need to contact one than did citizens in central Kiruna (differences significant at the $p < .05$ level). In the remote areas, more than 70 per cent of the questioned people agreed, as compared with less than 50 per cent in the other two.

Citizens in the remote areas also perceived more strongly that they were not treated equally (difference from central Kiruna at the $p < .10$ level). Obviously, these aspects were perceived according to the citizens' specific regional experience. Citizens in the remote areas have a longer distance to travel to contact local officials, and the local bureaucracy is much harder to comprehend from a distance. Citizens in the remote areas felt they were not treated equally in comparison to the citizens in central Kiruna, which was reflected in their responses regarding the 'fair' distribution of local services (see above).

In sum, the perceptions of local politicians and administrators were most negative in the remote areas, followed by central Kiruna, and were least negative in Gnosjö. The next step now is to understand whether these different views of local politicians and administrators translate directly into differences in political trust.

Some of the strongest municipal differences are indeed indicated by the questions about trust for local politicians and whether the municipality 'works in the interest of citizens like yourself'—the North/South differences were significantly different at the $p < .0001$ level. For example, less than 25 per cent in Gnosjö thought that the local government did little or nothing in the interest of people like themselves, whereas in the North this group was 60 per cent (Kiruna central) and 70 per cent (Kiruna remote). In terms of trust in local politicians, the difference was also very pronounced and was one of the strongest indicators of citizens' political perceptions analysed so far. In Gnosjö, less than 40 per cent had little or no trust in their local politicians, whereas in central Kiruna, the same group was much larger at 75 per cent and in the remote areas with over 80 per cent. These differences are significant at the $p < .0001$ level and correspond to an eta coefficient of .30.

These different perceptions and views from citizens are reactions to the political realities that citizens experienced in their municipalities. There is not enough space for a fuller argument here;[9] the short version is that the one-party dominance in Kiruna over several decades produced a more and more ignorant and elitist approach by local politicians, and finally led to corruption scandals.[10] The basic fact about these scandals was that local politicians and administrators used public money for private purposes, building up privileges and protection for their own positions. As a result, in interviews with local leaders, citizens, association members and local politicians just a few years after the scandals surfaced, it was noticeable that in the Northern regions there was a lot of frustration with local politicians, or what the Swedish call 'politikerförakt' (disrespect for politicians), which was even more strongly developed in the remote areas. In Gnosjö, by contrast, political power has been more balanced and no single party has stayed in office for long periods of time. Local government has mainly changed hands between the Moderates and the Christian Democrats (or a coalition between the so-called bourgeois parties). There has never been a corruption scandal in Gnosjö, and when I asked citizens and politicians about it, both groups could not even imagine something like that happening in their municipality, despite being aware of the national and regional scandals around them. The reasons are that local politics is conducted more pragmatically in Gnosjö, politicians seem to be in touch with their citizens and their power is subject to widespread checks and balances.

In other words, the differences in political realities and in the resulting political trust between the North (K) and the South (G) are very strong. It is important that all of these variables: satisfaction with services, satisfaction with political contacts, and various aspects of political trust, move in tandem with each other and reveal the same regional pattern. Most importantly for the overall argument in this chapter, they reveal the same regional pattern as identified earlier with generalized trust. In fact the differences in political perceptions and trust are stronger than the regional differences in generalized trust. The fact that the variation in the causal variables are higher than the variation in the dependent variable (generalized trust) supports the idea that political aspects influence generalized trust (and not the other way around). In sum, observations and the analysis of aggregate survey data indicate that the provision of local services and experiences with local politicians are strongly related to political trust in local politicians. In addition, there is a positive relationship between these experiences of local politics and generalized trust. However, these findings at the aggregate level have to be tested at the individual level, and other potential sources for differences in generalized trust need to be considered as well.

Other Regional Sources for Generalized Trust

It is possible that regional differences in generalized trust could be caused by factors other than those related to local government. I will test the following three alternative hypotheses; namely, whether different parental practices, differences in structural and economic disadvantage, or variations in societal life such as associational membership might be behind variations in generalized trust. In the following regression model, all of these influences will be tested with individual-level measurements of families, socio-economic resources and associational memberships.

The measurement of family socialization taps whether the respondent thinks that his/her parents have been cautious with strangers. For measuring structural and economic disadvantage, the level of income of each respondent is combined with employment status. In other words, the lowest socio-economic status score (one) is given to a person who is unemployed and all the higher socio-economic status groups vary according to their income level (two to seven). The measurement of associational membership adds all the memberships of each respondent from a list of 27 different associational types. Respondents with several memberships have high scores, whereas respondents with low or no memberships have low scores.[11]

Turning to the first potential alternative explanation, it is clear that the variation in associational membership is not explained by variations in generalized trust. Whereas the northern regions indicate low levels of generalized trust, it is actually the southern region of Gnosjö that reveals a lower density of associational networks than the two regions at Kiruna. How can this be explained? The answer is that in Kiruna many associations have developed because the local government has provided support and financial help to them. In Gnosjö on the other hand, most of the activities in free churches and cultural groups were organized by the local citizens themselves, who do not usually ask for governmental support. The outcome is that while both municipalities have a fairly strong network of voluntary associations, Kiruna's is the slightly stronger one. The relationship between associational membership and trust, in short, does not support the expectations from social capital theory. How does the relationship look at the individual level?

Table 8.2 shows the results of three regression models. The first model in column 1 represents the basic trust model with the important personal characteristics as controls. The results for the alternative explanations, which are represented in column 2, suggest all of them—except for associational membership—have an influence on

Table 8.2 Sources of generalized trust

Dependent Variable: Generalized Trust

Variables	Previous Model with basic controls Standardized Coefficient (T value)	Model with additional sources of trust Standardized Coefficient (T value)	Complete model with political trust Standardized Coefficient (T value)
Age	-.02 (.1)	-.04 (-.7)	-.7 (-1.3)
Education	.12*** (2.9)	.04 (.9)	.02 (.3)
Gender	-.06 (-1.4)	-.00 (-.1)	.00 (.09)
Region: Kiruna (central)	-.18**** (-3.7)	-.17** (-3.3)	-.09 (-1.4)
Region: Kiruna (remote)	-.27**** (-6.1)	-.13*** (-2.4)	-.07 (-1.2)
Parents in past		.21**** (4.3)	.24**** (4.7)
Socio-economic Status		.20**** (3.4)	.18*** (2.9)
Associational Membership		.7 (1.3)	.08 (1.5)
Political Trust			.27**** (5.0)
Number of cases	633	383	322
R Square (adjusted)	.08	.13	.23

Note: Statistical significance tests: *p<.10; **p<.05; ***p<.01; ****p<.001.

generalized trust (which we expected given the aggregate differences). Turning to the other explanations, the family turns out to be the most important factor related to generalized trust. An open and trusting family environment obviously matters for the development of generalized trust. Socio-economic status is also an important determinant of generalized trust, and it seems that its inclusion diminishes the intra-Kiruna differences, even though the North-South divide remains. How can this remaining difference be explained? We are ready for a test of the political variable *vis-à-vis* the other factors. If we accept political trust as one of the best measurements of the political realities described, then we need to test the effect of integrating it into the explanatory model of generalized trust.

Column 3 shows that the most important factor for generalized trust among those selected is related to politics and political trust. Individuals with low political trust exhibit less abstract trust in their fellow citizens, and *vice versa*. I have already shown above how negative political trust results from political conditions marked by uneasy citizen-politician relationships and contacts, and dissatisfying service delivery in the regions. Hence it is not surprising that we find more individuals with low political trust in those regions where these political conditions are more problematic. The point to note is that the inclusion of political trust eliminates the remaining regional influences (shown with the regional dummy variables). The bivariate correlation between these two variables, political and generalized trust, is $r = .38$ in the whole sample ($p <. 0001$). At the same time, we find a similar relationship between political and generalized trust within each regional sample (results not shown here) which demonstrates that this relationship exists at the collective (or regional) as well as at the individual level. This is a remarkable result in the context of the argument elaborated I have made above. If we accept that the variable of political trust captures differences in political conditions as explained earlier, these results show that such political conditions are the most important determinants of generalized trust in these regions of Sweden.

Conclusion

One of the main questions that the social capital literature poses is, under what circumstances, and how, do trust and norms of reciprocity become generalized and institutionalized? Generalized trust is a complex attitude and is therefore clearly influenced by multiple factors. Regional density of associational membership does not explain regional variations in generalized trust, at least in a Swedish context. An open and outwardly trusting family environment during one's childhood is important for building generalized trust, as are one's personal socio-economic circumstances. In addition, there is another dominant factor that has been identified in this chapter. This analysis of three Swedish regions demonstrates that we cannot understand generalized trust without examining local politics and local government. This finding opens up a new research agenda in which social capital is conceived of not merely as a social variable determined by history, but rather as a variable that can be strongly influenced by political performance and government action. Regional scales and local governmental action seem particularly important for generalized trust because they are both close to people's everyday-life experiences, and 'distant' enough to be generalized to other situations and other groups of people.

What is the evidence for this argument? First, based on observations and statistical aggregate data analysis, significant differences in the political realities of the three regions were found. These differences in local politics are closely linked to citizens' political trust, evaluation of local services, satisfaction with local politics and evaluation of contact with local politicians. In other words, political trust is a response to the multifaceted local political conditions in each region.

Second, the regional differences in political trust move in tandem with weaker, but still significant, regional differences in generalized trust. Moreover, using political trust as an indicator of the different political conditions, it was demonstrated that this was the most important determinant of generalized trust at the individual level (controlling for other factors that were identified as being potentially influential on generalized trust).

Why is local politics so important for generalized trust? First, local politicians are in some ways strangers, but at the same time are known to the public to a degree. Second, local politicians are directly accountable and responsible to the public and serve as a model for them. If citizens feel they are not treated fairly and respectfully by local politicians and the local system, they will relate these experiences to their dealings with strangers or other people who are not known. Good experiences with local government can be generalized to other people who are not personally known. However, if citizens perceive their politicians act unfairly, dishonestly, and in an irresponsive manner, they feel less secure and discouraged to trust others.

Robert D. Putnam has shown that levels of social capital influence the performance of Italian regional institutions. He ultimately traced the social capital differences in Italian regions to the character of political power in Northern and Southern Italy during the Middle Ages. In his story, it was the oppressively powerful character of the Norman kingdom that extinguished any kind of 'desire for self-government' and led to a depletion of trust in the South, while the experience of progressive city-states in the North led to civic community. Indeed, state structures and institutions can have an impact on trust, yet while Putnam stresses the path-dependency of such a historical influence, I argue here that contemporary local governments (and possibly national governments) also have an influence on their citizens' generalized trust. This, then, might have the potential to change the path-dependency that was created centuries ago. In other words, I stress that above and beyond the long-term influences, there are important short-term influences in the way in which politics influences generalized trust.

Certainly, many questions remain unanswered, and the role of governments and state institutions for the building of generalized trust requires more research. What is the influence of state institutions compared to regional and local political conditions? Which aspects of the citizen-politician relationship are most influential for trust? How can lost trust be rebuilt, or is the positive role of local government limited to maintaining pre-existing levels of generalized trust? To answer all of these questions, we need more studies that compare regions and nations over longer periods of time. Longitudinal studies will better elucidate the causal flow of the argument that was advanced in this chapter. On the other hand, in-depth case studies of villages, cities, regions and nations can deliver a better understanding of the causal mechanisms between politics and trust. This chapter I believe takes one step towards that goal.

Notes

1. Department of Politics, McGill University, Montreal. The completion of this project was supported by a Grant provided by The Aspen Institute

Non-profit Sector Research Fund. I am especially indebted to Bertil Öström and Stefan Larsson, who helped me tremendously during my field research in Kiruna and Gnosjö respectively. Furthermore, I thank Larry Bartels, Siddhartha Baviskar, Sheri Berman, Nancy Burmeo, Jonathan Krieckhaus, Michele Micheletti and Sven Steinmo for helpful comments on earlier drafts of this chapter.

2. However, at the micro-level Stolle found little evidence that membership in voluntary associations creates generalized attitudes and values such as trust (Stolle 2001a, 2001b).

3. The third connection might be that citizens compare their political opinions and ideas to those of politicians, and decide whether they trust them more or less also according to which party is in office. This is particularly true for national politics and trust in politicians at the national level (see Listhaug 1995; Matton 1999). This third, more ideological dimension of the relationship, which reflects party politics, is less strongly developed at the local level even though it plays a role in political trust. However, there are no consistent measurements of political self-placement or similar indicators in the data set.

4. The citizen questionnaire to schoolchildren's parents was handed to pupils in major local schools; students took them home and asked their parents to fill them up. The children brought the completed questionnaires back to school where I picked them up. The response rate varied between 60 per cent and 75 per cent, depending on the region. In cases of blue-collar and white-collar workers, I distributed the questionnaires in the factories and companies and returned to pick them up. The response rate for these was 65 pre cent on an average.

5. The generalized trust scale consists of six questionnaire items, including standard survey questions on generalized trust. For details of the measurement and wording see the appendix in Stolle 2001a, p. 237ff.).

6. The findings of regional differences in generalized trust are confirmed by a further look at other related indicators that correlate highly with generalized trust, such as tolerance, belief in the basic honesty of people as well as in their goodness and kindness, and even, to a degree, optimism (see Stolle 2000).

7. There is a possibility that citizens with leftist political orientations place higher demands on local services than citizens with rightist political orientations. Swedish election data demonstrates that left political orientations are more prevalent in the North, whereas right political orientations are more developed in the South. It is possible that these political views determine some of the level of satisfaction with services, not the actual service performance itself. This is a subject for further study, and I thank Michele Micheletti for pointing this out.

8. Service evaluations in Gnosjö and central Kiruna are significantly different at the $p < .02$ level.

9. But see Stolle (2000) for a fuller treatment.

10. Significant political changes characterized the 1990s in Kiruna Kommun when Kiruna Partiet, especially under its leader Lars Törnman, became an important challenger to the political dominance of Kiruna's Social Democratic Party. As a consequence, local power has been shared between the two parties since.

11. I am aware that this item does not do full justice to the hypothesis that associational membership creates trust. A lot of research has been done on these questions, and it is clear that we need to make distinctions between different types of associations, the time spent in an association and other aspects of associational membership.

References

Banfield, E.C. 1958. *The Moral Basis of a Backward Society.* New York: The Free Press.

Berman, S. 1997. 'Civil Society and Political Institutionalization', in B. Edwards and M. Foley (eds.), *Social Capital, Civil Society and Contemporary Democracy: A Thematic Issue of the American Behavioral Scientist* 40(5): pp. 562–74.

Boix, C., and Posner, D. 1998. 'Social Capital: Explaining Its Origins and Effects on Government Performance'. *British Journal of Political Science* 28(4): pp. 686–95.

Brehm, J., and Rahn, W. 1997. 'Individual Level Evidence for the Causes and Consequences of Social Capital'. *American Journal of Political Science* 41: pp. 999–1023.

de Tocqueville, A. (1835) 1961. *Democracy in America.* New York: Schocken Books.

Erikson, E.H. 1963. *Childhood and Society.* New York: Norton.

Fukuyama, F. 1995. *Trust: The Social Virtues and Creation of Prosperity.* London: Hamish Hamilton.

Hooghe, M., and Stolle, D. (eds.) 2003. *Generating Social Capital: Civil Society and Institutions in Comparative Perspective.* New York: Palgrave.

King, G., Keohane, R.O., and Verba, S. 1995. *Designing Social Inquiry: Scientific Inference in Qualitative Research.* Princeton: Princeton University Press.

Levi, M. 1998. 'A State of Trust', in V. Braithwaite and M. Levi (eds.), *Trust and Governance.* New York: Russell Sage Foundation.

Lipset, S.M., and Schneider, W. 1983. *The Confidence Gap.* New York: The Free Press.

Listhaug, O. 1995. 'The Dynamics of Trust in Politicians', in H.D. Klingemann and D. Fuchs (eds.), *Citizens and the State*. Oxford: Oxford University Press.

Matton, J. 1999. 'Förtroende—ett instiutionellt dilemma. En studie av medborgerliga attityder'. Uppsats, Göteborg Universitet.

Newton, K., and Norris, P. 1999. 'Confidence in Public Institutions: Faith, Culture or Performance?' Paper prepared for delivery at the 1999 Annual Meeting of the American Political Science Association, Atlanta, Georgia., 2–5 September 1999.

Nye, J.S., Zelikow, P.D., and King, D.C. (eds.) 1997. *Why People Don't Trust Government*. Cambridge: Harvard University Press.

Petro, N. 2001. 'Creating Social Capital in Russia: The Novgorod Model'. *World Development* 29, 2: pp. 229–44.

Putnam, R.D. 1993. *Making Democracy Work*. Princeton: Princeton University Press.

Putnam, R.D. 2000. *Bowling Alone*. New York: Simon & Schuster.

Rothstein, B. 2000. 'Trust. Social Dilemmas, and Collective Memory'. *Journal of Theoretical Politics* 12(4): pp. 477–503.

Rothstein, B. 1999. 'Förtroende för andra och förtroende för politisk institutioner', in S. Holmberg and L. Weibull (eds.), *En ljusande framtid*. Göteborg Universitet, SOM report.

Rothstein, B., and Stolle, D. 2003. 'Social Capital, Impartiality and the Welfare State: An Institutional Approach', in M. Hooghe and D. Stolle (eds.), *Generating Social Capital: Civil Society and Institutions in Comparative Perspective*. New York: Palgrave, pp. 191–210.

Sides, J. 1999. 'It Takes Two: The Reciprocal Relationship between Social Capital and Democracy'. Paper presented at the Annual Meeting of the American Political Science Association, Atlanta.

Skocpol. 1996. 'Unravelling from Above'. *American Prospect* 25: pp. 20–25.

Smith, T. 1997. 'Factors Relating to Misanthropy in Contemporary American Society'. *Social Science Research* 26: pp. 170–96.

Stolle, D. 2000. 'Communities of Trust: Social Capital and Public Action in Comparative Perspective'. Princeton University, Doctoral Dissertation.

————. 2001a. 'Clubs and Congregations: The Benefits of Joining an Association', in K. Cook (ed.), *Trust in Society*, volume II, in the Russell Sage Foundation Series on Trust, pp. 202–44.

————. 2001b. 'Getting to Trust: An Analysis of the Importance of Institutions, Families, Personal Experiences and Group Membership', in P. Dekker and E.M. Uslaner (eds.), *Politics in Everyday Life: Social Capital and Participation*. London: Routledge.

Tarrow, S. 1996. 'Making Social Science Work Across Space and Time: A Critical Reflection on Robert Putnam's Making Democracy Work'. *American Political Science Review* 90: pp. 389–97.

Uslaner, E.M. 2002. *The Moral Foundations of Trust*. Cambridge: Cambridge University Press.

Wuthnow, R. 1997. '*The Role of Trust in Civic Renewal*.' Working Paper No. 1, The National Commission on Civic Renewal, University of Maryland.

9

Putting Social Capital to Work:
Agency and Development

Anirudh Krishna[1]

Introduction and Methodology

Does social capital help to improve development performance in the Third World? This chapter undertakes a critical examination of the social capital view and compares it with alternative formulations.

Performance is compared for four different sets of development activities across 60 villages in the state of Rajasthan in India. Located in the districts of Ajmer, Bhilwara, Rajsamand, Udaipur and Dungarpur, these villages were studied through fieldwork conducted from 1998 to 2000. Getting in and out of these villages and locating and meeting people was not difficult as I had lived and worked in these areas for 12 years from 1981 to 1993.

A combination of case-studies and statistical methods was employed for studying trends in these villages (Ragin 1987). Sixteen villages were investigated as case studies, and all 60 villages were studied through quantitative analysis of survey data. Villagers I knew in Rajasthan helped me form a team of 16 field investigators, with an equal number of men and women. These investigators helped me interview 1,898 villagers, selected by random sampling from the residents of these 60 villages (average population: 1,254). Focus-group interviews were also conducted in each village, and additional information was gathered from government departments' annual reports and by interviewing 105 city-based professionals, including government officials, party politicians, doctors, lawyers and bankers; people who have regular contact with villagers in these areas.

Section 2 presents an index of development performance that is appropriate for villages in this region. Village scores on this index serve as the basis for comparing alternative explanations of collective action and development, which are explored in section 3. A locally relevant measure of social capital is presented in this section, and variables corresponding to other bodies of explanation are also operationalized here. Case-studies as well as regression analysis are employed in section 4 to examine the correspondence between development performance and these alternative explanations. Conclusions and recommendations for action are offered in section 5.

Comparing Development Performance

Agriculture is the principal occupation of over 90 per cent of the villagers in Rajasthan.[2] Even though nearly all households depend upon the land, it however provides neither a bountiful nor an assured existence. Average productivity has risen only marginally, if at all, over the past 40 years, there are huge swings in yield from year to year and there is severe drought at least twice every decade, when crops fail and drinking water is hard to find.[3]

Livelihood stability is, not surprisingly, a principal development requirement of people in this region. Activities that enable them to raise crop yields sustainably and to improve the availability of fodder and drinking water at all times are highly regarded by villagers (Agrawal 1999). More than 90 per cent of those interviewed ranked soil and water conservation and pasture development activities as one of the three foremost development needs of their village, in addition to safe drinking water and education and health facilities.

A programme of integrated watershed development was launched in 1991 to assist villagers in achieving these aims. Prior to the launch of this government programme, few villages had done much to develop common lands or to conserve soil and moisture on private lands; neither was technology well-known that could enable villagers to improve the productivity of these resources reliably and cheaply; nor were most villagers in a position to work free of cost for the entire number of days needed to implement these schemes. External support in the form of appropriate technology and supplementary resources was required, and the state government provided these means starting 1991.[4]

Villages eligible for programme benefits share roughly similar starting conditions: less than one-third of their arable area is irrigated by any water-source, and nearly half of all households are classified as poor, earning incomes lower than what is required for purchasing basic nutritional requirements. Among the nearly 1,500 villages that joined the programme, 60 were selected that had participated in this programme continuously since it started in 1991. Villages participating in the programme from among the five selected districts of Rajasthan were ranked High, Middle and Low in terms of their achievements in watershed development, and I randomly selected an equal number of villages from each of these three categories. Both the smaller sample of 16 villages and the larger sample of 60 villages were selected in this manner.

Fodder production has increased ten-fold in some of these villages, crop yields have trebled and they fluctuate much less from year to year, and the water level in village wells has risen by more than 40 feet in some cases. In other villages, however, these changes are far less significant (CTAE 1999).

Performance with respect to common land development was compared using the following indicators:

1. *Quantum of work*: measured in terms of the percentage of village common land that was developed under the programme.
2. *Protection and Survival*: measured in terms of seven-year survival rates for trees and shrubs planted during programme implementation. Approximately 1,00,000 trees were planted on an average in each village, and survival rates vary from 12 per cent (in Kunda village) to 64 per cent (in Sangawas village).
3. *Productivity*: seen in terms of the quantity of fodder and firewood harvested from common lands in the previous year, measured as headloads harvested per capita. 18 headloads of fodder grass and dry sticks were collected by every resident of Sunderchha, for example, and 14 headloads by every resident of Nauwa, but residents of Ghodach harvested only three headloads each, and residents of Balesariya, Palri and some other villages harvested nothing at all.

4. *Diversification*: considered in terms of the number of activities, other than common land development, that were undertaken by the Users Committee of each village.

Information for coding these items was obtained from the records of the Watershed Development Department. Information on protection, survival and productivity was also collected through site inspections and focus group interviews. A village's score on any of these four indicators is closely correlated with its score on the other three measures.[5] A Common Land Development Index (CLDI) was constructed by taking a simple sum of scores over these four items.[6] Mean village score on this Index is 1.68 (out of four points), and standard deviation is 0.81. These CLDI scores provide our first measure of development performance.

Poverty reduction is a second important development objective for villagers. On an average, 44.5 per cent of households are poor in the villages of this region.[7] The figure is as high as 87 per cent in Dooka village of Dungarpur district. In 29 of the 60 villages, the majority of households are poor, i.e., they have incomes that are too low to acquire their minimum nutritional requirements.

No direct measures are available of the number of people who escape poverty each year. I rely instead upon the number of villagers assisted under the official programmes—Integrated Rural Development Programme (IRDP) and two others[8]—that provide assets and training to poor villagers. With their asset base increased in this manner, it is expected that the poor should be able to earn larger amounts. Not all persons assisted under these programmes have achieved substantial or sustainable income increases, and assistance has in many cases failed to bring about any significant improvement. Incorrect identification of beneficiaries, insufficient extension and follow-up, inappropriate selection of activities and misappropriation of funds by officials are mentioned as reasons for these failures.[9]

Be that as it may, and regardless of whether it is a success or a failure overall, IRDP represents quite often the only chance that the poor have for overcoming the limitations of their situation. Their credit-worthiness is low, and they have hardly anything to mortgage to banks and other lenders. The sum of Rs 16,000 (US$ 400) that is provided in grants and cheap loans—and which IRDP beneficiaries use to procure cows, buffaloes, machines and stock-in-trade—cannot usually be acquired by them in any other manner. IRDP has failed in many cases no doubt; but until something better comes their way, it often represents the only chance the poor have for enhancing their asset base.

The variable POVASSIST measures for each village the number of grants per hundred villagers over the past five years. Among the villages that have the highest scores on this variable are Sema (5.8), Sangawas (5.7) and Nauwa (4.9). The mean score for all 60 villages is 2.75, and the standard deviation is 1.17.

Employment generation is the third major economic concern of villagers. Continuing poverty abatement depends to an extent on the wages provided by public construction projects. 45 per cent of all villagers—i.e., 857 of 1,898 persons interviewed—asserted that wages earned in this manner are necessary for their families to subsist from year to year.

Employment-creation programmes have grown rapidly in the rural areas over the past 20 years. Between 1989 and 1997, 720 million man-days of employment were generated by a single state programme, the *Jawahar Rozgaar Yojana* (Jawahar Employment Scheme, or JRY), which amounts to six days of employment for every worker in the rural labour force (GOR 1999). Additional employment opportunities are provided by other state programmes—the Drought Prone Areas Programme and the Desert Development Programme, the Employment Assurance Scheme, the Million Wells Scheme and others—that are intended, just as JRY is intended, as much for constructing community assets as for providing wages to those who might otherwise starve. The idea is to spread employment out thinly so that all villagers have at least some chance of making the necessary income supplements, and so JRY projects are mostly of small size and short duration.

The variable EMPPROV measures man-days of employment generated over the previous three years per-capita village population.[10] The mean village score is 2.39, implying that over the three past years, employment opportunities were provided by the state to every villager—man, woman and child—for an average of nearly two-and-a-half days.

A fourth criterion of development performance mentioned by villagers relates to the *quality of health, education and water supply services*. Infant mortality in rural India is upward of 150 per 1,000 live births, and millions of villagers are struck every year with tuberculosis, polio, malaria and dysentry, diseases that have nearly disappeared from the industrialized world. The quality of health services they receive is a major concern for most villagers, as is the quality of education and water supply services.

A focus group of villagers was consulted to rank the quality of health, education and water supply services in their village compared to neighbouring villages. A five-point scale was used for this purpose. The variable QUALSERV combines the scores for all the three services of health, education and water supply. The highest range of scores, 11–13 points, is achieved by two of the 16 case-study villages; Sema and Nauwa. The lowest range of scores, 5–8 points, is achieved by three case study villages; Kundai, Palri and Sare.

Analysis

We now have four separate measures of development performance that relate to different and unrelated activities. Common land development, poverty assistance, employment generation and service quality relate to different aspects of the quality of development performance. Nonetheless, it is striking to find that the same group of case-study villages—Nauwa, Sangawas, Khempur and Sema—are consistently among the top 10 performers for each of the four different measures of development performance. Conversely, Sare, Hajiwas, Balesariya and Kundai occupy the bottom third in each of the four sets of rankings.

Among the larger group of 60 villages also, there are some that perform uniformly highly in all four activities considered above, and others that perform uniformly poorly. Village scores for the four separate development programmes are highly correlated with each other, as seen in table 9.1.

Table 9.1 Four development indicators: Pearson correlation coefficients

	CLD	POVASSIST	EMPPROV	QUALSERV
CLD	1.00	0.632	0.678	0.662
	(0.0)	(0.0001)	(0.0001)	(0.0001)
POVASSIST		1.00	0.524	0.484
		(0.0)	(0.0001)	(0.0001)
EMPPROV			1.00	0.457
			(0.0001)	(0.0001)
QUALSERV				1.0
				(0.0)

Note: n=60; significance levels are in brackets.

Correlations among the four development variables are high and statistically significant. Further, these variables load commonly on a single factor, which accounts for 76 per cent of their combined variance.

Table 9.2 Development performance: Factor pattern

Cld (Livelihood Stabilization)	0.820
Povassist (Poverty Assistance)	0.691
Empprov (Employment Provision)	0.843
Qualserv (Quality of Basic Services)	0.712

It would appear from these results that proponents of the social capital view might be right: regardless of programme choice, some villages perform well and other villages perform poorly. Results of correlation as well as factor analysis indicate that some underlying propensity exists which is associated with high performance by some villages and low performance by others.

It is not clear, however, whether this underlying propensity can be equated with social capital. To be useful conceptually and in practice, social capital must be observed and measured *independent* of the phenomenon one is trying to explain. Alternative explanations must also be considered and evaluated alongside the social capital hypothesis.

Three sets of alternative explanations are presented in the following section, and variables corresponding to each of these views are evaluated in section 4. To facilitate statistical comparison, the four separate development indicators are combined, since they are so closely associated, into a single *Index of Development Performance*, which is constructed by aggregating the scores received on each of the four separate scales.[11] The mean village score on this index is 48 points, and the standard deviation is 20.6.

Explaining Results: Three Alternative Views

The Institutionalist View

According to one school of thought, villages located within this relatively small area—of roughly 150 kilometres north-to-south and about the same distance east-to-west—and sharing a similar policy framework and market structure, should not differ very much in terms of development results. Since the right institutions produce the right results—and the wrong institutions produce the wrong results—the same mix of right and wrong institutions should produce the same mix of right and wrong results (Brehm and Rahn 1997; Levi 1996; North 1981; Tarrow 1996). Significant inter-village differences should not exist—and if they do, then it is only because institutions make an unequal impact; for instance, if some villages are remotely located or otherwise disconnected from institutional effects.

This institutionalist view is tested in section 4 by considering six separate independent variables. The variable, DISTMKT, measures the distance in kilometres to the market town that villagers visit most frequently. All else being the same, villages located further away from market towns and government offices should be comparatively less influenced by these institutions. The variable INFRASTR is also considered which combines scores for levels of facility related to transportation, communications, electrification and water supply. In addition, literacy is measured to test the hypothesis of Dreze and Sen (1995) which expects economic development to be closely related to educational achievement in communities. LITERACY is calculated as the sample percentage of persons in each village who have had five or more years of formal education.

Two other structuralist views are also tested. First, the hypothesis by Wade (1994) proposing relative need as a cause of collective action is tested by considering two variables. DRYLAND measures the percentage of village land that is not irrigated by any other source except seasonal rainfall. The higher the proportion of dry land in the village, it can be conceived that the greater is the need for villagers to seek livelihood stability, poverty assistance and employment generation. Similarly, the higher the percentage of below-poverty households in a village, i.e., the greater the value of PERCPOOR, the more the need to reach out for help to programmes of the state.

Finally, stratification and caste are considered because these are regarded by some analysts to affect the potential for collective action in Indian villages (e.g., Dumont 1970). The variable N_CASTES is a measure of the number of different caste groups that reside in any village. This variable provides one measure of the extent of homogeneity within the population of a village. The variable CASTE_DOM measures the proportion of village households that belong to the most numerous caste group, corresponding to the hypothesis of Srinivas (1987) that villages where the dominant group is larger will act collectively more often and more effectively than others. Both of these variables have been generated from information obtained during the field survey.

Variables reflecting these structural views are juxtaposed against other variables that correspond to bottom-up views of influence and performance. Social capital is looked at first among these variables.

The Social Capital View

Social capital has been defined by Putnam as 'features of social organization such as networks, norms and social trust that facilitate coordination and cooperation for mutual benefit' (1995: 67). Putnam et al. (1993) rank social capital in Italian regions according to a measure of density of membership in formal organizations. It must be noted, however, that this is a proxy measure of social capital; it is not directly concerned with norms or with trust but looks, instead, at certain manifestations that accompany social capital in this setting. It is not obvious whether social capital will be manifest in other cultures in a similar fashion.

Institutions do not have 'an ontological status apart from the human activity that produces them' (Berger and Luckmann 1966: 57). Varying forms of human activity develop to deal with different needs and compulsions of life in different ecological and cultural settings. Networks, roles, rules, procedures, precedents, norms, values, attitudes and beliefs are different among people who have different patterns of life. Measures of social capital that are relevant for one set of cultures can be irrelevant for others.

Density of formal organizations is a particularly inappropriate indicator for Rajasthan villages. Hardly any formal organizations have been set up voluntarily by villagers in Rajasthan, and nearly every formal organization in these villages is companion to a state agency and executor of its programme. Joint Forest Committees are looked after by the Forest Ministry. The Women's Development Ministry is responsible for *Mahila Mandals* (women's groups). The Sports and Education Ministry officials sets up new *Yuva Mandals* (youth groups) every year. Officials are judged by the numbers of groups they can set up every year. Governments and donor agencies prescribe targets. Villagers are coerced into joining. There are benefits to be availed. People sign up to get the benefits; the target is achieved; then everyone goes home.

Formal organizations in this context do not, therefore, provide any reliable indication of voluntarism and cooperation among villagers.

However, several informal networks exist, and many villagers attend these networks regularly.

A locally relevant scale for measuring social capital in Rajasthan was devised by Krishna and Uphoff (1999) that relies upon assessing participation in informal networks. We started by considering the types of activities with which people of this area are commonly engaged. Not all activities observed in this area are valid for investigating dimensions of cooperation and coordination. Social capital exists 'in the *relations* among persons' (Coleman 1988: 100–101), and only those activities are valid for comparing social capital that inhabitants of this area regard appropriate to carry out collectively rather than individually. Six survey questions, corresponding to six such activities, were used for measuring social capital in this context. Responses to these six questions were found to be highly correlated with one another, and factor analysis supported the proposition that these were manifestations of a single underlying factor. Some modifications were made to this scale based on reviewers' comments, and a modified form of this scale is used for the present investigation, which has the following six components:

1. *Membership In Labour-Sharing Groups*: Are you a member of a labour group in the village, i.e., do you work with the same group very often, sharing the work that is done either on your own fields, on some public work or for some private employer? Responses were coded as 0 for 'no' and 1 for 'yes'. These responses were aggregated for all individuals interviewed in each surveyed village, thereby measuring the proportion of villagers participating in such networks. 1,522 of the total number of 1,898 respondents interviewed in Rajasthan (more than 80 per cent) gave a 'yes' response to this question, though this proportion varied from a high of 98.5 per cent (in village Sadariya) to a low of 73 per cent (in village Sinhara).

2. *Dealing with Crop Disease*: If a crop disease were to affect the entire standing crop of this village, then who do you think would come forward to deal with this situation? Responses ranged from 'Everyone would deal with the problem individually', which scored 1, to 'The entire village would act together', which scored 5. Individuals' responses were averaged for each surveyed village. The highest average response score came from village Balesariya (3.07), while the lowest was from village Sema (1.11). This item and the next relate to

the cognitive maps that people have concerning the breadth of mutual support networks in their village.

3. *Dealing with Natural Disasters:* At times of severe calamity or distress, villagers often come together to assist each other. Suppose there was some calamity in this village requiring immediate help from the government, e.g., a flood or a fire, who in this village do you think would approach the government for help? Responses varied from 'No one', which scored 1, to 'The entire village collectively', which scored 5. Averaged villager responses varied from a high of 4.64 (in village Chawandiya) to a low of 2.58 (in village Sodawas).

4. *Trust:* Suppose a friend of yours in this village faced the following alternatives: which one would he or she prefer?
   — To own and farm 10 units of land entirely by themselves (which scored 1)
   — To own and farm 25 units of land jointly with another person (which scored 2)

   The fourth item scales the factor of trust in terms of an empirical referent that is valid for these agrarian communities. The second alternative would give each person access to more land (12.5 instead of 10 units), but they would have to work and share produce interdependently. The question was framed so that the respondent was not making an assessment of his or her own level of trust, but rather of how trusting other people in the village were in general. Average villager responses ranged from a high of 1.76 (in village Chautra), showing a high level of mutual trust, to a low of 1.05, showing a virtual absence of interpersonal trust (in village Chachiyawas).

5. *Solidarity:* Is it possible to conceive of a village leader who puts aside his own welfare and that of his family to concern himself mainly with the welfare of village society? Responses ranged from 'Such a thing is not possible', which scored 1, to 'Such a thing happens quite frequently in this village', which scored 3. Averaged individual responses ranged from a high of 2.26 (in village Balesariya, once again) to a low of 1.23 (in village Kunda).

6. *Reciprocity:* Suppose some children of the village stray from the 'correct' path, for example, they are disrespectful to elders, they disobey their parents, are mischievous, etc., who in this village feels it right to correct other people's children?

Four alternatives were posed: 'No one', which scored 1; 'Only close relatives', which scored 2; 'Relatives and neighbours', which scored 3; and 'Anyone from the village', which scored 4. Averaged individual responses ranged from a high of 3.45 (in village Khemaroo) to a low of 1.70 (with village Sema once again occupying the lowest spot).

These six items load highly on a single common factor (table 9.3), indicating that villages that have high scores on any one manifestation of social capital also tend to have high scores on the other five manifestations observed here. This common factor is highly correlated with each of these six items,[12] and the individual items are also are closely correlated to each other.[13]

Table 9.3 Social capital: Factor pattern

Membership in labour-sharing groups	0.64131
Dealing with crop disease	0.68887
Dealing with natural disasters	0.74042
Trust (sharing land)	0.74162
Solidarity	0.84012
Reciprocity	0.84192

Because these are so closely correlated with each other, village scores on the six separate items were aggregated to form the Social Capital Index (SCI).[14] Mean score on the SCI is 38.8 points (out of a possible 100 points) and standard deviation is 23.6. Eight villages have scores of 75 points or more, including three of the sixteen case-study villages. Balesariya, with 88 points, leads this list, and Sunderchha (82 points) and Nauwa (74 points) come next. Twelve villages have scores of 25 points or lower, including four of the sixteen case-study villages: Kundai (21 points), Sare (20 points), Ghodach (18 points) and Sema (13 points).

In addition to looking at the institutionalist variables and at the SCI, one other set of variables is also considered for analyzing development results. These variables correspond to the *agency view* of social capital, set forth by Berman (1997, 1997a).

The Agency View

What enables the effect of social capital, it is asked, to flow from grassroots-level associations and localized social networks into decision-making at higher levels? How exactly does social capital existing among members of community organizations affect the performance of regional and national institutions?

Berman considers the example of inter-war Germany. Civil society organizations, which were 'organized primarily along group (and class) lines rather than across them', not only failed 'to contribute to republican virtue, but in fact subverted it'. This 'fragmented but highly organized civil society ... proved to be the ideal setting for the rapid rise to power of a skilled totalitarian movement'. 'Without the opportunity to exploit Weimar's rich associational network ... the Nazis would not have been able to capture important sectors of the German electorate so quickly and efficiently.' (Berman 1997: 414–22)

Dense social networks are not enough, therefore, to achieve more effective and more accountable government. 'Associationism,' Berman (1997a: 564) concludes, is 'a *politically neutral multiplier*— neither inherently good nor inherently bad'. Whether associationism weakens or strengthens institutional performance depends, in Berman's view, on the nature of the mediating links.

In the Western contexts studied by Berman, party organizations are expected to provide such linkages.[15] Since political parties are relatively weakly organized in rural areas in India (Kohli 1990; Sabharwal 1997; Weiner 1989), other agency types should also be considered to test the agency hypothesis.

Six different agency variables, corresponding to an equal number of agency forms, are considered here. These agency types are common among villages in this region, and each is regarded by some body of literature as being effective for serving the common objectives of Indian villagers. The effectiveness, utility and range of functions of each type of agency differ from village to village, however, and I look to these variations for developing scales for comparing agency strength.[16]

Each caste group in a village is organized into an association, though the strength of these associations varies from village to village. The variable STR_CASTE assesses this by averaging survey responses for each village as to how strong or weak these associations are in any particular village. Survey responses are considered for a set of three questions related to the salience, effectiveness and continuity of caste associations. Villages where caste associations were relatively more salient—where villagers met more often with their caste fellows, where caste leadership was more effective and where its effectiveness was expected to continue into the future—received higher scores on this scale.

The variable STR_PANCH was similarly constructed to scale the strength of village councils (*panchayats*) (Kurien 1999; Mathew 1994).[17] The variable STR_PCR similarly reflects the strength of patron-client linkages in each village (Kothari 1988). Another such variable STR_PARTY gauges the strength of political parties as perceived by respondents of any particular village. Notice that this variable does not relate to the strength of any particular political party. It is intended, instead, to take stock of the extent of allegiance, loyalty and influence in relation to political parties in general.

The remaining two agency variables, STR_NEW and STR_VC, require a little more explanation. I found during field work that a number of young leaders have come up in villages, and who have benefited from the expansion of education in the last few decades. Such new leaders are present in almost every village, and they perform a number of tasks on behalf of villagers that require mediation with state and market agencies. 1,308 (or 69 per cent) of the 1,898 villagers interviewed in Rajasthan said they seek the assistance of this type of agency (and no other) when they need to procure employment on government construction works; 1,248 said that such leaders helped them get bank loans or subsidies from poverty reduction programmes of the government; and 1,253 (66 per cent) said they consulted such leaders regularly whenever they needed to procure seeds or fertilizer from the market. To assess the capacity of such new leaders in any village, three survey questions were asked relating to their existence, utility and frequency of contact by villagers. A fourth question assessed their range of effectiveness in terms of numbers of activities performed. Village scores on the variable STR_NEW were derived by summing up individuals' response scores to these four questions and taking the average of this score for each village.

Another agency form that was found to exist in all these villages is the informal Village Council.[18] This body is different from the village *panchayat*, and it is not recognized by the administration or the courts. It is chaired by respected elders from all caste groups in the village. Some of these elders are also leaders of their respective caste associations. When they sit on the Council, however, they play a different (and more collaborative) role, and deal with issues that concern the entire village and not just a particular caste. The

strength of Village Councils is assessed in terms related to familiar-
ity, frequency, range of activities and attendance at meetings. Four
survey items were considered for constructing the scale for the variable STR_VC, which was derived by summing across responses averaged for each village.

Correlation coefficients were calculated between the SCI and each
of these measures of agency strength. Table 9.4 reports these results.
Apart from the Village Council, which is significantly, though not
highly, correlated with the SCI, none of the other agency variables
has a correlation coefficient which is either statistically or substantially significant. The absolute size of each of these coefficients is
quite small and—more importantly—just one of these correlation
coefficients is significant at the 0.05 level.

Social capital is neither an effect nor a cause of the strength of
different types of agency, these data indicate, and (with the partial
exception of STR_VC) the two sets of variables can be considered as
separate and unrelated independent variables. While social capital
reflects the nature of relations within a community, i.e., it is a collectively possessed resource, agency strength is related to a different set of capacities that particular individuals possess.

Social capital and agency strength are both high in some villages.
In most villages, however, there is no correlation between social
capital and the strength of any particular agency type. As a result,
these villages are unable to convert their stocks of social capital into
flows of benefits, as we shall see in the next section.

Social capital represents a potential—a propensity for mutually
beneficial collective action. But potential needs to be activated, and
agency is important for this purpose. Local-level resources, however plentiful, need to be marshalled strategically and directed toward

Table 9.4 Correlation between social capital and agency strength

Agency Variable	Correlation Coefficient with Social Capital Index	Significance Level
STR_PCR	−0.24	0.12
STR_PARTY	0.06	0.63
STR_PANCH	−0.06	0.65
STR_NEW	0.19	0.13
STR_VC	0.45	0.05
STR_CASTE	−0.05	0.68

incentives available within the broader institutional environments of state and market. When the intermediate links are weak, as they are when agency is not capable, social capital does not translate readily into good performance.

Explaining Development Performance

Development performance is examined for the full group of 60 villages with the help of regression analysis. These statistical results are illuminated using case-study data collected for 16 representative villages.

Table 9.5 gives the results of regression analysis conducted to assess the significance of the separate bodies of explanation. Model 1 tests all of the institutional and agency variables in association with the dependent variable, the 100-point Index of Development Performance, DEVINDEX. Not one of the agency variables is individually significant, and none of the variables corresponding to structural theories, including stratification, relative need, and commercialization and modernization, respectively, is significant either. Only literacy matters. However, the fit of this regression equation is very imperfect. R^2 is only 0.12 (and adjusted R^2 is almost zero). The F-probability of 0.186 indicates that a regression model consisting of these structural and agency variables is not a good predictor of values of DEVINDEX.

Table 9.5 OLS regressions on development performance: DEVINDEX is the dependent variable

	Model 1	Model 2	Model 3
1. Intercept	22.4	−60.2**	−47.2*
	(15.7)	(24.70)	(22.9)
INDEPENDENT VARIABLES			
(A) Societal Variables			
DRYLAND	0.09		
	(0.19)		
2. PERCPOOR	0.79	0.61	0.52
	(3.48)	(3.21)	(3.24)
3. DISTMKT	3.21	0.30	0.27
	(0.39)	(0.36)	(0.37)
4. INFRASTR	−0.24		
	(4.77)		

Ncastes	0.15		
	(0.97)		
Castedom		−0.001	0.002
		(0.05)	(0.04)
Literacy	1.14*	0.65*	0.52*
	(0.44)	(0.37)	(0.24)
(B) Agency Variables			
Str_Pcr	−0.14		
	(0.68)		
5. Str_Panch	1.45		
	(3.89)		
Str_Party	0.97		
	(5.39)		
Str_Caste	0.25		
	(4.41)		
Str_Vc	−0.78	−0.89	−0.69
	(4.82)	(4.9)	(4.77)
Str_New	0.87	1.12	0.61
	(2.68)	(2.7)	(2.64)
(C) Social Capital		1.10*	0.35
(SCI)		(0.34)	(0.36)
(D) Interaction			
(Sci*Str_New)			0.08***
			(0.009)
N	60	60	60
R^2	0.12	0.28	0.43
Adj-R^2	0.04	0.21	0.37
F-ratio	1.56	3.39	6.27
6. F-probability	0.186	0.01	0.0001

Note: Standard errors are reported in parentheses. *$p<=.05$ **$p<=.01$ ***$p<=.001$.

Model 2 drops most of these non-significant structural and agency variables and adds the SCI to the equation. R^2 improves; it now has a value of 0.28, and the SCI has a significant coefficient, in addition to literacy, which remains significant as before.

Model 3 retains all of the variables of Model 2. Additionally, an interaction term is added that is calculated by multiplying together SCI with Str_New, the variable that measures the capability of new leadership in each village. Once again, literacy remains significant. The SCI loses significance, however, and the interaction term is revealed to be highly significant. R^2 improves further to 0.42, and the F-statistics also improve considerably, indicating that Model 3 fits much better with the data at hand. The interaction of social capital and agency is highly significant for development performance.

Social capital and the capacity of new leaders both matter for development performance, and they matter in interaction with each other.[19] It is the multiplication of these two variables in any village that is critically related to its level of development performance. A village that has the median score of 40 points on the SCI, for example, and where STR_NEW has the low value of 4 points, scores 25 points lower on development performance when compared to another village where social capital is at the same level but agency is strong (STR_NEW = 12 points). Similarly, if we compare two villages that have the same score for agency strength (say STR_NEW = 10 points), the village that has the higher social capital score (80 points) achieves 40 points more on development performance than the other village where the SCI is only 30 points.

The higher the value of social capital, the greater the effect made by differences in agency strength. Conversely, the greater the agency variable, the more the difference in performance due to social capital. Social capital and agency interact with one another, and development performance is significantly and substantially influenced by the interaction term. Villages like Nåuwa are developing rapidly; while villages such as Balesariya, where new leaders are less effective, i.e, where STR_NEW is low, and other such as Ghodach, where new leaders are effective but social capital is low, are falling behind.

The five high-performing case-study villages—Nauwa, Sangawas, Gothra, Khempur and Sema—all have high levels of social capital, and also have capable new leaders, reflected in high village scores on the variable STR_NEW. It is this combination of high social capital and capable agency that is most clearly associated with high development performance.

High social capital is necessary for high development performance (all high performance villages have medium to high social capital), but it is not a sufficient condition (some low performing villages also have medium or high social capital). Similarly, capacity of new leaders is also necessary for high development performance, but it is not sufficient by itself (capacity is high even among some low performing villages). However, both these factors are together sufficient for high development. Development is high in all those villages where social capital is medium to high and where agency strength is also medium to high. Development is not high in villages where even one of these factors is low.

Social capital matters in each case, but it's effect is refracted; it is magnified or reduced, depending upon agency capability. Having a high level of social capital enables communities to take up multiple tasks involving mutually-beneficial collective action. But merely because citizens can act collectively with greater facility does not mean that their actions will always have the intended impact.

In terms of democracy and development, especially where the state is the target of collective action by communities—i.e., where the result is not entirely or even mainly within citizens' control—it is hardly certain that collective action will not end up being a wasted effort. To succeed in achieving their goals, citizens must also at a minimum be well-informed about the processes of decision-making in the state and must be able to gain access to the officials who make and implement these decisions.

Agency matters because information about state institutions and government programmes is not widespread among villagers and also because few channels are available that enable villagers to connect effectively with market and state institutions. Communications between villager and state and villager and market are weak. Capable agents help villagers overcome these obstacles to effective collective action. Social capital is made more productive when such agents exist in the villages.

How Can Development Performance be Improved?

Communities vary in terms of their *capacity to participate* in development initiatives, as the foregoing analysis demonstrates, and results from even the best-designed programmes are likely to differ depending upon the relative capacity of participating villages. Instead of focussing their energies exclusively on developing newer and better programmes and implementing these from the top down, as they have done for so many years, development agencies ought to consider as well the capacities that emerge from the bottom-up and that enable villagers to succeed in multiple development enterprises.

Recall that a single root propensity enables villagers to perform well in multiple development enterprises. Villagers that do well by way of poverty assistance, for instance, also tend to do well in regard to livelihood sustainability, employment provisions and population control. Stimulating the growth of factors associated with this root propensity will be valuable, therefore, for assisting multiple aims of national economic development.

Analysis reveals that social capital, capability of new agents, and literacy are significantly and consistently associated with high development performance. Enhancing the levels of these three factors is likely, therefore, to stimulate faster-paced development.

Literacy is already on the rise. Especially in the past two decades, villagers are increasingly sending their children to school. Nearly 70 per cent of villagers between 18 to 25 years have been educated for five years or more, which is more than double this proportion among the 35 to 45 age group (Krishna 2000). Development in the future is likely to benefit from the investments in education that are being made by current generations.

What can be said about enhancing social capital and agency strength? Social capital may or may not be easy to build up over the short term. The evidence in this regard is mixed and so far inconclusive. Putnam et al. propose that social capital is accumulated only very slowly. 'History determines,' they claimed, and 'historical turning points ... have extremely long-lived consequences' (1993: 179). Analyses undertaken in other parts of the world indicate that social capital may not be a historically fixed endowment, and that it might be possible to build up stocks of social capital within relatively short spans of time (e.g., Hall 1997; Schneider et al. 1997).

The issue is far from closed, however, and resolving it with any reasonable conviction will require undertaking a careful analysis of comparative data collected systematically over a long period of time. This kind of analysis has not been undertaken so far. The concept of social capital has gained popularity only very recently, and social scientists have utilized mainly cross-sectional data to make their cases for and against the utility of this asset.

Though it is not clear whether the stock of social capital can be enhanced significantly in the short term, the productivity of this asset can be definitely increased by investing in measures that help to raise agency capacity. The flow of benefits can be increased by investing in programmes that involve leadership training, increased awareness of constitutional rights and government programmes, and easier access to offices of the state. Villages that presently engage at low levels with state programmes and market operations can be assisted to enhance their capacity to participate. Social capital can be made more productive—and development performance improved—through measures that seek to enhance agency capacity.

Notes

1. Associate Professor, Sanford Institute of Public Policy, Duke University, Durham, North Carolina.
2. 1,450 of 1,898 respondents contacted in 60 Rajasthan villages reported cultivation as their primary source of income, and another 294 reported agricultural labour.
3. Maize yields in Udaipur district rose to a high of 1,528 kilogrammes per hectare in the year 1967–68 but fell to 458 kilogrammes in 1968–69, less than a third of what it was a year ago. Twenty years later less than half of even this amount was harvested in a drought year. In 1987–88, yields were a mere 211 kilogrammes per hectare (Government of Rajasthan 1991).
4. I was the founder director of this programme and of its implementing agency, the Rajasthan government's Department of Watershed Development. For a more detailed account of this programme and of its numerous achievements, both dismal and outstanding, see Krishna (1997).
5. A single common factor is found that is closely associated with all of these four measures of performance in livelihood stabilization activities. Factor loading is as follows: Quantum of work (0.720), survival (0.806), productivity (0.837), diversification (0.850). Communality is 2.76, implying that the underlying factor accounts for about 70 per cent of the combined variance of the four individual items.
6. An alternative index weights the individual items by their factor scores and it is highly correlated (correlation coefficient = 0.94) with this Index.
7. Poverty data were taken from the records of the District Rural Development Agencies (DRDAs), which maintain an updated list of poor households in each village. The poverty cutoff is defined as annual income below Rs 11,000 (US\$ 260), which is calculated as the income with which a person can just about afford to eat the minimum requirement of 2,400 calories per day.
8. Training of Rural Youth for Self-Employment (TRYSEM) and Development of Women and Children in Rural Areas (DWACRA).
9. Dreze (1990), Swaminathan (1990), and Yugandhar and Raju (1992) make the general case; Ahuja and Bhargava (1989) make a similar case for Rajasthan.
10. Considering three-year figures here (and five-year figures for poverty reduction) helps smooth the random fluctuations that can arise from year to year.
11. Each of these scores is standardized to have a range from zero to one, so that each has an equal weight in the index. The four-point aggregate is transformed to have a range from zero to hundred, which makes it easier to interpret regression results, reported later in this chapter.

12. Individual correlation coefficients are all significant at the 0.0001 level with a value of 0.65 or higher; Cronbach's Alpha coefficient = 0.91. The single common factor accounts for 3.68, or about 61 per cent of the combined variance of the six individual items.

13. Correlation coefficients are all 0.85 or higher, and significant at the 0.01 level.

14. Each item is given an equal weight within the Index, which is obtained by summing across the scores after first dividing each variable by its range, so that each item has a maximum range of one. A further transformation results in an index that has a range from zero to hundred. This latter transformation is useful at a later stage for interpreting regression results. An alternative index was constructed by weighting the individual items with their factor scores. The two indices are highly correlated with one another (0.98), indicating that this index is robust against alternative weighting schemes, and there is no special merit in preferring one index over the other.

15. For Italy it is also claimed that parties play much of the role for which Putnam gives credit to social capital. 'Sports clubs, choral societies, cooperatives and cultural associations have been organized by and for two major political parties, the Communists and the Christian Democrats,' claim Foley and Edwards (1996: 42) for the Emilia–Romagna region. Tarrow (1996) enlarges this claim to include other regions as well.

16. Each scale presented below is used for comparing a particular type of agency across villages. Since they rely upon different items, however, scores on one scale cannot be compared with scores on another. Political party strength cannot be compared with, say, the strength of caste associations in any village; their units of measurement are too different. But villages are compared to see if strength of political parties is related as a variable to economic development. Villages are also compared in respect of five other modes of agency—caste associations, panchayats, new leaders, village councils and patron-client links.

17. A *panchayat* is a unit of local government in India that is elected usually by residents of from one to five villages, depending on population size. According to some observers, *panchayats* are hardly effective units of governance, and they function, instead, merely as 'implementing agencies of a centralized state' (Mayaram 1998).

18. The term, Village Council, is mine. Villagers themselves refer to these bodies as *Gaon-ki-Panchayat,* or villagers' *panchayat* as opposed to the other one that is *Sarkari,* or the government's, *panchayat.* Persons who sit on these bodies are spoken of as *purana netas* (old leaders).

19. Though some independent variables are correlated with each other, for instance, STR_CASTE is correlated with CASTEDOM, and literacy with PERCPOOR, pairwise correlation among the independent variables is

not greater than 0.5 in any case. The value of the Condition Index is
24.68 for model 1, indicating moderate multicollinearity, and less than
15 for Models 2 and 3, indicating low collinearity. White's general test
does not reveal the presence of any significant heteroskedasticity.

References

Agrawal, A. 1999. *Greener Pastures: Politics, Markets and Community Among
a Migrant Pastoral People*. Durham: Duke University Press.
Ahuja, K., and Bhargava, P. 1989. 'Long-Term Impact of Integrated Rural
Development Programme'. Jaipur: Institute of Development Studies,
mimeo.
Berger, P.L., and Luckmann, T. 1966. *The Social Construction of Reality: A
Treatise in the Sociology of Knowledge*. Garden City, New York:
Doubleday.
Berman, S. 1997. 'Civil Society and the Collapse of the Weimar Republic'.
World Politics 49: pp. 401–29.
Berman, S. 1997a. 'Civil Society and Political Institutionalization'. *American
Behavioural Scientist* 40 (5): pp. 562–74.
Brehm, J., and Rahn, W. 1997. 'Individual-Level Evidence for the Causes
and Consequences of Social Capital'. *American Journal of Political Sci-
ence* 41 (3): pp. 999–1023.
Coleman, J.S. 1988. 'Social Capital in the Creation of Human Capital'. *Ameri-
can Journal of Sociology* 94: pp. 95–120.
CTAE. 1999. 'Integrated Watershed Development Project. Impact Evalua-
tion Report 1991–1997'. College of Technology and Agricultural Engi-
neering, Rajasthan Agricultural University, Udaipur.
Dreze, J. 1990. 'Poverty in India and the IRDP Delusion'. *Economic and
Political Weekly* 25 (39).
Dreze, J., and Sen, A. 1995. *India: Economic Development and Social Op-
portunity*. New Delhi: Oxford University Press.
Dumont, L. 1970. *Homo Hierarchicus: An Essay on the Caste System*. Chi-
cago: University of Chicago Press.
Foley, M.W., and Edwards, B. 1996. 'The Paradox of Civil Society'. *Journal
of Democracy* 7 (3): pp. 38–52.
GOR. 1999. *Progress Report: Eight Five-Year Plan: 1992–1997*. Jaipur: Plan-
ning Department, Government of Rajasthan.
Hall, P. 1997. 'Social Capital in Britain'. Paper prepared for Bertelsmann
Stiflung Workshop on Social Capital, Berlin, June 1997.

Kohli, A. 1990. *Democracy and Discontent: India's Growing Crisis of Governability*. Cambridge, U.K.: Cambridge University Press.

Kothari, R. 1988. *State Against Democracy: In Search of Humane Governance*. Delhi: Ajanta Publishers.

Krishna, A. 2000. 'Social Capital, Collective Action, and the State: Understanding Economic Development, Community Harmony, and Political Participation in Rural North India'. Doctoral dissertation, Department of Government, Cornell University.

Krishna, A. 1997. 'Participatory Watershed Development and Soil Conservation in Rajasthan, India', in A. Krishna, N.T. Uphoff and M.J. Esman (eds.), *Reasons for Hope: Instructive Experiences in Rural Development*. West Hartford, Connecticut: Kumarian Press, pp. 255–72.

Krishna, A., and Uphoff, N. 1999. 'Mapping and Measuring Social Capital: A Conceptual and Empirical Study of Collective Action for Conserving and Developing Watersheds in Rajasthan, India', in *Social Capital Initiative Working Paper*, no. 13. Washington, D.C.: The World Bank.

Kurien, G. 1999. 'Empowering Conditions in the Decentralization Process: An Analysis of Dynamics, Factors and Actors in Panchayati Raj Institutions From West Bengal and Karnataka, India', in *Working Paper Series*, no. 228. The Hague, Netherlands: Institute of Social Studies.

Levi, M. 1996. 'Social and Unsocial Capital'. *Politics and Society* 24: pp. 45–55.

Mathew, G. 1994. *Panchayati Raj: From Legislation to Movement*. New Delhi: Concept Publishers.

Mayaram, S. 1998. 'Panchayats and Women: A study of the processes initiated before and after the 73rd Amendment in Rajasthan'. Jaipur: Institute of Development Studies, mimeo.

North, D.C. 1981. *Structure and Change in Economic History*. New York: Norton.

Putnam, R.D. 1995. 'Bowling Alone: America's Declining Social Capital'. *Journal of Democracy*: pp. 65–78.

Putnam, R.D., Leonardi, R., and Raffaella, Y. N. 1993. *Making Democracy Work: Civic Traditions in Modern Italy*. Princeton: Princeton University Press.

Ragin, C.C. 1987. *The Comparative Method: Moving Beyond Qualitative and Quantitative Strategies*. Berkeley: University of California Press.

Sabharwal, S. 1997. 'On the Diversity of Ruling Traditions', in S. Kaviraj (ed.), *Politics in India*. Delhi: Oxford University Press: pp. 124–40.

Schneider, M., Teske, P., Marschall, M., Mintrom, M., and Roch, C. 1997. 'Institutional Arrangements and the Creation of Social Capital: The Effects of Public School Choice'. *American Political Science Review* 91 (1): pp. 82–93.

Srinivas, M.N. 1987. 'The Indian Village: Myth and Reality', in M.N. Srinivas, *The Dominant Caste and Other Essays*. Delhi: Oxford University Press, pp. 20–59.

Swaminathan, M. 1990. 'Village-Level Implementation of IRDP: Comparison of West Bengal and Tamil Nadu'. *Economic and Political Weekly* 25 (13).

Tarrow, S. 1996. 'Making Social Science Work Across Space and Time'. *American Political Science Review* 90: pp. 389–97.

Wade, R. 1994. *Village Republics: Economic Conditions for Collective Action in South India*. San Francisco: Institute for Contemporary Studies.

Weiner, M. 1989. *The Indian Paradox: Essays in Indian Politics*. New Delhi, London: Sage Publications.

Yugandhar, B.N., and Raju, B.Y. 1992. 'Government Delivery Systems for Rural Development: Malady-Remedy Analysis'. *Economic and Political Weekly* 27 (35).

III
New Directions and Cul-de-Sacs

III
New Directions and Cul-de-Sac

10

Passive Membership in Voluntary Organizations: Implications for Civil Society, Integration and Democracy

Dag Wollebæk/Per Selle[1]

Introduction

The most unique characteristic of the Norwegian voluntary sector is neither its high level of participation, nor the dominant role of cultural associations over welfare-oriented organizations. First and foremost, associational life in Norway is characterized by the enormous numbers of *passive members*, i.e., persons who are affiliated with one or more association, but spend next to no time participating in their activities. More than 70 per cent of the population holds membership in one or more association, with an average of 2.4 affiliations per member. But only one-third of them spend more than one hour a week volunteering or participating when their entire involvement in organizations is added together (Wollebæk et al. 2000).

However, as participation rates decline, 'tertiary organizations' replace 'classic secondary associations' in most Western countries (Putnam 1995a; Skocpol 1999; Maloney 1999). Passive membership is becoming the rule rather than the exception in organized civil society elsewhere, too.

This development necessitates a better understanding of passive support, about which strong opinions are expressed in social literature, based on *a priori* ideas of what this phenomenon represents. This chapter attempts to contribute to the empirical basis for such opinions. We use data from a country where passive membership has a long history in order to cast light on what may be underway in other societies. We suggest that the current anxieties concerning the future of democracy if activity rates should drop can be assuaged by taking a closer look at what passive support really means.

Passive Support Reconsidered

Despite their vast numbers, passive members are attributed a rather marginal role by advocates of the virtues of participation. Their assertion is that in a true democracy, citizens should be able to actively take part in civic matters, at least on the local level (Pateman 1970; Macpherson 1977). Regular elections and the existence of formal rights are by themselves not sufficient for democracy, but need to be supplemented by opportunities for direct democratic influence. Thus, passivity is read as an expression of the massive number of individuals restricted from actively taking part in civic and political life.

On the other hand, pluralists emphasize how a diverse range of associations may act as representatives on the political scene, regardless of the activity level of the participants (Almond and Verba 1963). National political systems are too large to allow face-to-face discussion between all citizens. Therefore, associations are institutional requirements if the combined values or interests of individuals are to be mediated. The members may sanction their representatives by means of either withdrawing their support to the association, to *exit*, or through *voicing* their preferences (Hirschmann 1970). Hence, in this perspective, the passive supporter is important not only as a source of numerical strength and legitimacy for associations, but also as a part of the democratic process. Furthermore, weak and multiple affiliations ensure that most members belong to several and overlapping networks. This implies that views will be moderated as a result of cross-pressures.

Robert D. Putnam's influential work on social capital is inspired by both strands of thought (1993; 1995a; 1995b; 2000). His view of associations as intermediary institutions between citizens and the state, and the weight he attaches to networks cutting across subcultural divides, reveals a clear inspiration from writers in the pluralist vein. His emphasis on the necessity of active participation for the socialisation into democratic virtues is, by contrast, influenced by participant-oriented approaches to democratic theory (Selle and Strømsnes, 2001). For Putnam, the primary role of associations is to provide social connections between their participants, which in turn produce and disperse trust and civic engagement. Thus, the core contributions of associations to democracy consist of the 'internal' effects on their members and volunteers, not the 'external' effects on the wider polity.

According to Putnam (1995b), America's stock of social capital is rapidly diminishing. The recent proliferation of tertiary organizations does little to alleviate this erosion of civic life, since social capital can only be formed and transmitted through direct interaction, from which passive supporters are deprived. Furthermore, tertiary groups are largely made up by vertical rather than horizontal connections. Their structure is better characterized as client-patron relationships than as interaction among equals, and 'two clients of the same patron, lacking direct contact, hold nothing hostage to each other' (Putnam 1993: 175). Therefore, due to the low level of active participation of members and the vertical organizational structure, tertiary associations contribute next to nothing to horizontal networks and social trust.

This leads Putnam to discard passive support as a source of social capital, and with it numerous politically oriented, value-based organizations. This conclusion may be too hasty. It rests on two assumptions that are not entirely obvious: one, that the associations' internal effects are more important to democracy than their external role, and two, that associations cannot have internal effects on passive supporters. The first is primarily a normative question pertaining to Putnam's preferred model of democracy, which is explicitly 'bottom-up' and clearly influenced by communitarian impulses. The second assumption is based on the view that passive members are disconnected and marginalized from the social and political systems their organizations represent. This is an empirical question which Putnam does not address. In fact, it has not been properly researched empirically since Almond and Verba's *The Civic Culture* (1963).

Almond and Verba, who are among Putnam's main influences, attribute an importance to passive membership which exceeds its external effects. In their classic study, passive members displayed significantly higher levels of civic competence than non-members across five countries. Passive supporters were also more supportive of democratic norms than outsiders, and shared a higher sense of political efficacy.[2]

The question arising from this is: does a sense of commitment, community or identification with a cause, creating trust between compatriots, linkages from citizens to society at large and crosscutting loyalties really presuppose face-to-face individual contact? We are not entirely convinced that this is the case, and suggest that insights from Almond and Verba's work in the 1960s may improve current theories pertaining to associations and democracy such as Putnam's version of social capital.

The theory of *imagined communities* can be used to illuminate how social capital might develop without extensive personal interaction (Anderson 1991; Newton 1999; Whiteley 1999). An imagined community is a group with which one feels a psychological affinity, even though it is too large to allow for face-to-face contact between all its members. Although the *nation* is given as the typical example of the imagined community,[3] the concept is transferable to other social systems with similar properties. The relations between a passive member and his/her association and between a citizen and his/her nation clearly share important characteristics. Face-to-face contact is impossible between every member in an association, as it is between every citizen of a nation, but their members/citizens may still feel affinity to a common set of symbols or values, or share a commitment to a cause. To the degree that individuals hold overlapping memberships in several associations their sense of identification and trust may be transferred to several contexts, and possibly to society as a whole.

Thus, passive members *belong to institutions within which large stocks of social capital are embedded*. If these ties are of some importance for the supporter, it is quite possible that the 'internal' effects of belonging are not reserved only for those who physically meet. In that case, a re-evaluation of the role of passive membership in the formation of social capital is in order. In short, we need more empirical knowledge about *how passive members relate to their organizations*. This task is undertaken below.

The Data

The analyses are based on a nationwide survey carried out by the Norwegian Centre for Research in Organization and Management

(LOS Centre) in 1998 as part of the '*John Hopkins Comparative Non-profit Sector Project*' (Wollebæk, Selle and Lorentzen 1998). The '*Survey on Giving and Volunteering*' is the most comprehensive data gathered on the involvement of individuals in voluntary associations in Norway. The survey was administered by means of mailed questionnaires to 4,000 randomly selected Norwegians aged between 16 and 85. The respondents were contacted four times—a postcard one week before mailing the questionnaire, the mailing of the questionnaire itself and two follow-ups. The last follow-up was carried out over the telephone. In all, we received 1,695 valid responses, which equals a response rate of 45 per cent (adjusted gross sample).

This response rate is somewhat lower than is the case for most mailed surveys in Norway. However, there is no systematic over-representation of active participants, and the bias towards the middle-aged and higher educated respondents is sought to be compensated by weighing the results.

Understanding Passivity

In another study (Wollebæk 2000; Wollebæk and Selle 2002), we demonstrated that participation in voluntary associations does appear to be related to the formation of social capital. However, Putnam's emphasis on face-to-face contact was given little or no support by the data. While those affiliated with associations consistently displayed higher levels of social capital (measured as social trust, civic engagement and breadth of social networks) than outsiders did, the difference between those spending little or no time participating and highly active participants was very small or altogether absent. The number of affiliations held by each individual (scope of participation) emerged as a much stronger predictor of social capital than the time-related intensity of the involvement. Furthermore, Putnam's penchant for associations with non-political purposes (such as culture, music, sports and leisure) was not encouraged by the data. Their members deviated from the population at large only if their affiliation was accompanied by a connection to an association with a more politicised purpose.

We believe these findings bring the *a priori* assumptions dominating the participant-oriented literature on participation in voluntary associations into serious question—that only active, personal participation is of value to democracy, and that only active members are socialised by their affiliation. It opens up a plethora of intriguing questions about the mode of this type of participation: what is the rationality behind passive support? Why do the numerous passive members consider it of value to belong at all? Once on the inside, how do they relate to their associations? Are they as alienated, indifferent and marginalised as Putnam would have it? Is it conceivable that passive membership is more than a residual category representing those deprived of direct social interaction, but rather a distinct mode of participation with particular properties?

Some of these questions are addressed below. The analyses are based on a series of questions concerning why the members chose to join, how they view the internal life of the association and their role in it, and in which arenas they think the association should primarily exercise its potential external democratic function. The responses are cross-tabulated with the level of activity and the type of association with which the member is affiliated.

The answers pertain only to the affiliation *the members considered to be the most important*. The indicator used to distinguish between active and passive supporters is their *self-reported* level of activity. What are the most common reasons for becoming a member, and how do passive members differ from active ones? Table 10.1 summarises the coded answers to an open-ended question about the main reason the respondents gave for becoming a member of the association they considered to be the most important.

The results show that the two highest-ranking reasons for active members to join an association are personal fulfilment (e.g., to keep in shape, or learn new things) and social contacts. Among passive members, on the other hand, economic or work-related advantages are the most important reason given for joining. However, this applies almost exclusively to union memberships. The second and third most important motives are to influence decisions and to gain membership benefits (including access to information).

Thus, personal and 'egoistic' motives generally rank above 'altruistic' causes for joining associations (such as 'helping others') among active and passive members alike. The motives among the passive members are more explicitly instrumental than among the activists, for whom opportunities for socializing predictably play a more important role. The most surprising finding, however, is that passive members are slightly more likely to join associations in order to influence decisions than active members. This is not due to the fact

Table 10.1 Most important reason for joining the organization, by type of organization and level of activity (per cent)

	Non-political, leisure		Non-political, religious		Semi-political		Political (parties/unions)		All memberships	
	Passive	Active	Passive	Active	Passive	Active	Passive	Active	Passive	Active
Economic advantages/work-related	2	2	(–)	2	2	5	69	69	26	15
Influence decisions	16	8	(16)	13	27	19	7	21	16	12
Membership benefits	12	10	(–)	4	28	27	9	7	15	11
Personal fulfilment	29	58	(–)	3	–	7	–	2	10	33
Social contact/social benefits	18	41	(7)	17	5	15	3	5	9	27
Help others	5	3	(9)	6	18	27	2	2	8	6
Previous experiences	12	4	(20)	–	7	1	5	–	6	2
Help own children	14	4	(–)	–	2	2	–	2	5	2
Social pressure	1	0.2	(–)	0.2	1	1	10	–	4	1
Special qualities of the organization	1	3	(–)	–	12	9	2	2	4	3
Religious conviction	2	1	(48)	72	1	–	–	–	2	7
Total*	112	134	(100)	117	103	112	107	109	105	119
N=	105	289	(11)	51	82	69	111	119	309	528

Note: (*) Total percentage exceeds 100 because some respondents provided more than one answer.

that political associations rely more on passive support than non-political associations do. It is especially within non-political and semi-political associations that political influence emerges as more important for passive members than for the more active ones, while the relationship is the other way round among members of political organizations.

Table 10.2 shows that in addition to the slight difference in the *weight* attached to political influence as a motive, there is also a difference in *scale* between passive and active participants.

When asked at which political level their association should primarily try to exert influence, active members tended to emphasize institutions in their immediate environment. Passive members, on the other hand, express a stronger interest in decisions at the national or international level. While twice as many of the active members emphasize living conditions in the local community compared to national or international agencies, the passive members consider the two arenas to be equally important. Among members in non-political associations, only passive supporters emphasize their role as actors on the national political scene, while passive members of semi-political associations are clearly more interested in influencing decisions on the international arena than the active members are.

These results underline that, perhaps even more so for passive members than for activists, associations may serve as institutional links between citizens and the larger political system. Whereas activists are strongly oriented towards the local community, passive members place more weight on issues of a larger scale. When regarding associations as networks providing links from the individual to decisions at the political scene, as the neo-Tocquevillian approach does, passive support may be at least as important as active participation.

With regard to the marginal role attributed to the passive supporter in Putnam's work, we might expect that passive members were fairly indifferent to the operations of the associations, and that activists would regard passive contributions as relatively unimportant. The results in table 10.3, which summarize the members' attitudes towards the internal life of their respective associations, show that this is clearly not the case.

Statements A through C aim at capturing the importance members attribute to the internal democratic structure of the association. The responses reflect that internal democracy is still, despite recent developments in the voluntary sector in Norway, a core value among

Table 10.2 Most important level of influence, by type of organization and level of activity (per cent)

	Non-political, leisure		Non-political, religious		Semi-political		Political (parties/unions)		All memberships	
	Passive	Active	Passive	Active	Passive	Active	Passive	Active	Passive	Active
Living conditions in local community	54	59	(54)	70	50	54	3	7	32	46
Municipal/county authorities	17	26	(15)	8	6	21	30	28	20	24
Companies	5	5	(-)	-	-	1	32	29	15	10
State authorities	22	6	(15)	13	17	17	33	35	25	16
International agencies	2	4	(15)	10	27	8	2	2	8	5
Total	100	100	(100)	100	100	100	100	100	100	100
N=	104	250	(13)	40	70	78	129	123	316	491
chi-square (sig.)	21.577		1.347		15.248		1.859		30.442	
	.000		.718		.004		.762		.000	

Table 10.3 Attitudes towards most important association (per cent, percentage difference agree-disagree in italics)

	Non-political, leisure		Non-political, religious		Semi-political		Political (parties/unions)		All members	
	Passive	Active	Passive	Active	Passive	Active	Passive	Active	Passive	Active
A. It is important to me that the organization is democratically structured	86	86	(83)	84	84	87	89	96	87	87
	+83	*+82*	*(+75)*	*+76*	*+82*	*+86*	*+89*	*+94*	*+84*	*+83*
sig.*	.834		.983		.957		.011		.093	
B. The leaders often act on their own, without regard for the members' views	23	20	(42)	23	8	17	26	31	22	22
	-28	*-46*	*(-17)*	*-45*	*-31*	*-51*	*-17*	*-28*	*-22*	*-32*
sig.	.013		.032		.002		.008		.000	
C. There is too little debate and discussion within the organization	20	21	(29)	30	13	26	25	34	21	25
	-13	*-35*	*(-13)*	*-17*	*-21*	*-24*	*-14*	*-23*	*-13*	*-29*
sig.	.000		.852		.028		.002		.000	
D. Being a passive member is also an important contribution to the activities of the organization	83	56	(79)	48	91	67	81	66	85	59
	+75	*+28*	*(+72)*	*+15*	*+90*	*+46*	*+74*	*+40*	*+80*	*+22*

sig.	.000	.000	.049		.000	.000	.000	.000	.000	.000
E. I'd gladly take part in specific activities initiated by the organization, but I rarely have the energy to attend regular meetings	55 +29	27 −33	(50) (+31)	11 −67	53 +38	15 −58	44 +18	27 −32	50 +28	24 −39
sig.	.000	.000	.000		.000	.000	.000	.000	.000	.000
N=	117–125	300–306	(12–14)	52–54	87–94	77–79	136–142	129–130	348–366	588–600

Note: Strongly/mildly agree and strongly/mildly disagree are collapsed into 'agree' and 'disagree' respectively.
(*) Significance tests based on chi-squares.

the members (Wallebæk, Selle and Lorentzen 2000a). More interest-ingly in this context however, passive members place no less weight on internal democratic structure than active members, except for a slight difference between the two groups among members of politi-cal associations. As reflected in the responses to statements B and C, active supporters express slightly more satisfaction with the way democracy works in their associations (disagree more with the state-ments) than passive members do. Still, even among passive support-ers the majority is content with the internal democratic processes.

The fact that passive members consider internal democracy to be important *and* are quite satisfied with the performance of these structures indicates that they are neither indifferent nor marginalized supporters of voluntary associations. In Hirschmann's (1970) terms, they have a potential *exit*-power if the association operates counter to their preferences.

That the exit of passive members is not inconsequential is clearly reflected in the responses given to statement D. Predictably, passive members consider their support to be more valuable than active mem-bers do. However, there is also a majority among the active mem-bers who think that passive memberships represent important contributions to the organizations. Based on the findings of a recent survey of local associations, passive members are also highly valued by the associations themselves. On a scale from 1 to 10, where 1 repre-sents full agreement with 'only active members are of great value to the association' and 10 full agreement with 'also passive members are of great value to the association', the average score was 7.2.[4]

Statement E is the only question to which the opinions of active and passive members differ substantially. A majority of the passive members who have an opinion agree that they would gladly take part in specific activities, but do not have the energy to attend ordinary meetings, while a majority of the active supporters with an opinion disagree. The propensity to participate actively when needed, but reluctance to enter into a binding obligation with the organiza-tion, reveals two important features of passive membership. First, passive members display what is probably the most *modern* atti-tude. While being able to exert some influence on the organization and step in when needed, the member also preserves her indi-vidual autonomy. Second, from the association's point of view, it indicates that the passive members represent a reserve of activists from which the association can draw when carrying out specific short-term activities.

The latter underlines the importance of viewing passive memberships dynamically (Selle and Strømsnes 2001). The passive member of this year might be the active member of yesteryear, or next year. Individuals drift in and out of different roles and functions in associations depending on their life situation, their motivation and current resources. Most of those that are passive at present have the potential for becoming active in the future, and furthermore, they are connected to the society at large by means of their organizations. The boundaries between passive and active participation are neither absolute nor insurmountable.

In summary, the reasons for joining given by passive members were less oriented towards social rewards than among the active members, while opportunities for political influence played a comparatively more important role among inactive supporters. Passive support is also related to a more politicized view of the association's role in democracy, while active members tend to emphasize conditions in their immediate surroundings. Passive members care as much as active ones about how the associations operate, do not see themselves as being marginalized in relation to internal processes and are prepared to take active part in specific activities if asked. Active members on the other hand value the contributions of passive support only slightly less than the passive members do themselves. Thus, the results suggest that passive members are *not alienated from, nor uninterested in, nor inconsequential for, the affairs of their associations.*

The results presented in this chapter demonstrate that passive support cannot be left out in any comprehensive analysis of participation in associations. Regardless of whether passive support is seen as an independent, intermediary or dependent variable, it needs to be taken more seriously in social science than what has been the case till now.

Discussion

We believe that Putnam's basic contention, that voluntary associations are important in the formation of social capital, is correct. However, one central tenet of Putnam's thesis, that *only face-to-face contact* in networks of secondary associations can generate these resources, finds little or no support in our empirical results.

The comparison of the motives and attitudes of active and passive supporters revealed a picture quite contrary to the impression given by Putnam. Passive members, who are not exposed to face-to-face contact are often more conscious about the importance of the affiliation, its potential for political influence and its democratic significance than their active counterparts. Passive members are not indifferent to the internal life of associations, and are prepared to take on active roles when necessary on a temporary basis. Their involvement is quite often rooted in a commitment to a cause, an interest in exerting influence and—like active members—a possibility of personal rewards.

Passive support may become more common in the years to come due to tendencies towards centralization and professionalization in Norwegian associations (Selle and Øymyr 1995). However, this is hardly a development which is limited to Norway (Skocpol 1999; Maloney 1999; Putnam 1995a). Considering the current changes in organized civil society in most of the Western world, it seems clear that the question of the value of passive membership will increase in importance in the years to come. These questions concern issues such as the extent to which the rule of voluntary associations should be evaluated: simply by the amount of direct interaction they generate, or whether other aspects of their activities are of equal or more importance.

We have argued that face-to-face contact is not as crucial in creating bonds between members, their organizations and society at large as some have suggested. Instead, *even passive affiliations* may have internal effects on those participating. We have also suggested that, given the current decline in membership-based internally democratic organizations, we need to look at other aspects of organized activity than just social integration at the micro-level when assessing the role of voluntary organizations in civil society.

A central issue here is how passive supporters be affected by their 'participation by proxy'. It is possible to distinguish between four understandings of the relationship between the passive supporter and his or her association: the association as *social system, imagined community, information system* and *network of political influence*. When regarding the passive member as part of a *social system*, it is implied that socialisation may take place even if he or she does not interact with other members within the context of the association. Many passive members are likely to socialize with activists in social settings other than the organization. While most members in tertiary associations, at least in the U.S., are recruited through direct marketing techniques (Maloney 1999), many are recruited through already existing social networks (Selle and Strømsnes 1998). Thus passive members can keep in touch with the association through their networks of contacts with activists. Although this is not always the case and though the related socialization is of a less intensive nature than for active participants, it should not be ruled out *a priori*. The finding that number of affiliations has a stronger effect on the breadth of social networks as well as on the number of friends suggests that this interpretation may not be entirely off the mark.

Second, the affiliation may develop a sense of identification with and commitment to a cause. As discussed above, associations relying on passive support resemble Anderson's (1991) idea of an *imagined community*, a concept referring to all social systems too large to allow face-to-face contact wherein members nonetheless share emotional ties to a community. Passive affiliations may foster a sense of affinity to a cause which the individual knows is not only important to himself or herself, but also to others. If the association is successful, the membership, regardless of activity level, conveys a sense of the value of cooperation for common purposes, of political efficacy and of a shared belonging to something important. Clearly, these virtues are all conducive to social capital.

Third, associations may function as *information systems*. Norwegian nationwide voluntary associations distribute almost five copies of journals and newsletters per person among the adult population (Hallenstvedt and Trollvik 1993). Furthermore, the information networks in the new tertiary associations founded in the past couple of decades, which rely almost entirely on passive support, are at least as comprehensive as in traditional voluntary associations (Selle and Strømsnes 2001). It is not unlikely that this function will become increasingly important with recent technological developments, such as the Internet. As pointed out by Selle and Strømsnes, tertiary associations are at the forefront in making use of these new opportunities for information dissemination. This implies that the passive member is not necessarily out of touch with the goings-on of the association, nor will he be in the future. The extensive networks of information disseminate knowledge about current issues and how the association relates to them. As such, they may serve as 'schools in democracy' and promoters of civic engagement—even though the members do not interact personally.

Finally, associations might serve as *networks of political influence*, even for those not actively involved. As demonstrated in section 4, passive members are not entirely marginalized with regard to internal decisions in the associations. They have the power to withdraw their support—to *exit*—which is clearly not inconsequential to the associations. If they hold multiple affiliations, as many do, they have the opportunity to exert influence on many arenas at the same time.

This 'contracting out' of the democratic participation function may be of no less significance for democracy than active participation. We noted above an observable difference in *scale* between active and passive supporters with regard to which issues they believe the association should address. While activists are strongly oriented towards living conditions in their immediate surroundings, passive members regard national and international issues as equally important. This indicates that the associations in many cases function as intermediary institutions between the citizen and the larger political system *even more* for passive members than for active ones. The small scale of many of the associations in which active participation takes place may inhibit them from having much bearing on political issues of a larger scale: 'Thus neighbourhood associations may thrive and be effective in advancing their interests locally, but such participation often has little or no political impact at the regional and national level' (Rueschemeyer, Rueschemeyer and Wittrock 1998: 13).

The idea that passive members' affiliations with extensive information networks, 'imagined communities' and networks of political influence leave them unaffected in terms of trust, social networks and civic engagement is an assumption which has not been supported by empirical results. Pending evidence to the contrary, the postulation that *only* face-to-face contact within voluntary associations has internal effects on members should not be accepted as anything more than an unproven hypothesis.

Is it the Other Way Around: Associations Institutionalize Social Capital?

A quite different understanding of the absent effect of face-to-face contact is that associations contribute to social capital, *but primarily as institutions in which norms and resources are embedded* (Selle and Strømsnes 2001).

The logic of this argument may be clarified by means of a contrafactual thought experiment. What would be the level of social capital if associations were absent? Regardless of whether those joining associations possess more social capital than non-joiners to begin with, associations contribute to the sustenance of social values and norms. This is especially true for those affiliated as members, but to some extent it spills over to non-members. In this view voluntary associations define important parts of the social environment regardless of whether one takes part in them or not. The existence of a multitude of visible voluntary associations is in itself evidence of the value and rationality of collaborative efforts, even for individuals who are not active in these efforts themselves. Thus the role of associations as generators or catalysts of trust, or networks of civic engagement, is subordinated to their role as institutions expressing and sustaining common values and resources. As Wollebæk et al. (2000a) show, the population not only trusts voluntary associations more than government or business, they also see them as an indispensable part of society.

Such a perspective implies a move away from the internal effects of associational life on participants to external effects on society at large. These external effects can be divided into two broad categories: *integration* and *democracy*. Their contribution to integration lies in the ability to create multiple and overlapping networks that reduce levels of conflict potential in society. This occurs because the loosely knit networks span existing cleavages and patterns of loyalty. In this perspective, the 'broad' voluntary sector characterized by extensive, multiple memberships but low activity rates, as exemplified by the Scandinavian countries (Dekker and Van Den Broek 1998), may be particularly well suited to institutionalize social capital because it creates weaker ties to multiple institutions (instead of) or in addition to (bridging social capital) strong ties to a few (bonding social capital). Dekker, Koopmans and Van Den Broek (1997) show that the highest levels of social trust are to be found in countries with voluntary sectors resembling the Norwegian one, i.e., the other Scandinavian countries and the Netherlands. This may well be a result of the 'broad' participation model prevalent in these countries, in contrast to the 'parochial' or 'active' models characterized by more intensive involvements found in the rest of Europe and North America.

If associations contribute to the sustenance of values of moderation and generalized trust among citizens, they also contribute to a stable democracy. A diverse range of associations is necessary for democratic pluralism, which can be viewed as a value in itself. Involvement in public discourse can convey a sense of political efficacy to members and non-members alike—a feeling that participation is not futile. The role of the passive supporter is not unimportant in this respect. A broad membership base, more or less regardless of activity level, is an essential source of legitimacy (and funding) for many associations with outward-oriented political purposes.

Viewing associations as institutionally-embedded stores of trust, norms and networks of civic engagement, rather than as generators, catalysts or vehicles, entails a quite different perspective from that of Putnam. Rather than focussing on the internal effects of participation on the active member (i.e., degree of socialization), it draws attention to external effects on the wider polity or society (pluralism and crosscutting cleavages). Less significance is attributed to the intensity of the involvement (or degree of face-to-face contact) as the main indicator of vibrancy of associational life, in comparison with the scope of participation (multiple, overlapping memberships).

Finally, we should not reject the value of associations with political purposes simply because they tend to be more vertical in structure than leisure-oriented associations. On the contrary, purely horizontal networks (if such power-neutral networks exist at all—see Mouzelis 1995) are insufficient if democratic pluralism as well as political and social cohesion are to be ensured (Rueschemeyer 1998; Berman 1997). In order to contribute to these ends, associations need to provide institutional links reaching beyond local communities into the political system. Thus, by definition, the networks need to be vertical in at least one sense of the turn.

This does not exclude or undervalue horizontal networks at the local level, which are still found in most externally-oriented, politically relevant secondary associations in Norway and other countries. Rather, we stress the fact that the desire for social connectedness through active participation in local non-political associational life should not lead us to neglect the role of associations as intermediary institutions—between the citizen or individual on the one hand, and the political system and wider society on the other. This function may indeed be of more consequence to democracy than bowling in any number of organized leagues.

Implications for Further Research

If social capital is to move beyond a theory of social connectedness, its emphasis on horizontal networks, non-political purpose and face-to-face contact needs to be challenged. This is not to say that face-to-face contact and socialization are unimportant, only that associations provide very little of both—compared to families, friends, schools and workplaces—for the vast majority of citizens.

Thus, we need to search elsewhere in order to locate the contribution of participation in associations to social capital. Abandoning intensity of involvement in favour of scope provides a good place to start. Associational memberships provide us with access to sources of knowledge, skills, information and opportunities to exert political influence. Perhaps most significantly, affiliation with an association, even when passive, may give rise to a sense of belonging and commitment to a cause. Neither of these virtues presupposes face-to-face contact, all of them are conducive to social trust and civic engagement, and all are strengthened by bonds to multiple networks.

Further studies should therefore address the dynamics through which involvement in associations contributes to social capital. This entails particular attention giving to passive membership, the implications of which have not as yet been adequately researched. We believe that the imported mechanism of face-to-face contact needs to be treated as a falsifiable hypothesis and not an incontestable truth. Otherwise it may well become a theoretical blindfold obstructing the view towards more fruitful avenues of thought and investigation.

Notes

1. Dag Wollebæk is a doctoral candidate in the Department of Comparative Politics, University of Bergen. Per Selle is Professor in the Department of Comparative Politics and Senior Researcher at the Stein Rokkan Centre for Social Studies, University of Bergen.

2. Maloney (1999: 113) cites one other study researching passive support, by Godwin (1992), who emphasises that even the most passive forms of participation (financial support through check-writing) '... reduces political alienation, as contributors believe their contributions make a difference. This, in turn, reduces the support for aggressive political participation'. This effect is related to the durability of involvement—the longer individuals remain in their passive roles, the more influence the affiliation has on their attitudes.

3. For example, Whiteley (1999: 31) shows that those who most strongly identify with the imagined community (express patriotism) are more likely to express a generalized sense of trust in other people than individuals whose patriotism is weaker.

4. N=2.168. The survey covered all associations in Hordaland County. The response rate was 60 per cent. The only types of associations deviating from the tendency are those active in song, music and theatrical activities, where the members' active participation is often required in order to carry out meaningful activities (average score 4.8). Passive members are most highly valued in language, teetotal, mission, and social and humanitarian associations, as well as in political parties (all with average scores above 8.0).

References

Almond, G., and Verba, S. 1963. *The Civic Culture: Political Attitudes and Democracy in Five Nations*. Princeton, NJ: Princeton University Press.

Anderson, B. 1991. *Imagined Communities: Reflections on the Origins and Spread of Nationalism (revised)*. London: Verso.

Berman, S. 1997. 'Civil Society and the collapse of the Weimar Republic'. *World Politics* 49 (3): pp. 401–29.

Dekker, P., Koopmans, R., and Van Den Broek, A. 1997. 'Voluntary associations, social movements and individual political behaviour in Western Europe', in J.W. Van Deth (ed.), *Private Groups and Public Life*. London: Routledge, pp. 220–41.

Dekker, P., and Van Den Broek, A. 1998. 'Civil society in comparative perspective: Involvement in voluntary associations in North America and Western Europe'. *Voluntas* 9 (1): pp. 11–38.

Godwin, R.K. 1992. 'Money, Technology, and Political Interests: The Direct Marketing of Politics', in M. Petracca (ed.), *The Politics of Interests*. Boulder, Colorado, CO: Westview Press.

Hallenstvedt, A., and Trollvik, J. 1993. *Norske organisasjoner*. Oslo: Fabritius Forlag.

Hirschmann, A.O. 1970. *Exit, Voice and Loyalty*. Cambridge, Massachusetts: Harvard University Press.

Macpherson, C.B. 1977. *The Life and Times of Liberal Democracy*. Oxford: Oxford University Press.

Maloney, W.A. 1999. 'Contracting out the participation function. Social capital and cheque-book participation', in J.W. Van Deth, M. Maraffi, K. Newton and P.F. Whiteley (eds.), *Social Capital and European Democracy*. London and New York: Routledge, pp. 3–24.

Mouzelis, N.P. 1995. *Sociological Theory: What went wrong. Diagnosis and remedies*. London and New York: Routledge.

Newton, K. 1999. 'Social Capital and Democracy in Modern Europe', in J.W. Van Deth, M. Maraffi, K. Newton and P.F. Whiteley (eds.), *Social Capital and European Democracy*. London and New York: Routledge, pp. 3–24.

Pateman, C. 1970. *Participation and Democratic Theory*. Cambridge: Cambridge University Press.

Putnam, R.D. 1993. *Making Democracy Work: Civic Traditions in Modern Italy*. Princeton, NJ: Princeton University Press.

————. 1995a. 'Bowling Alone: America's Declining Social Capital', *Journal of Democracy* 1: pp. 65–78.

————. 1995b. 'Tuning in, Tuning out: The strange disappearance of social capital in America'. *Political Science and Politics* 28 (4): pp. 664–83.

————. 2000. *Bowling Alone: The Collapse and Revival of American Community*. New York: Simon & Schuster.

Rueschemeyer, D. 1998. 'The Self-Organization of Society and Democratic rule: Specifying the Relationship', in D. Rueschemeyer, M. Rueschemeyer and B. Wittrock (eds.), *Participation and Democracy: East and West. Comparisons and Interpretations*. Armonk, New York, and London, U.K.: M.E. Sharpe.

Rueschemeyer, D., Rueschemeyer, M. and Wittrock, B. (eds.) 1998. *Participation and Democracy: East and West. Comparisons and Interpretations*. Armonk, New York: M.E. Sharpe.

Selle, P., and Strømsnes, K. 1998. 'Organized Environmentalists: Democracy as a key value?'. *Voluntas* 9: pp. 319–43.

Selle, P., and Strømsnes, K. 2001. 'Membership and democracy', in P. Dekker and E.M. Uslaner (eds.), *Social Capital and participation in everyday life*. London: Routledge.

Selle, P., and Øymyr, B. 1995. *Frivillig organisering og demokrati. Det frivillige organisasjonssamfunnet 1940–1990*. Oslo: Det Norske Samlaget.

Skocpol, T. 1999. 'Advocates without members: The recent transformation of American civic life' in T. Skocpol and M.P. Fiorina (eds.), *Civic Engagement in American Democracy*. Washington, D.C./New York, NY: Brookings/Russel Sage Foundation.

Whiteley, P.F. 1999. 'The origins of social capital', in J.W. Van Deth, M.
  Maraffi, K. Newton and P.F. Whiteley (eds.), *Social Capital and Euro-*
  pean Democracy. London and New York: Routledge, pp. 3–24.
Wollebæk, D. 2000. 'Participation in voluntary associations and the formation of social capital'. Bergen: LOS Report, June 2000.
Wollebæk, D., and Selle, P. 2002. 'Does participation in voluntary associations contribute to social capital? The impact of intensity, scope and
  type'. *Non-Profit Voluntary Sector Quarterly*.
Wollebæk, D., Selle, P., and Lorentzen, H. 1998. '*Undersøkelse om frivillig*
  innsats. Dokumentasjonsrapport'. Bergen: LOS Center Notat 9834.
————————. 2000a. *Frivillig innsats*. Oslo: Fagbokforlaget.
————————. 2000b. 'Giving and volunteering in Norway. A brief summary of
  results from a national survey'. Bergen, Oslo: LOS Centre/Institute for
  Social Research.

11

Social Capital and Economic Development:
A Plea for Mechanisms

Gaute Torsvik[1]

Social Capital and Economic Development

Many analysts convey great expectations to the concept of social capital. In a recent paper from the World Bank, social capital is termed the 'missing link' in theories of economic development.[2] Another influential author on social capital, Robert D. Putnam, believes it will play a vital role in our understanding of economic development:

> Social capital is coming to be seen as a vital ingredient in economic development around the world. Scores of studies of rural development have shown that a vigorous network of indigenous grassroots associations can be as essential to growth as physical investment, appropriate technology, or (that nostrum of neo-classical economists) getting the prices right (Putnam 1993b: 38).

A good explanation of differential economic success must satisfy two requirements. First, the explanatory variables must be clearly defined. Second, it must be specified how these variables interact in the production process; the *mechanisms* that these variables work through must be specified. It is my opinion that the social capital idea falls short of both standards. There is no coherent definition of

social capital, and the mechanisms through which social capital is supposed to work are not spelled out with sufficient rigour and clarity.[3]

There is no unified understanding of exactly what social structures one is referring to when one uses the concept social capital.
In a critical review of the social capital idea, Fine (1999) writes that
social capital 'has to be something over and above other types of
capital but, as such, it seems to be able to be anything ranging over
public goods, networks, culture, etc.'. Fine also refers to Narayan
and Prichett (1999), who write, 'social capital, while not all things to
all people, is many things to many people', an assertion Fine char-
acterizes as an understatement (Fine 1999: 5).

Given the unclear and incoherent definitions of social capital, it
is not surprising that the literature is even more vague when it
comes to specifying the mechanisms that link social capital and
production. Those who write on social capital agree on a broad set
of ideas. They agree that social capital is important for economic
development because it facilities efficient use of information and
the creation of trust, goodwill and cooperation in a society. The
result of all this ambiguity is that the machinery of social capital
resembles a black box. Certain not-so-well defined social variables
called social capital enter on one side of the box, and on the other
side we find a more efficient governance structure and higher production. What is going on inside the box is only hinted at and
therefore, to a great extent, left in the dark. This paper is an attempt
to open up a small part of this box.

The remaining part of this section gives a brief review of the
literature on social capital and economic development. It is not my
objective to give a detailed review of this literature.[4] The review is
meant to provide readers with enough information to ground my
contribution in the existing literature, and to put me in a position
where I can state my object of concern more precisely.

Consider two economically underdeveloped communities A and
B. Suppose it turns out that standard economic variables, such as
the amount of physical capital, human capital, access to natural
resources and harbours etc., can explain only a small part of the
differences in economic performance between the two communities.[5] To capture more of the variation in productivity we decide to
measure the amount of social capital in A and B. How do we proceed; what do we measure? Should we take a narrow local perspective and focus on the social structures within each community, or

should we broaden our perspective and take into account various governmental institutions that encompass local communities? The literature does not give a clear answer. The breadth of what is included in 'social capital' varies from one study to another.

A narrow measure of social capital concentrates on the degree of horizontal contact between individuals in a community. This is how Putnam defines social capital. In the quotation above, he links social capital to 'a vigorous network of indigenous grassroots associations'. In his work on regional differences in public sector efficacy in Italy, he identifies social capital with the density of civic engagements such as football clubs and choral associations (Putnam 1993a).

Others have considered a broader notion of social capital. Coleman (1988, 1990), for example, includes other elements of the social fabric into a community's social capital. He sees social capital as a variety of different entities with two things in common: (*i*) they consist of some aspects of the social structure, and (*ii*) they facilitate certain actions of actors within the structure. This broader concept of social capital includes vertical as well as horizontal associations among members in a community. In vertical associations it is important to assess the patterns of hierarchical relations and the power distribution among citizens.

The most encompassing notion of social capital includes the government, the political system, and formalized institutions and relationships more generally, such as the rule of law, civil and political liberties, etc. Grootaert (1998) traces the focus on formal institutions, and their impact on the rate and pattern of economic development, back to the 'new institutional economics' of North (1990) and Olson (1982).[6] Collier (1998) refers to the notion of social capital that includes the organization of the government as 'governmental social capital', as opposed to 'civil social capital' typified by the work of Putnam.

All the notions of social capital I have mentioned so far identify social capital with the various components of social structure in a community. They differ, as we have seen, with respect to the breadth of the concept; that is, with respect to the scope of social components they include.[6] There is another branch of the literature that associates social capital directly with beliefs and behavioural dispositions, such as norms of cooperation and trust. Paldam and Svendsen (1998) for example, define social capital as the 'level of mutual trust between members in a group' (Paldam and Svendsen 1998: 3). Knack and Keefer (1997) also identify social capital with trust in general, and this interpretation seems to be in line with Fukuyama's use of the same concept (Fukuyama 1995). I think this is an unproductive way to define social capital. First, I cannot understand why we need the term social capital if it is just a more fancy way of referring to mutual trust. Second, to make social capital a useful concept, we must define it in terms of its sources, not in terms of its outcome. Trust is endogenous to certain elements of the social structure. Social capital ought therefore to be defined in terms of the measurable variables that create mutual trust and cooperation within a community.

My discussion is based on the narrow concept of social capital. My object of concern is the bearing 'civil social capital' has on economic development: why will a dense network of horizontal associations facilitate economic activities? An advantage with a narrow perspective is that it gives us a relatively precise interpretation of social capital and this makes it easy, at least in principle, to measure it. It is therefore possible to test whether or not this notion of social capital captures social structures that are essential for economic development.

Narayan and Prichett (1999) investigate the empirical link between social capital and household income in different villages in Tanzania. They measure social capital as the 'quantity and quality of associational life'. Their results indicate that this notion of civil social capital is indeed important for understanding economic development. Based on their empirical findings they conclude: 'a village's social capital has an effect on the incomes of the households in that village, an effect that is empirically large, definitely social and plausibly causal' (Narayan and Prichett 1999: 871).

My critique of Putnam (1993b), Narayan and Prichett (1999), and others who apply the concept of civic social capital, is that they do not discuss with enough care and rigour *why* we should expect civil social capital to enhance economic production. These authors allude to different explanations, but they do not develop the formal structure of the mechanisms they mention. Narayan and Prichett (1999), for example, mention five different reasons why a high quantity and quality of associational life can facilitate economic activities. All five reasons are discussed within the length of a page.

One of the explanations they mention is that social capital can create trust and cooperation among those who live in the village. Trust and cooperation is indeed central to the idea of civil social capital. The hypotheses is that communities with a high density of tight and inclusive networks of individual contact will experience an atmosphere of mutual trust; trust which enables individuals to cooperate and work together more efficiently. The hypothesis is illustrated schematically in figure 11.1.

Figure 11.1 Communities with a high density of inclusive networks of individual contact

SOCIAL CAPITAL   →   TRUST   →   PRODUCTION
Measured as the density,
inclusiveness, strength
and vitality of horizontal
associations in a community.

My objective is to dig deeper into this hypothesis to untangle its inner machinery. We need to know *why* social capital enhances trust and production. We must, in other words, make more explicit the mechanisms that social capital works through. As we can see from figure 11.1, there are two links (arrows) that must be explained:

• How can civil social capital (as defined above) create trust?
• How can trust enhance production?

In the next section I discuss trust and economic activities. I show that trust is important for production because it reduces or eliminates transaction costs. My next argument is that the kind of trust needed to enhance production can be based on two different sources. Trust can be based on reciprocity and the maximization of enlightened self-interest, or it can be based on prosocial motivation. I argue that civil social capital can produce both 'types' of trust. It is important to distinguish these mechanisms, not only as a logical exercise, but also to understand and predict the consequences for policy decisions. In the last section of the paper I apply this framework to illustrate how development policies utilising social capital can have totally different impacts, depending on the basis of trust.

Trust and Production

In a complex and confusing real world it is often impossible to regulate transactions by complete contracts. Buyers and sellers rarely have symmetric information about the goods they trade. Neither can individual behaviour easily be verified and enforced so as to ensure compliance.[7] This is the case even if trade takes place within the framework of a well functioning legal system, but even more so if, as is the case in many developing countries, there is no objective third party to enforce compliance. It is in this environment that transaction costs becomes an issue.

Transaction costs arise when selfish individuals trade in the face of asymmetric information and monitoring problems.[8] Every economic agent has to be on the alert, looking out for the possibility that other individuals will behave opportunistically to increase their economic gains at his expense. Resources will be used to increase the available information and to improve monitoring and enforcement of transactions. Put in another way, asymmetric information, monitoring problems and enforcement problems expose traders to economic behavioural risks that can impede efficient trade.[9]

It is not hard to find evidence that behavioural risk and transaction costs are important elements of real life transactions. Kollock (1994) refers to an interesting study of the market for rubber:[10]

> Rubber is an interesting commodity in that at the time of sale it is impossible to determine its quality. It is not until months later, after exhaustive processing, that the buyer can determine whether the grower took the extra time and expense to insure a high-quality crop. Within this situation the buyers are not motivated to pay the high price of unknown quality and the growers are not motivated to produce high quality goods as there is no simple objective way of displaying the care they took. The participants are faced with a type of Prisoner's Dilemma that is the result of asymmetric information (Kollock 1994: 314).

These problems arise more generally in situations in which agents are unable to observe all relevant dimensions of others' actions before they choose their own actions. The fear of opportunism, due to asymmetric information and lack of compliance, is obviously a problem in credit transactions. Will a creditor behave so as to maximize her ability to repay the loan? Will she repay the loan if she is able to do so? The same questions arise in insurance, in the management of common resources and when efficient trade involves relation-specific investments. If the behavioural risk dominates, there will be too few credit and insurance transactions, common resources will be mismanaged, and there will be too little investment.

It is in the environment of behavioural risks and transaction costs that trust becomes an important 'asset'. Trust, as I use the term, refers to certain behavioural dispositions that eliminate behavioural risks. Saying that there is mutual trust among traders is the same as saying that everyone is confident that no one will behave opportunistically. Trust can therefore reduce (or eliminate) transaction costs and enhance economic production. An example illustrates the notion of trust I am interested in, and the role it plays in economic activities.

Consider an isolated exchange where Mary can trade with John. John makes his choice after Mary has made an irrevocable decision whether or not she will trade with him. This is a non-anonymous relationship, so Mary's decision is in part based on her expectation of John's behaviour. Mary knows that John has two options, either to cooperate (*C*) or defect (*D*). If Mary decides to trade and John chooses *C*, both receive a decent surplus. If Mary chooses to trade and John chooses *D*, then John increases his own earnings but Mary makes a loss. No trade gives both zero profits. Note that the numbers in the figure below denote the income each of them gets for different strategy combinations (the numbers are the amount of money each of them gets for different outcomes).

The transaction exposes Mary to a behavioural risk. By trading she places herself in the hands of John who might behave

Figure 11.2 Behaviourial risks in transactions

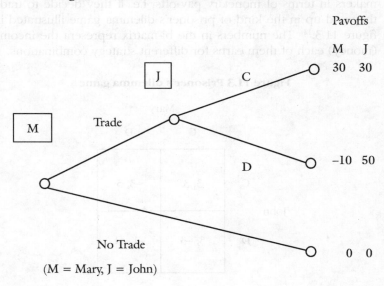

Pavoffs

M J

30 30

−10 50

0 0

(M = Mary, J = John)

opportunistically to increase his income at Mary's expense. Clearly, if this is the only trade they engage in and Mary believes that John is motivated solely by a desire to maximize his monetary income, she will not trade with John. We could say that Mary *trusts* John if she, despite the behavioural risk involved, expects John to behave well (choose *C*) and therefore decides to trade with him. I think, however, that it is fruitful to give trust a more restrictive meaning and distinguish between two cases. One possibility is that the exchange relation is framed by a well functioning judicial system that can effectively enforce all parties to fulfil their role in the trade. This is the complete contract assumption the neo-classical model implicitly builds on. In that case Mary's reliance on John would not be based on trust. To give room for trust we must take away the third party that guarantees compliance.[11] Suppose there is no outside enforcement of any agreement between Mary and John, but Mary nevertheless believes that John will abstain from economic opportunism, and she decides to trade with him. In that case we can say that Mary *trusts* John.

We can rewrite the story above slightly and transform it into a more familiar framework. Let Mary and John make their decision simultaneously, and let both be exposed to behavioural risk. If they decide to trade, both players can choose either to cooperate (*C*) or defect (*D*). Suppose *D* is the dominant action for both decision makers in terms of monetary pay-offs, i.e. if they decide to trade they end up in the kind of prisoner's dilemma game illustrated in figure 11.3.[12] The numbers in the bi-matrix represent the income (money) each of them earns for different strategy combinations.

Figure 11.3 Prisoner's dilemma game

		Mary	
		C	D
John	C	3, 3	−3, 5
	D	5, −3	−1, −1

Again, it makes sense to restrict the notion of trust to situations in which there are no third parties that can enforce cooperation. There is mutual trust among those involved if both individuals are confident that none will behave opportunistically and defect if they decide to trade. Mutual trust makes it possible to obtain the cooperative solution.

The general insight is that trust can solve social dilemmas that arise in the presence of economic opportunism and behavioural risks. Trust is therefore an important economic asset when transactions are governed by incomplete contracts. This observation is, however, not particularly helpful. All we have done so far is to conclude that trust refers to certain behavioural dispositions illustrated by the examples above. This begs a more fundamental question: Where do these behavioural dispositions that can solve social and economic dilemmas come from? Before I proceed to discuss the origin of trust, I want to make the reader aware that trust, as it is defined in the examples above, is not necessarily productive.

To see why, suppose Mary and John are two producers. Their collective profit is maximised if they cooperate and behave like a monopolist (both choose *C*). However, the cooperative outcome is not stable without trust; each has an incentive to deviate and underbid the monopoly price in order to 'steal' customers from the other. From the perspective of the society, trust among the producers is now a bad thing, because it enables them to collude against the public. This is the negative, the anti-competitive face of trust that Adam Smith warned against. The general point here is that mutual trust and cooperation among one group of citizens might have negative effects on other groups and on society as a whole. Trust and cooperation can increase the effectiveness of all types of collective actions; the problem is that increasing the success of some collective endeavours, such as rent seeking, economic crime or outright violence, will reduce the overall welfare in society.[13] The countervailing effects of trust tell us that we have to be more specific when we discuss trust and production. In what follows I focus on the 'anti- transaction-cost' effect of trust, and not on the 'anti-competitive' effect of trust.

Sources of Trust

Why should Mary trust John in the first example, and how can mutual trust emerge in the second? To take the obvious first, trust, cooperative trade and increased production is out of the question if it is common knowledge that this is an isolated transaction and both are selfish materialists. To make room for trust we have to depart from these assumptions. There are two alternative routes. We can hold on to the assumption of material egoism, but introduce repeated trade; or we can introduce individuals who are motivated by other considerations than their own material gains and losses.

Repeated Play, Reciprocity and Trust

Even completely selfish individuals can choose to cooperate in social dilemmas typified by the game illustrated in figure 11.3. What cooperation requires in this case is that the game is repeated over and over, and that both players follow a norm of reciprocity and that they are not too impatient. Even if Mary and John care only about their own income, they might choose to cooperate if the payoff matrix in figure 11.3 represents just one exchange in a sequence. The point is that if they engage in a sequence of transactions it can be in their enlightened self-interest to cooperate. This can be shown formally in a rigorous game theoretic framework, but doing so would take us into technical details that are irrelevant for the points I want to make.[14] All we need to understand is the logic that lies behind this notion of trust. This logic has been characterized very well by David Hume:

> ...I learn to do service to another, without bearing him any real kindness, because I foresee, that he will return my service in expectation of another of the same kind, and in order to maintain the same correspondence of good office with me and others. And accordingly, after I have serv'd him and he is in the possession of the advantage arising from my action, he is induc'd to perform his part, as foreseeing the consequence of his refusal. (David Hume, *A Treatise of Human Nature*, quoted from Binmore (1994: 261).

A credible threat by others to punish individuals who exploit a cooperative norm will prevent everyone who is sufficiently far-sighted from breaking the norm. Cooperation based on repeated play and reciprocity is extensively discussed in game theoretic models.[15] I shall say more about the nature of 'reciprocity-based trust' in the next section where I discuss the link between social capital and trust.

Prosocial Motivation and Trust

I have talked about trust that is grounded in prudent and forward-looking individuals. Alternatively, trust can be based on what Batson

(1995) and others call prosocial motivation. With prosocial motivation I think of different reasons that make us direct effort and energy toward benefiting others. In the example illustrated in figure 11.2 Mary realizes of course that John earns more money if he deviates from cooperative behaviour. She might nevertheless trust John and choose to trade with him if she thinks he is motivated by other considerations than his own material gains and losses. There are various forms of prosocial motivation that are worth keeping apart.

One alternative is altruistic motivation. For an altruist, benefiting another person is an end in itself. Suppose Mary and John have altruistic concerns for each other. When they play the game illustrated in figure 11.3, they do not focus solely on their own material outcome; they care also about the material outcome for the other. Hence, the numbers in the bi-matrix do not represent individual preferences. More specifically, assume that both Mary (M) and John (J) have preferences that can be represented by the following utility function: $U_i(m_i, m_j) = m_i + \alpha m_j$, where $0 \leq \alpha \leq 1$, $i = j = M, J$ and $i \neq j$; m_i and m_j is the amount of money player i and j gets and α is the parameter that captures the strength of their altruistic concerns. If $\alpha = 0$ both are complete egoists, if $\alpha = 1$ they are complete altruists in the sense that they care just as much about the others income as they care about their own income. It is easy to check that this kind of altruism creates enough trust to establish cooperation in the prisoner's dilemma game in figure 11.3 if $\alpha \geq 1/3$.[16]

Another kind of prosocial motivation is principlism. With principlism I think of the possibility that individuals act so as to uphold a moral principle.[17] Maybe Mary trusts John because she knows that he behaves according to some principle of impartiality and therefore will not exploit the fact that Mary has made a commitment to trade with him. Or consider figure 11.3 and suppose that both players behave according to Kant's categorical imperative. Both of them act as if the maxim of their action were to become, through their will, a universal law of nature. In this case the outcome of the game would be trade and cooperation (C, C). The numbers in the bi-matrix have no bearing on the actions taken by individuals who behave according to Kant's categorical imperative. People who are guided by moral principles do not even consider the economic gains of deviant behaviour, their ethics are deontological and their behaviour driven by duty.

A third kind of prosocial motivation is grounded in individuals' concern about their social status. Maybe it is to stretch the point to say that peoples' care for social status is a prosocial motivation. An egoistic concern about what others think about us is not a very desirable trait, and it is hardly the first motivation that comes to our mind when we think of prosocial motivation. But, and this is what I am concerned about here, people who care about their social status can be trustworthy. Individuals who care sufficiently about their social status, i.e. what others think about them, will go a long way to behave appropriately in their social interactions.

Let me summarize. The kind of trust needed to get efficient trade in the examples above can be based on two different mechanisms. Material egoists might trust each other if they interact repeatedly, follow a norm of reciprocity and are sufficiently concerned about the future. Alternatively, trust can be based in various forms of prosocial motivation. I have mentioned three forms that refer to motivational concerns that can generate trust and cooperation in transactions where the monetary pay-offs are as in a prisoner's dilemma, even if this is a single transaction.

Social Capital and Trust

Let us return to the social capital idea as it was illustrated in figure 11.1. Now, since trust can emerge through two different mechanisms, it follows that social capital can, at least in principle, affect trust in two different ways. A high 'quality and quantity of voluntary associations', which, according to the definition I use, indicates a high level of social capital, can create trust either by making the reciprocity mechanism work more efficiently, or by broadening individual motivation. The possibilities are illustrated in figure 11.4.

Figure 11.4 illustrates what is possible in principle; but a more interesting question is: How likely is it that social capital fosters both types of trust? Can a strong and active civic society, a community in which people have regular contact through informal and voluntary networks, produce the kind of trust that builds on repeated interaction and reciprocity? Can such a community produce the other kind of trust, i.e. trust that builds on prosocial motivation? I think the answer to both of these questions is yes.

Social Capital and Reciprocity

Let us first discuss if and how social capital can affect trust based on repeated interaction, reciprocity and individuals' maximisation of

Figure 11.4 Social capital and trust

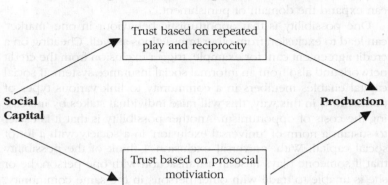

their enlightened self-interest. Recall that in this case individuals are truly selfish materialists. They refrain from opportunism (if they do) because prudent calculations reveal that it is in their enlightened self-interest to behave well. Thus, trust can be established if, and only if, the discounted sum of future losses in income adds up to more than the short-term gain of opportunism (see note 15). The expected long-term loss in income that follows from opportunism is therefore an important variable. The magnitude of this loss depends on two factors. It depends on how likely it is that opportunism or deviant behaviour is detected, and it depends on how severely such behaviour is punished. Hence, everything that increases the probability of detecting opportunism, or increases the punishment that follows, makes it easier to sustain trust and cooperation based on repeated interaction and a norm of reciprocity.

One of the externalities generated by social interaction is a knowledge about other agents' economic behaviour. More knowledge about individual behaviour makes it easier to detect opportunism. Furthermore, it is reasonable to assume that the more civil social capital there is in a community, the harder opportunism can be punished. Most models of reciprocity-based cooperation work by denying access to future transactions to anyone who deviates from the informal agreement of cooperation. It is realistic to assume that the cost of being excluded is more sweeping the tighter individuals are integrated within social networks. I can think of two reasons why this could be the case. Both rest on the idea that social capital can expand the domain of punishment.

One possibility is that opportunistic behaviour in one 'market' can lead to exclusion from other transactions as well. Cheating on a credit agreement can, for example, trigger exclusion from the credit network and also from an informal social insurance system. If social capital enables members in a community to link various types of transactions in this way, this will raise individual stakes by increasing the costs of opportunism. Another possibility is that it is easier to sustain a norm of 'universal exclusion' in a society with a lot of social capital. With 'universal exclusion' I think of the possibility that if someone plays false in a transaction with one person, he or she is unable to trade with other persons in the same community. Universal exclusion can be based on a norm that requires sanctions to be imposed not only on the one who originally violated the cooperative agreement, but also upon those who failed to punish the violators and so on.

Based on these arguments I conclude that social capital can make it easier to sustain reciprocity-based trust. It is easier to detect and punish fraudulent behaviour if individuals are tightly interwoven into civil networks. As a corollary of this conclusion we should expect tight personal networks of traders to arise in markets where agents are particularly exposed to behavioural risks. It is interesting to note that Kollock (1994) detects this pattern in an experimental study.[18] Greif, Milgrom and Weingast (1994) explain the emergence of merchant guilds in late medieval Europe as one way to generate cooperation through the universal exclusion of 'cheaters'.

Trust and Prosocial Motivation

Can social capital contribute to the other kind of trust? Will individuals who are tightly interwoven in social networks tend to be more altruistic, impartialistic or care more for their social reputation than more detached individuals? Consider the formal representation of altruistic preferences in section 3. The question is: Will individuals who live in communities where people are tightly embedded in social networks tend to have a higher value of α than those who live in communities where there is less contact among members?

This question takes us far away from the standard rational choice model. In the standard approach individual motivation is assumed to be independent of social institutions; individual values and preferences are taken as given. Institutions might play a role in that model as well, but only to the extent that they change individual incentives and opportunities. The preceding discussion of civil social capital and trust based on reciprocity fits very well into the standard model. That discussion presumes that individuals maximize their enlightened self-interest independent of their social environment. The only reason why a dense social network matters for trust and cooperation is because it increases the 'costs' of behaving opportunistically. The other possibility, the idea that individuals' motivation is a function of the social structure, is a much more radical thought. It does not fit into the standard economic paradigm. Consequently, the possibility that social capital can create trust by changing individuals' motivation is never discussed in economic models. This is unfortunate. It is an interesting hypothesis and it should not be excluded by assumption.

It is also a difficult question. We do not know enough about human nature to predict exactly how our motivation is moulded by social structures. This, however, does not imply that our motivation is fixed and independent of social institutions. It is, I believe, realistic to assume that altruism and other forms of prosocial dispositions are nurtured in a process of communal living. The density of social networks might therefore influence to what extent prosocial motivation guides our behaviour. In an experimental study of prosocial motivation, Dawes, van de Kragt and Orbell (1990) find evidence that point towards this conclusion. They report that the condition that seems to be most important in inciting prosocial motivation is group identity:

> Our experiments have led us to conclude that cooperation rates can be radically affected by one factor in particular, which is independent of the consequences for the choosing individual. That factor is group identity. Such identity—or solidarity—can be established and consequently enhance cooperative responding in absence of any expectation of future reciprocity, current rewards or punishment, or even reputational consequences among other group members (Dawes, van de Kragt and Orbell 1990: 99).[19]

A dense network of horizontal contact in a community will probably increase the sense of group identity among members. It is also realistic to assume that individuals' concern for social status or social reputation increases with the amount of civil social capital. A social reward mechanism will only work as long as individuals' actions are observable in the community. Furthermore, it seems realistic to assume that the more connected we are to other individuals in a community, the greater is our concern about what they think about us.

I could have speculated further on if and how civil social capital affects prosocial motivation, but elaborating more on this issue would take me away from the point I want to make in this chapter. My aim is to uncover some of the problems that hide behind the notion of civil social capital. It suffices therefore to show that trust *can* rest on two different mechanisms, and that civil social capital *can* produce both kinds of trust. In the introduction I argued that it is important to distinguish between the two trust mechanisms, not only as an exercise in analytical reasoning, but also to make sound policy decisions. Let me explain this point now.

Social Capital and Development Policies

The point with this section is to show that development policies utilizing social capital can have differential impacts depending on the basis of trust. I illustrate the point with two examples.

Roscas

Consider a village in a poor country. Those who live there cannot borrow money from formal credit institutions in a well-functioning credit market (they lack collateral, are illiterate, are intimidated by the formal loan procedure, etc.). As a substitute for formal lending they organize informal rotating savings and credit associations (Roscas). N number of individuals get together and form a Roscas. At each meeting the members put a fixed amount of money into a 'pot' and the funds are allocated randomly to one of them. When they meet for the nth time ($n < N$), everyone must contribute the fixed amount, but those who have already won the pot can no longer participate in the lottery. The behavioural risk in a Roscas is that the incentive winners have to withdraw from the association. Consider for example the first winner of the pot; he saves a lot of money if he quits after the first meeting (he saves ($N - 1$) times the individual contribution at each meeting). Since it is unlikely that this relationship can be governed by a complete contingent enforceable contract, it follows that a Roscas will be established only if the members *trust* each other.

I have argued above that there are two sources of trust. Trust can emerge between members who are material egoists if there is a sequence of Roscas ahead and if opportunism implies exclusion from all credit arrangements in the future. This is the reciprocity mechanism. Alternatively, the members might trust each other because it is common knowledge that they are not motivated solely by material considerations. Altruism, adherence to a norm of impartiality, or a concern for social reputation, are prosocial motivations that can prevent early winners from withdrawing from the Roscas, even if there are no Roscas planned for the future.

Why is it important to distinguish between the two trust mechanisms? Because the outcome of policy decisions depends on what kind of trust there is between the members. To see this, suppose some aid benefactor decides to locate a formal credit programme in the region. The programme aims at reaching individuals who otherwise cannot get loans from formal credit institutions. The programme is, however, of limited size and cannot provide loans to everyone in the area, but it distinctly increases each member's probability of getting funds from outside of the Roscas.

A negative effect of such a credit programme is that it can undermine the sustainability of the Roscas institution. The crux is that this is a problem only if the trust that exists among the members builds on the reciprocity mechanism. It is easy to understand why. Consider the person who wins the pot at the first meeting. He is selfish, but before the credit programme was announced he calculated that the long-term costs from being excluded from future Roscas surpassed the money he would save from withdrawing from the present Roscas. The announced credit programme alters his equation. It reduces the long-term costs from exclusion since it opens up an alternative source of funds. This problem does not arise if trust is based on the prosocial motivation mechanism.

Informal Insurance

Here is another example that illustrates the same phenomenon. This village is on the coast. The people who live here are fishermen. There are two types of fishermen. Some fish close to the shore; they use small nets and have no boats. Some have small canoes and are able to fish a bit further out. The amount of fish each fisherman gets during a day is uncertain, a random variable. At the end of the day all the fishermen meet in the harbour where they share the total catch. Since this 'share system' provides insurance against daily fluctuations in individual catches, it is a welfare-improving institution. It is unlikely that this practice is regulated by a formal insurance contract that can be enforced by a third party. It must build on mutual trust. Those who are lucky one day will share with those who are less fortunate only if they trust others to share when they are in opposite positions. Again, the trust needed to sustain informal insurance can rest on two sources.

Consider again donors who want to help the people who live in the village. The donors observe individuals who are tightly integrated in social networks. They conclude that there is a lot of social capital in the village, which explains why there is trust and cooperation among the fishermen. The donors do not ask what kind of trust there is among the fishermen. They do not ask *how* social capital contributes to building trust, whether it is through the reciprocity mechanism or through the changing motivation mechanism (see figure 11.4). This turns out to be a mistake.

The donors decide that the best way to increase the standard of living in the village is to give the group with canoes bigger boats. With bigger boats they are able to get further out, and, being able to fish further out, they will get fish with certainty every day. The donors are of course aware that this policy only helps one group in the village, but they do not consider that as a problem, since there is a well-established redistribution or insurance system in the village. This justification is valid if, and only if, the trust that exists among the fishermen is trust that is based on prosocial motivation. The donors make a fatal mistake if the informal redistribution or insurance institution is based on egoism and the reciprocity mechanism. The reason is that the group that is given the bigger boats will catch fish with certainty every day. They will therefore withdraw from the insurance system, since they do not benefit from it anymore.

Discussion

These examples demonstrate that trust based on repeated interaction and reciprocity is more fragile than trust based on prosocial motivation. In the first case trust hinges on individual calculations of enlightened self-interest, and everything that reduces the long-term loss, or increases the short-term gains, of opportunism can destabilise cooperation. I have argued that social capital plays a positive role here since it increases the costs of opportunism and raises individual stakes. The problem in both the examples is that the development policies considered undermine the economic value of social capital. A formal credit system is an alternative to an informal system, and even if the formal institution can serve only a small fraction of the population it lowers everyone's costs of being excluded from future Roscas. A formal credit system can therefore destabilize the Roscas institution and reduce aggregate welfare in the community. Can this problem be avoided?

To reduce the problem we must somehow restore individual stakes in the informal system. One way to do this is to link participation in the formal credit programme to behaviour in the informal credit system. A formal credit programme would not destabilize an informal Roscas system if opportunism in a Roscas implies a zero probability of being accepted in the formal programme. The problem is of course to establish this link between behaviour in informal networks and involvement in formal programmes. Lack of information is obviously a problem, and so is lack of commitment and enforceability. One way to get around these problems would be to also use a group-based system in the formal credit programme. Suppose credit is provided only to individuals who can establish a group of at least five people who are mutually responsible for repaying the loan. In this case one would expect opportunism in a Roscas to carry negative consequences over to the formal credit institution, since no one would like to form a group with one who cheated on an informal agreement. Group-lending systems have recently gained much popularity in developing countries. It is usually argued that a group-based system will improve incentives *within* formal credit institutions. My argument indicates that another desirable aspect of group-based formal institutions is that they do not undermine the positive effect social capital has on trust and cooperation in informal systems.

Concluding Remarks

The aim with this paper has been to demonstrate how important it is to spell out the formal structures of the mechanisms that link civil social capital and economic development. It is not sufficient to allude in a vague manner to trust and cooperation. We need a clear definition of social capital and an explicit specification of what trust is and why it is important for production. This puts us in a position to point out different sources of trust and to discuss how social capital affects these sources. I have followed this formula. I have shown that the kind of trust needed to enhance production can be based in reciprocity or in prosocial motivation, and that it is reasonable to expect civil social capital to foster both kinds of trust. I have shown the importance of keeping these two kinds of trust apart in order to make sound policy decisions. At a more general level these examples illustrate how important it is for social scientists to be mechanism-oriented. Only if we understand the mechanisms that produce different social phenomena can we say anything sensible about how the phenomena will change as the environment changes.

Notes

1. Professor of Economics, University of Bergen. An earlier version of this paper was presented at the World Bank–CMI conference on 'Local Level Institutions and Social Capital'. I thank Kjetil Bjorvatn, Johs Hjellbrekke, Guri Lowrie, Anders Molander, Sanjeev Prakash, Fred Scroyen and Bertil Tungodden for their comments.
2. Christiaan Grootaert, 'Social Capital: The Missing Link'.
3. I am not the first to criticise the concept of social capital for being vague and incoherent; see for example Fine (1999) and Collier (1998).
4. For a helpful annotated bibliography on social capital, see Feldman and Assaf (1998). For an informative discussion of social capital and economic development, and the historical antecedents of the concept, see Woolcock (1998)
5. This is not an unrealistic scenario. Many empirical studies of regional differences in economic productivity have found that variation in the standard economic variable accounts for only a small part of the variance in productivity and income. Hall and Jones (1999) find that output-per-worker in the five countries with the highest output-per-worker in 1988 was 31.7 times the output-per-worker in the five countries with the lowest output-per-worker. Of this huge difference in output per worker, physical capital and human capital contributed difference factors of 1.8 and 2.2 respectively, leaving a factor of 8.3 to what they call the 'social infrastructure'.
6. All the definitions of social capital I have mentioned differ from another influential view associated with Pierre Bourdieu (see for example Bourdieu [1986]). Bourdieu also identifies social capital with certain characteristics of social networks. His focus is, however, on the distribution of social capital between different groups of individuals, how networks can change and affect the distribution of social capital, and

how and to what extent social capital is correlated with other kinds of capital (e.g. human capital and physical capital). So while Bourdieu (see also Loury [1977]) is concerned with the distributional aspects of social capital, Putnam for example focuses more on how social capital affects the overall efficiency of political and economic governance in a community.

7. In economic literature, there is a distinction between *adverse selection* problems that can arise when seller and buyer have asymmetric information about some relevant quality of the good, and *moral hazard* problems that can arise when there is asymmetric information about some action taken after the trade agreement is made. There is also a useful distinction between things that can be observed within the trading relationship but not verified outside, and things that are both observable inside and verifiable outside. I have suppressed these and other details in order to focus on the main point in this paper.

8. A key reference in transaction-cost literature is Williamson (1975); see also Hart (1995) for a discussion of recent contributions to this literature.

9. Behavioural risks are ignored in the neo-classical model, either because the model implicitly assumes that all trade can be regulated by complete contracts, or because it assumes that even if individuals are driven by material selfishness, they do not pursue their interests with guile.

10. The problem Kollock describes is one of hidden information and adverse selection. Akerlof (1970) was the first to show that the market system might work inefficiently when there is asymmetric information about the quality of a product: we might then observe that low quality products drive high quality products (for example rubber) out of the market.

11. One possibility is that the judicial system is imperfect. This is the case in many developing countries. But, as I have said before, since most transactions take place in a much more complex and confusing world than our example indicates, it becomes practically impossible to write and enforce complete contracts even if traders operate within a well-functioning legal system.

12. This example could be interpreted as a formalization of the situation Kollock describes in the quotation above.

13. See Olson (1982) and Gambetta (1993) for more about the downside of trust.

14. I will use the Prisoner's Dilemma game in Figure 11.3 to sketch the formal argument of reciprocal cooperation. Suppose both players are material egoists. Suppose also that both of them get a pay-off of 0 if they choose not trade with each other. There is a unique Nash equilibrium if they play this game only once and choose to trade, namely (D,D). In this case, if they can choose whether to trade or not, they decide not to trade, and both receive 0 profits. Suppose now that this game is repeated infinitely many times (or a finite number of times but with an uncertain end-period). Let $\delta \in (0,1)$ be their common discount

factor. Suppose both follow this strategy: *In period t choose trade and cooperate if—in every period preceding t—both have cooperated if they traded. If not, that is if there exists a period t'<t with trade and defection, choose defect in every period with trade in the future.* Let us check if trade and cooperation can be realized as the outcome of a sub-game perfect equilibrium (loosely this means: let us check if trade and cooperation can be an outcome if we constrain ourselves to look at Nash equilibria which are supported by credible threats of punishment). Suppose we enter period *t* and there has been trade and cooperation in every period preceding *t*. If Mary chooses to defect she earns 5 in this period and 0 in every future period (the best she can do if both follow the strategy above, is to stay away from John). Defection gives a total surplus of 5. The cooperative alternative generates a surplus of 3 in each period forever:

$$\sum_{t=0}^{\infty} \delta t 3 = [\delta/(1-\delta)]3$$

It follows that trade and cooperation is the better alternative, given the strategies above, if $\delta > 5/8$. Furthermore, it is easy to acknowledge that the strategy above includes a credible punishment: choosing defect in every period they decide to trade is indeed Nash Equilibrium. No trade is therefore a credible outcome if there is a deviation from the cooperative norm. We can conclude that trade and cooperation is a sub-game perfect outcome as long as the players are not too impatient, that is as long as the weight on the future is δ sufficiently high.

15. See for example Chapter 5 in Fudenberg and Tirole (1991); for a more philosophical and encompassing discussion see Binmore (1994).
16. Suppose the game in Figure 3 is played only once. If *M* chooses *C* she gets utility $3 + 3\alpha$ if *J* chooses *C*, and $5\alpha - 3$ if *J* chooses *D*. By choosing *D* she gets utility $5 - 3\alpha$ if *J* chooses *C*, and $-1 - \alpha$ if *J* chooses *D*. This is a symmetric game so *J* evaluates the outcomes equivalently. Cooperation is a Nash Equilibrium if playing *C* is a better alternative than *D* given that the other player plays *C*, that is if $3 + 3\alpha \geq 5 - 3\alpha \Rightarrow \alpha \geq 1/3$. In fact *C* is a dominant strategy for $\alpha \geq 1/3$.
17. See Batson (1995).
18. A study by Geertz (1978) of the bazaar economy found that the more uncertainty associated with transactions, the tighter were the bonds that linked buyers to sellers.
19. See Batson (1995) for a critical discussion of the experiment done by Dawes and his associates.

References

Arrow, K. 1974. *The Limits of Organization*. New York: W.W. Norton.

Akerlof, G. 1970. 'The Market for "Lemons": Quality Uncertainty and the Market Mechanism'. *Quarterly Journal of Economics* 84: pp. 488–500.

Batson, D.C. 1995. 'Prosocial Motivation: Why Do We Help Others?', in A. Tesser (ed.), *Advanced Social Psychology*. New York: McGraw-Hill.

Binmore, K. 1994. '*Playing Fair. Game Theory and The Social Contract*'. Cambridge, Massachusetts: MIT Press.

Bordieu, P. 1986. 'The Forms of Capital', in J. Richardson (ed.), *Handbook of Theory and Research in the Sociology of Education*. Westport, Connectieut: Greenwood Press.

Coleman, J. 1988. 'Social Capital in the Creation of Human Capital.' *American Journal of Sociology* 94 (supplement); pp. 95–120.

Coleman, J. 1990. *Foundations of Social Theory*. Cambridge, Massachusetts: Harvard University Press.

Collier, P. 1998. 'Social Capital and Poverty'. *The World Bank Social Capital Initiative Working Paper No. 4*.

Dawes, R., van de Kragt, A. J. C., and Orbell, J. M. 1990. 'Cooperation for the Benefit of Us—Not Me, or my Conscience', in J.J. Mansbridge (ed.), *Beyond Self-Interest*. Chicago: University of Chicago Press.

Elster, J. 1998. 'A plea for Mechanisms', in P. Hedstrøm and R. Swedberg (eds.), *Social Mechanisms: An Analytical Approach to Social Theory*. Cambridge: Cambridge University Press.

Feldman, T.R., and Assaf, S. 1998. 'Social Capital: Conceptual Frameworks and Empirical Evidence. An Annotated Bibliography' *The World Bank Social Capital Initiative Working Paper No. 5*.

Fine, B. 1999. 'The Development State is Dead—Long Live Social Capital'. *Development and Change* 30: pp. 1–19.

Fudenberg, D., and Tirole, J. 1991. 'Game Theory' Cambridge, Massachusetts: MIT Press.

Fukuyama, F. 1995. *Trust. The Social Virtues and the Creation of Prosperity*. London: Penguin.

Fukuyama, F. 1997. 'Social Capital'. Tanner Lectures, Brasenose College, Oxford: Mimeo Institute of Public Policy, George Mason University.

Gambetta, D. 1988. '*Trust: Making and Breaking Cooperative Relations*'. Oxford: Basil Blackwell.

Gambetta, D. 1993. *The Mafia: A Ruinous Rationality*. Cambridge, Massachusetts: Harvard University Press.

Geertz, C. 1978. 'The Bazaar Economy: Information and Search in Peasant Marketing'. *American Economic Review* 68: pp. 28–32.

Greif, A., Milgrom, P., and Weingast, B. 1994. 'Coordination, Commitment, and Enforcement: The Case of The Merchant Guild'. *Journal of Political Economy* 102: pp. 745–76.

Grootaert, C. 1998. 'Social Capital: The Missing Link.' *The World Bank Social Capital Initiative Working Paper No. 3.*

Hall, R.E., and Jones, C. 1999. 'Why Do Some Countries Produce So Much More Output Per Worker Than Others?' *Quarterly Journal of Economics* 114: pp. 83–116.

Hart, O. 1995. *Firms, Contracts, and the Financial Structure.* Oxford: Oxford University Press.

Hart, O. and Holmstrom, B. 1987. 'The Theory of Contracts', in T. Bewley (ed.), *Advances in Economic Theory.* Cambridge: Cambridge University Press.

Knack, S., and Keefer, P. 1997. 'Does Social Capital have an Economic Payoff? A Cross-Country Investigation.' *Quarterly Journal of Economics* 112(4): pp. 1251–288.

Kollock, P. 1994. 'The Emergence of Exchange Structures: An Experimental study of Uncertainty, Commitment and Trust.' *American Journal of Sociology* 98: pp. 313–45.

Loury, G. 1977. 'A Dynamic Theory of Racial Differences' in P.A. Wallace and A.A. LaMond (eds.), *Women, Minorities, and Employment Discrimination.* Lexington, Lexington Books: Lexington Books.

Luhman, N. 1979. '*Trust and Power.*' Chichester: John Wiley.

Lyons, B.R., Mehta, J. 1997. 'Contracts, Opportunism and Trust: Self-Interest and Social Orientation.' *Cambridge Journal of Economics* 21: pp. 239–57.

Narayan, D., and Prichett, L. 1999. 'Cents and Sociability: Houshold Income and Social Capital in Rural Tanzania.' *Economic Development and Cultural Change* 47: pp. 871–97.

North, D. 1990. '*Institutions, Institutional Change and Economic Performance.*' New York: Cambridge University Press.

Olson, M. 1982. *The Rise and Decline of Nations: Economic Growth, Stagflation, and Social Rigidities.* New Haven: Yale University Press.

Paldam, M., and Svendsen, G. T. 1998. 'Is Social Capital an Effective Smoke Condenser?' Working Paper From Aarhus University.

Putnam, R. with Leonardi, R., and Nanetti, R. 1993a. *Making Democracy Wok: Civic Traditions in Modern Italy.* Princeton, N.J.: Princeton University Press.

Putnam, R. 1993b. 'The Prosperous Community: Social Capital and Public Life.' *The American Prospect* 13: pp. 5–22.

Williamson, O. 1975. *Markets and Hierarchies: Analysis and Antitrust Implications.* Free Press: New York.

Woolcock, M. 1998. 'Social Capital and Economic Development: Toward a Theoretical Synthesis and Policy Framework.' *Theory and Society* 27: pp. 151–208.

12

Surfing for Online Connectedness:
Is the Internet Helping to End Civic Engagement?

Tommy Tranvik[1]

Introduction

In any modern large-scale democracy, technological systems for social communications are essential for facilitating collective action and social control. And since social communication is crucial for democracy, and technology is crucial for social communication, the question is: How are technology and democracy related? Will technology enhance our sense of community, solidarity and identity? Or will it cause social isolation and political apathy? Modern information and communications technologies (ICTs)—particularly the Internet—are now the target of these questions. One important issue is the effect of Internet technologies on social connectedness and civic engagement—on social capital.

Cyberlibertarianism, the ideology of Internet pioneers and enthusiasts, holds that the Internet is inherently democratic, and that digital technology will change our notions of community, revitalize civic society and contribute to the rise of social capital by creating '…"electronic neighbourhoods" bound together not by geography

but by shared interests' (Dyson et al. 1994: 9). 'Electronic neighbourhoods' (or virtual communities) are digitally constructed social
spaces where people come together to gossip, chat or discuss the
great collective issues of the day. They are, in short, cyberspace's
equivalent to Putnam's (1993) 'horizontal networks of associations',
which he credits for fostering norms and habits of civic engagement
(ergo, social capital). If this is true, virtual communities may have
similar healing effects on democracy that Putnam argues offline
'horizontal networks of associations' have.

The 'young' Robert D. Putnam (pre-2000), however, does not
think so: since the Internet is based on long-distance screen-to-screen,
rather than intimate face-to-face interaction, it cannot produce social
capital (see, for example, Putnam 1995a; 1995b). This view seems
to be informed by a quasi-communitarian vision of the good society—small-scale relationships make large-scale coordination and
cooperation possible. But the 'older' Putnam (post-2000) is less certain that the Internet is bad for social capital. The conclusion is
nevertheless pessimistic: 'If the primary effect of computer-mediated
communication is to reinforce rather than replace face-to-face relationships, however, the Net is unlikely in itself to reverse the
detoriation of social capital' (Putnam 2000: 180). And he is right, of
course: there is no easy technological fix to problems of social
capital formation (and we should not be looking for one). But being unable to reverse a social trend is not the same as making things
worse: the Internet may contribute to social cooperation and coordination even if it is not the answer to all our collective action
problems. The study of technology, democracy and social capital,
therefore, is messier than Putnam makes it out to be.

I will address this messiness stepwise: first, by pinning down
how Putnam's framing of social capital relates to traditional perspectives on civil society, and how Putnam relates ICTs to social
capital generation. Second, by introducing (although rather tenta-
tively) what Putnam does not provide: a perspective for analysing
the relationship between technology, society and democracy. Third,
by employing this perspective to explain the characteristics of digital social spaces—virtual communities. And, finally, to present some
general findings about the nature of social bonding going on within
virtual communities. My argument, in brief, is that the Internet—
consisting mainly of software code instead of bricks, mortar, steel
and concrete—is a flexible technology: a technology that engages

people in designing communities where values, norms and rules of
interaction are decided on by the participants themselves. By taking
part in shaping these spaces, social capital may be generated, but in
a different way than in the physical world.

Civil Society, Social Capital and the Role of ICTs

Civil society, according to standard definitions, is a channel for exercising political power, particularly for those who lack access to
coercive power (the state) or to great economic resources (the market). In a North European context, the separation of civil society,
the state and the market is somewhat problematic because of 'cor-
porative pluralism': that the elites of voluntary associations, interest
groups, political parties and the state bureaucracy negotiate the
settlement of collective issues and jointly administer the implementation of whatever is decided. The priority of voluntary associations, therefore, is system capacity to influence the authoritative
allocation of collective resources. System capacity orientation, however, is balanced by a membership-based, decentralized and democratic internal structure. These features spell citizen effectiveness;
the members of the organizations control the strategic policy decisions. It is this balance between system capacity and citizen effectiveness that makes it possible for the voluntary associations to combine state-centric power aspirations with a degree of organizational
and political autonomy. But, as recent research on voluntary associations in Norway (see, for instance, Selle and Øymyr 1995) shows,
the combination of external influence and internal democracy may
be changing: traditional membership associations face a recruitment
crisis, and new technocratic and non-democratic associations are
gaining momentum. Since these new associations lack a balance
between system capacity and citizen effectiveness, the big unknown
is whether they will maintain the same degree of relative autonomy
from state and market as the old-fashion associations have.

What seems to make civil society tick, then, is power struggle
and interest representation in cooperation and/or conflict with the
state and the market. But this was before Putnam's *Making Democracy Work* (1993) appeared, and his notion of social capital entered
the scene: '... features of social—networks, norms and trust—that
enable participants to act together more effectively to pursue shared
objectives' (Putnam 1995a: 665). Contrary to old-fashioned civil society

perspectives, Putnam holds that social conflicts, power struggle and interest representation may be detrimental to democracy because it will make it harder to nourish norms of mutual trust and cooperation essential for solving collective action problems. If you want to explain the success or failure of political society, according to Putnam, you must therefore disregard the political: it is sport clubs, bowling leagues, mutual aid societies, bird-watching societies and the like—every association that is explicitly non-political—that makes democracy work.

The problem of Putnam's approach, and what it boils down to, is *a biased interpretation of scale*: social capital is generated through horizontal networks of intense face-to-face interaction. It is, in other words, the quality and structure of small-scale institutions that is essential. But how do small-scale institutions relate to large-scale democratic stability and performance? The answer Putnam (1993: 243, footnote 45) provides is that '... the structure of the situation is more important than personal character'. It is the way we interact, not with whom we interact, that is central to Putnam: daily face-to-face interaction with loving and caring friends, family and fellow bird watchers foster norms of generalized trust. When the institutional context scales up from small to large, and we need to cooperate with strangers, we are able to do so if our relations with these strangers have the feel and touch of smallness (horizontal, face-to-face): personal trust is translated into generalised trust because of interactional resemblance across different institutional settings. This means that it is the scaling capacity of social capital—the way it can move from small to large social settings and back again without altering its properties—that enables people to resolve their differences in a peaceful and effective manner. And nothing is 'rotten in the state of Denmark' as long as small-scale communities are conflict-free, power-agnostic and interest-blind spheres of social activity. Consequently, the system capacity orientation of civil society associations—that they are here to make a large-scale difference—is played down, and the citizen effectiveness perspective—a feeling of participation best nurtured on a small scale—is pushed to the centre of attention.

Thus, the Putnamian approach to social capital, civil society and democracy raises a few vital questions:

1. *Small vs. large scale*: Is the absence of conflicts on a small scale good for democracy, or may the structural resemblance of conflicts across localities cause large-scale integration and cooperation?

2. *Social vs. unsocial capital*: Is the exercise of power—even if perfectly democratic—possible without causing distrust, resentment and conflict?

3. *System capacity vs. citizen effectiveness*: Is it more important to take part in local community matters (citizen effectiveness) than to be engaged in the great collective issues of the day (system capacity orientation)? Is small-scale involvement more important than large-scale awareness?

4. *Community vs. association*: Is the integral experience of community living more central to democracy than the partial interest representation of associations? How close need the relations between associations and community be in order to foster norms of civic engagement?

5. *Political vs. non-political organizations*: Can democracy be properly understood by overlooking cleavage-based organizations, representing segmented interests, that aim at exercising political power?

6. *Trust vs. distrust*: How much trust and cooperation is too much? How much distrust and conflict is enough?

This is not the place to address these questions, but some of them will pop up as I go along—although in a slightly different manner of framing. The first item on the agenda is to forge a link between ICTs, civil society and social capital.

ICTs are important for sustaining a strong civil society and a democratic polity. Tocqueville, for instance, discovered that in America in the 1830s a wide range of newsletters, newspapers, journals and periodicals—not constrained by fees, taxes or regulations—competed for an audience. But Tocqueville was not impressed by the content of these publications, noting that journalists seemed to be inadequately educated and mostly interested in '...exposing weakness in the character of others' (Tocqueville 1990: vol. 1, 197). It was the pluralistic structure of ICTs that was important to Tocqueville. Democracy was sustained because no single elite, journal or editor controlled the political agenda or shaped public opinion. Newspapers, Tocqueville argued, also provided a social glue by drawing minds together dispersed across great geographic distances around a programme of beliefs and actions. These invisible social links made it possible for an individualistic and large society to form and nurture civic associations and uphold a democratic order.

The 'young' Putnam, following Tocqueville's lead, finds positive correlations between newspaper reading and social trust, group

membership and voter turnout, but the same correlations are negative for television viewing. Again, it is the structure of interaction,
not the content of programmes, that explains these negative correlations: 'There is reason to believe that deep-seated technological
trends are radically "privatizing" and "individualizing" our use of
leisure time and thus disrupting many opportunities for social-capital
formation' (Putnam 1995a: 74). Critics, however, claim that Putnam
attacks television in black-and-white terms: '...as though there is
one television experience, rather than multiple channels and
programmes, and one audience, rather than different types of viewers' (Norris 1996: 475). Watching the news, for instance, may be
positively correlated with levels of political knowledge, voter turnout and participation in voluntary organizations. But even if valid,
this critic misses the point: like Tocqueville, Putnam's focus on the
institutionalized patterns of social life—how habits and roles, patterns of power and control—are shaped and reshaped by ICTs. The
question is not 'what kind of information is consumed?', but 'how is
this information consumed?' This is stressed by the 'old' Putnam in
his analysis of the nature of social bonding on the Internet:

> Computer-mediated communication is, to be sure, more egalitarian,
> frank and task oriented than face-to-face communication. Participants in
> computer-based groups often come up with a wider range of alterna-
> tives. However, because of the paucity of social cues and social com-
> munication, participants in computer-based groups find it harder to reach
> consensus and feel less solidarity with each other....Computer-based
> groups are quicker to reach an intellectual understanding of their shared
> problems ... but they are much worse at generating the trust and reci-
> procity necessary to implement that understanding (Putnam 2000: 176).

This means that Putnam is not too concerned about the information
transmitted 'on top' of these relationship structures. And rightly so,
probably: in a democracy it makes little sense—and it might even
be dangerous talk—to claim that one type of content is more democratic than others. One of the oldest tricks in the book of political
manipulation, of course, is to get your own views accepted as
'properly democratic' and to make sure that all other views are
labelled 'undemocratic'. Consequently, Putnam is on the right track
while his critics are not (although I suspect that Putnam supposes that
the 'proper' content is produced so long as the structure of relationships is 'right'). Nevertheless, Putnam's analysis of ICT-generated
social practices is rather shallow (see Putnam 2000: 166–80). He

argues, for instance, that telephony and the Internet have similar effects—they cause greater small-scale orientation (people tend to use these ICTs to keep in touch with people they already know). But the relationship structures that are enabled by the telephone and the Internet may be very different (one-to-one versus many-to-many interaction). According to Putnam's own logic, they should therefore produce different conditions for social capital formation because social capital (or the lack thereof) depends on how people relate to each other. What Putnam needs but does not provide, then, is a scheme for connecting technological design and patterns of social activity.

Technology and Democracy

Such a perspective has not much to gain from conventional wisdom—that technology is tool-like. According to the technology-as-tool perspective, we first decide on a socially desirable goal, and then we find a technology to help us realize that goal. In this view, our only worry is to understand the political, economic or social actors and processes shaping the construction and use of technical artifacts (see, for instance, Bijker 1995; Jasanoff et al. 1995; Bijker and Law 1992; Bijker, Hughes and Pinch 1987; MacKenzie and Wajcman 1985). The problem with this instrumentalist and social constructionist approach is that technology seems to be ready to bend over backwards to satisfy our commands (so-called 'interpretive flexibility').[2] But an increasing body of cross-disciplinary literature points to the opposite: technology is a structure that tends to produce path-dependence and 'interpretive inflexibility' (demonstrated, for instance, by the fact that technologies—new and old—are often highly controversial, yet are very hard to change or dislodge). And as technologies are interconnected in complicated ways, predictable control with our technical environment seems relatively elusive (see, for example, Arthur 1994; Collingridge 1980; Ellul 1980, 1964; Mumford 1971; Schwarz and Thompson 1990; Winner 1986, 1977). Technologies may therefore exert a negative influence on democracy, it is argued, because they have a tendency to determine future social developments, imparing the ability of citizens, politicians and technical experts to envision alternative technological and social futures. Plurality and diversity, the nuts and bolts of liberal democracy, is traded away for economic growth, material well-being and the 'easy living' of technical standardization.

This position may seem a bit deterministic, and, in a sense, it is: we are not always free to choose the design of the technical and material structures that our lives depend on. But technology does not strictly determine human decisions: technology is not exactly an innocent bystander but, by the same token, people are not neutral either. The point is that there seems to be a connection between our preferred design of society and technology: we like and trust technologies that are likely to support our vision of the good society. This means that social, political and economic structures play a part in shaping technology, but whether the design is determined by technical imperatives or socio-cultural factors, or both, the end result is pretty much the same: flexible use of technology, by and large, is ideological mumbo jumbo because technology is a method for use (that is why you need a manual in order to programme your VCR: the VCR determines how you do things but not the programmes you tape[3]). And this is the value of technology: it makes us do things in a fixed, predetermined way because it is practical, relatively effortless and cost-effective.

Even if flexibility is not a very common technological feature (technology is usually used in only one particular way), the notion of flexibility is not useless. But it needs some refinement: a flexibile technology does not predetermine the social structure of its operating environment—it supports different visions of how technological life should be lived. In flexible technology, plurality and diversity are built-in qualities of the method of use itself (Tranvik, Thompson and Selle 2000). At the same time, social dependency and entrenchment is crucial: we need some assurance that the technology we put an effort into developing today will still be around tomorrow and the day after. Otherwise, we will not bother to engage in technological decision-making. Entrenched flexibility is therefore the structural feature we are looking for. This, I will argue, is the most striking characteristic of the Internet.

The Structure of the Internet and Social Capital

There are several ways of explaining the strange and novel structure of the Internet (for example, by tracing the different social and technical influences that shape the basic technologies and applications, see Abbate 1999; Hafner and Lyon 1996). But the easiest way of doing it is in terms of access to two important technical resourses—information-processing power and bandwidth (communication capacity).

Traditionally, information-processing power has been a scarce resource. In the 1970s, transistors—the electronic switches which process information in computers—were expensive to make and had to be economized with. This gave rise to hierarchically organized mainframe systems, where access to processing power was carefully portioned out to a few trusted employees (Lebow 1995). In much of the same way, the short supply of bandwidth governed the organization of telephone, radio and television networks. The result was a concentration of processing power and bandwidth in the hands of a limited numbers of large companies. The users, on their part, had few opportunities to influence the services offered and settled for standardized ones. *Entrenched inflexibility*, therefore, was the name of the game.

The Internet, however, is not governed by the necessity to economize with processing power and bandwidth. This is mainly due to two technical trends, usually referred to as the 'law' of microelectronics (Moore's 'law') and the 'law' of digital networking (Metcalfe's 'law'). The 'law' of microelectronics states that as the power of silicon chips increase (doubling every 18 months), their production costs drop. The social significance is that increasingly powerful computers are becoming less and less expensive. The 'law' of digital networking states that as the number of network computers increase arithmetically (due to the 'law' of microelectronics), the value of the network increases exponentially (Brand 1999; Kelly 1998; Gilder 1994). To put it simply: it is more valuable to be connected to a large network (multiple sources of information) than to a small one. Just as important, the 'law' of digital networking has an effect on bandwidth through increasing returns dynamics: since each new node craves for more bandwidth, it makes sense to invest in technology that supplies this bandwidth (Tanenbaum 1996). And, because of the sheer amount of resources committed to the network and the number of people depending on it, we cannot get rid of it even if we wanted to. The Internet is therefore entrenched. But the Internet is also flexible because it puts most of the human and technical intelligence on the hosts and not on the network. In almost every other communications system, the intelligence is on the network. The novelty of the Internet is that its users control the network, while for other ICTs it is the network that controls the users (however, since the Internet is not carved in stone but in software, it may change in ways that leaves users with less control than they enjoy today. For a discussion of this possibility, see Lessig 1999). Thus, *the Internet is globally entrenched and locally flexible.*

These properties of entrenched flexibility, sceptics argue, may spell 'the tragedy of the digital commons': since the network does not control its users, irresponsible behaviour is encouraged and everyone is worse off than they would have been had there only been someone there to guide and direct their actions. But the distribution of control may provide for self-constrained sociability, especially if people congregate in voluntary virtual communities. These online organizations often regulate excessive individual behaviour just as or more effectively than states and markets do (in fact, states and markets have not proved particularly effective in regulating the Internet).

In virtual communities, individual behaviour is regulated through informal, collective decision-making: participants decide the rules of interaction (netiquette, for instance), what subjects to discuss and how to treat those who break the rules of the community (Harasim 1993). This means that virtual communities emerge when '...enough people carry out those public discussions long enough, with sufficient human feeling, to form webs of personal relationships in cyberspace' (Rheingold 1993: 5). A virtual community, therefore, is established when participants start to think of themselves as a group sharing some common purpose, and when boundaries are drawn between the 'inside' and the 'outside' (but, of course, a group is not the same as a community). Thus, duration and dedication are key features. What constitutes 'a member' is equally fuzzy but, again, duration seems to be important: you are a member when you (and the other participants) think of yourself as one. At any rate, both terms—'community' and 'member'—are used in a more liberal and knockabout way online than offline (or in the academic literature on communities). A virtual community, then, is a system of coordinated 'channels' where the 'viewers' provide the 'programming' themselves. And it is by participating in establishing, developing and governing virtual communities that Internet users may foster some of the norms of trust and reciprocity that Putnam finds essential for making democracy work.

Despite this structural resemblance between online and offline communities, Putnam (1995a: 74) is far from enthusiastic about the democratic effects of the Internet: '...electronic technology enables individual tastes to be satisfied more fully, but at the cost of the positive social externalities associated with more primitive forms of

entertainment ... The new 'virtual reality' helmets that we will soon
don to be entertained in total isolation are merely the latest extension
of this trend'. Putnam's concern is that 'virtual reality' may subject
people to individual hedonism rather than to 'the common good'.
Again, Putnam's vision of scale is at the centre of things: isolation or
integration is a function of geographical distance—small scale is
biased towards intimacy and stability, while large scale is biased
towards isolation and volatility. Since social capital needs time to
grow, the stability of smallness is more suited for this purpose than
the volatility of largeness. What Putnam seems to overlook is that
distance may be social and cultural as well, and that socio-cultural
distance is not easily bridged by geographic proximity. This is particularly important when looking at the Internet: because most members of virtual communities do not share the same geography, these
communities are often organized around and differ from each other
by socio-cultural distance. Moreover, the inter-group conflicts produced by this distance are essential for fostering in-group cohesion,
loyalty and voice. Virtual communities may therefore be hubs of
connectedness comparable to the way Tocqueville thought that newspapers focussed the attention of geographically dispersed readers
on a single set of values and beliefs. To understand why, we need
first of all to know what kind of space a virtual community is.

Symbolic and flexible space   In a technical sense, a virtual community is a set of social relationships that operate within specified
locales—the server hosting a bulletin board service (BBS) or a Usenet
newsgroup, for instance—that provide a computer-generated image of physical space: a fabricated reality consisting of digital code
which is converted into text, pictures, video-clips, etc. The illusion
of community space is augmented by the graphical user interface
which pops up on the computer screen when you log on to a
virtual community, and the sense of physical presence that is created by so-called avatars—digital, online representations of real
persons (also, each collection of digitalized information, a web-site
for example, has a unique address). Accordingly, virtual communities are symbolic, i.e., code-based and flexible. The downside of
this digital construction of space is that virtual communities are
fragile. Digital codes representing community space may vanish if,
for example, the server hosting them goes out of service, are cracked
or if the person(s) operating the service quits. The upside is that it is

a relatively easy technical job to re-establish a community service if it has gone down.

Still, some virtual communities are based on geographic affiliation. Such networks are growing in popularity because they draw on pre-established, real-life community experiences (for analyses of municipal and city networks, see Tsagarousianou, Tambini and Bryan 1998). Nevertheless, these communities provide the same illusion of real space and physical proximity as other communities do.

Cultural symbolism   Community-specific cultural symbolism is the nuts and bolts of virtual identity formation. In Internet Relay Chat (a multi-user synchronous chat line) culture, for instance, lack of nonverbal cues are compensated for by typing 'stage directions' to indicate actions or emotions. For example, *squeeze* and *smooch* indicate a user's actions toward another user (Fernback and Thompson 1995). If you do not recognize or know how to use these symbolic cues in conversations, you are not regarded as a member of the community (see also 'The Jargon File' at *http://catb.org/~esr/jargon/html*). Consequently, it is claimed that without a specific and shared set of textual symbols as a substitution for verbal language the users would not constitute a community.

Cultural symbolism, then, is the social glue of a virtual community. But culture also depends on the motivation for establishing a community. For virtual communitarians, for example, the interest and motivation for community-building stems from a desire to recreate a romanticized vision of *Gemeinschaft*—a community of equal and like-minded individuals. The norm, however, is interest-satisfaction: creating a space where people enjoying a common set of interests or hobbies can meet to discuss whatever they find gratifying (see, for example, Raymond's [1999] account of the Linux community). For typical surfers, what seems to be in demand is not necessarily the homogenity of Gemeinschaft-like or interest-based communities, but the ability to traverse a culturally diversified space. Hence, cultural rules of a community may be egalitarian but rather exclusive (virtual communitarians), inclusive but achievement-oriented (interest satisfaction), few and malleable (surfers).

Historical records and collective memory   'Real world' communities often store written records of their history. These records serve as a pool of knowledge and experience and provide a sense of common destiny that tend to reinforce the members' committment to shared objectives. Virtual communities, on the other hand, rarely keep historical records. This is mainly due to practical problems (insufficient electronic storage capacity and the administrative costs of keeping up-to-date archives). However, postings are usually stored for some time after being submitted, and some communities provide searchable archives of prior discussions. Also, most virtual communities operate a FAQ (frequently asked questions) service containing important information about the community. Both FAQs and stored postings are forms of historical records. Although they give no long-term chronological presentation of community history, they are important in socializing members into the cultural and symbolic context of the communities. In this respect, they provide a sense of common destiny. But, as in 'real world' communities, the best source of historic capital is the unwritten, collective memory of older members. Their knowledge and experience serve as a 'community scrapbook', and is vital for teaching new members the ways of the community.

So, to summarize, virtual communities create an illusion of physical proximity and presence. Community-specific symbolism defines the boundaries of the community; for example, between 'real' members, new members and visitors. Historical records are scarce, but the collective memory of older members is instrumental for the socialization of new members.

Types of Virtual Communities and the Nature of Digital Bonding

So far we have mapped the spatial characteristics of virtual communities. But this does not tell us much about the concrete, social characteristics of these communities. The next step therefore is to look at what virtual communities are doing and how they are going about it.

According to cyberlibertarian ideology, virtual communities are (or should be) guarded spaces of digital property that can be bought and sold according to market value:

> ...these cyberspaces will not all be the same, and they will not all be open to the general public. The global network is a connected 'platform' for a collection of diverse communities, but only a loose, heterogeneous community itself. Just as access to homes, offices, churches and department stores is controlled by their owners or managers, most virtual locations will exist as distinct places of private property ... And

the 'externalities' associated with variations can drop; what happens in one cyberspace can be kept from affecting other cyberspaces (Dyson et al. 1994: 9–10).

In this view, community is property and no one can surf the Internet without trespassing or paying for access. Social bonding based on solidarity and common interests, moreover, is replaced by individualistic, impersonal and contractual relationships: the citizen is overtaken by the consumer. And as digital space is divided into spheres of private property, horizontal interaction is replaced by social segregation: the rich over here, the poor over there and the bird watchers in the middle. The cyberlibertarian vision of virtual community, however, is in a minority position. Most commercial companies have realized that this is not the way to do business on the Internet. Instead of carving virtual space into spheres of private property, the trend for quite some time now has been to use the open culture of virtual communities as a platform for commercial activity. This means that instead of virtual communities being private assets exploited by economic actors, we need more subtle answers for: (1) which types of virtual communities exist, and (2) how these communities affect the people involved.

First things first: types of virtual communities. Because of the distributed structure of the Internet, it is difficult to produce a comprehensive typology of virtual communities. But, as a crude guide, there seem to be four main types of virtual communities: economic, functional, territorial and extra-territorial.

Economic communities   These communities may or may not be commercially motivated, but they are usually not based on territoriality. The characteristic feature, however, is that the communities are organized around activities related to the production or distribution of goods and services. One obvious example are commercial companies—especially software vendors—that build and maintain websites where producers and consumers congregate to discuss, criticize or obtain/provide advice on the products sold by these companies (Hagel and Armstrong 1997). Even if such communities—at least indirectly—are profit-seeking (for instance, they raise brand awareness and/or promote customer loyalty), they may also foster a sense of consumer solidarity and so-called 'smart shopping': that collectives of consumers are more likely to discover the importance of non-economic values for market behaviour than 'atomized' buyers (for an analysis of 'smart shopping', see Micheletti 2000). But the most famous examples of economic communities are non-commercial ones—most notably those labelled 'free software' or 'open source', for example, the Apache and Linux communities. Open source is community-building based on collaborative production of public domain software: software that is not copyrighted, and, therefore, not owned by anyone. The philosophy of Apache or Linux-like communities is a blend of technical instrumentality and a strong sense of social purpose: open source turns out the best software and software codes should belong to 'the people', e. g., the software users. Instead of 'smart shopping', it is 'smart production' (for a presentation of open source ideology and organization, see Raymond 1999).

Functional communities These communities may or may not be based on territoriality, but their main characteristic is that they are organized around a common set of geography-independent solidarities, interests or leisure activities. Most virtual communities are of a functional kind, but I will briefly present a couple of examples: BRAINTMR, a Boston based brain-cancer support group, and the Internet newsgroup *alt.support.cancer* are two of the hundreds of health-related communities in the U.S. alone. Such communities dispense medical information and provide moral support for members (patients and family members, but also for other interested parties like researchers and doctors, for instance). Among the diverse group of functional communities, we also find task-specific and tightly-focussed digital places—places where you go to for specific types of information: financial advice, travel information, music recommendations, software expertise, etc. These communities provide voluntary services—usually for free—that are often of a very high quality. The classical example of a functional community, however, is The WELL (Whole Earth 'Lectronic Link)—a conference site initiated by people in the San Francisco Bay Area (see Hill and Hughes 1998; Hafner 1997; Rheingold 1993). The WELL is a typical non-focussed community—a community that is devoted to all kinds of topics. Functional communities with a more social and political bite include, for instance, 'Netslaves' (*http://www.netslaves.com/weblogs*), a site for disgruntled 'proletarians' of the dotcom economy.

Territorial communities What distinguishes these digital spaces from the functional ones is that territorial communities build a virtual environment on top of geographically delimited locations, and that activities are focussed around local community issues. Public authorities, for example, pay a growing attention to the possibilities of territorial communities—mainly municipalities eager to boost a lack of interest in local party politics and community issues. It is also expected—a bit optimistically perhaps—that these virtual environments may help create a stronger sense of real-life community and foster offline responsibility, and that this may help reduce some of the social problems (youth gangs, criminality, drug abuse, etc.) troubling metropolitan areas (for example, by promoting cooperation between police offices, neighbourhood associations, non-profit groups, and public housing managers). The success of such services, however, is uncertain. In Norway, the experience has been that local authorities lack committment and financial resources to create vibrant community networks (the technical and administrative responsibility for running online community services are often outsourced to commercial companies that sometimes promote their own rather than the community's interests), and public interest has so far been lukewarm. In the U.S., most online community services are run by volunteers—usually aided by local schools and universities—and this model seems to work somewhat better than the Norwegian one, especially in socially deprived areas (see Nardi and O'Day 1999).

Extra-territorial communities Extra-territorial digital spaces are a mix of functional and territorial communities: an electronic forum for the aggregation of geography-bound solidarities and interests, like, for example, when municipal networks are connected to establish online services for discussing issues of common interest. The best example of extra-territorial communities is the aboriginal videoconference networks. In a continuing series of videoconferences, land rights, language perservation, and traditional and contemporary aborigine music have been discussed among the Warlpiri aborigines of Australia, the Scandinavian Saami, Alaskan Inupiat, Canadian Inuit and the Little Red Cree nation in Alberta, Canada. The aim is to knit together closer cultural ties between minority groups and to coordinate political initiatives on the international level.

Virtual Communities and Social Interaction

This—and similar—orderings of virtual communities do not, of course, do justice to the complexity of the phenomenon and the exact nature of their activities. It may also be difficult to decide whether a community belongs to this or that category. However, to my knowledge, all virtual communities are biased towards one of them. So, on the basis of this typology, let us turn to the second question: how are people involved in virtual community activity affected by it? How and to what extent is social capital production going on? Here, little systematic research has been done. The research that has been done consists mainly of case studies, and it is difficult to evaluate how representative the findings are. On the other hand, these studies provide some insight into the social mechanisms of virtual communities. Keeping these shortcomings in mind, a few main lessons emerge:[4]

1. Typed, non-verbal communication and the lack of physical presence force people to express themselves in a frank and direct way—mainly because typed messages need to be short and to the point. This gives communication an informal character that invites people (even the shy ones) to participate, but those with good typing skills have an edge.

2. The direct and open mode of discussion remove the barriers of communication and facilitate interpersonal bonding because participants get a feeling of interacting with people that have no 'hidden agenda'.

3. Open and frank communication (and the lack of physical presence) may amplify feelings of trust or animosity: the intensity of hate or love seems to be more intense online than in real life. This may account for the frequent eruption of 'hate speech' and 'flame wars'. However, these phenomena rarely occur within virtual communities.

4. Virtual communities are often fragile constructions. A few unpleasant participants (sometimes just one, depending on how large the community is) can cause a great deal of 'bad blood' and distrust—even to such an extent that the community disintegrates. This may explain why many virtual communities exercise a 'low tolerance' policy towards 'hate speech' and personal abuse.

5. The size of virtual communities is an important variable: a small community is usually integral, egalitarian and consensus oriented, while a large community is often inclusive, interest-based and task-oriented (this seems to apply regardless of the focus of the community).

6. The degree of participation and engagement may vary a great
    deal: some members are active all the time, some periodically
    and still others rarely take part in discussions.
7. The long-term success of a community depends on a core group
    of highly-motivated and dedicated participants. The process of
    succession (when old, trusted members withdraw, and new
    ones need to take over their responsibilities) is a critical junc-
    ture in the life of a community since there are usually no well-
    defined rules governing this process.
8. Communities that require members to disclose their real-life
    identities are the most successful ones and the community works
    better if members have a chance to meet in person at least once
    in the lifetime of the community.
9. Virtual communities cannot substitute for the loss (or lack) of
    'the real thing'. Even if there are examples of the opposite, the
    communities that work best (the most durable ones) seem to
    tap into resources generated by real-life community experiences.
    But since the intensity and scope of interpersonal relationships
    may be enhanced, virtual communities harbour the potential
    for adding value to offline communities. This seems to confirm
    statistical evidence presented by, among others, Pew Internet
    and American Life Project (*www.pewinternet.org*) and Net Value
    (*www.netvalue.com*)—the Internet facilitates small-scale con-
    nectedness.
10. Virtual communities that do not—for various reasons—tap into
    real-community identities and solidarities need a strong moti-
    vating force to stay vibrant over time (as in 'we at Linux hate
    Microsoft'). In these communities, the level of activity tends to
    vary a great deal (sometimes the community is dormant, some-
    times it erupts in activity). But even in dormant periods, the
    community performs a 'lighthouse' role for the members: it pro-
    vides a focus for social or political awareness.
11. The main value of virtual communities is that they give members
    a sense of social connectedness. The fear that these communi-
    ties may increase the feeling of social isolation and 'distance to
    society' seems to lack significant support.
12. The use of hyperlinks facilitates 'community shopping', which
    means that people surf from one electronic context to the next
    (this form of individual cyber-mobility is highly praised). There is,
    however, little evidence that the majority of community members

behave any less responsibly because of it, but it is likely that cyber-mobility has an effect on membership turnover rates.

13. A barrier against 'community shopping' and cyber-mobility is that few of the assets that have been accumulated in one digital location (for instance, time invested in shaping the community and one's standing as a member) can be transferred to the next (contrary to real life where many assets can be transferred between localities: money, education, reputation, work experience, belongings, personal networks, etc.). Exit may therefore be a less attractive strategy than voice or loyalty (at least, less attractive than we are inclined to believe).

14. 'Community shopping' and cyber-mobility may facilitate bridging rather than bonding social capital: the ability to get along with people different from oneself. The individualism of cyberlibertarians may therefore 'break the spell' of closely knitted and segmented virtual communities.

Even if these preliminary findings point to a possible positive relationship between virtual community membership and social capital formation, there is one last issue that we need to look into: how virtual community membership and Internet usage are related to the exercise of good citizenship (in a Putnamian sense). Are community members and Internet users more or less likely to engage in offline politics, community activities and organizational life? I suspect that members of the so-called hacker culture are less likely to trust the government than other Internet users (and non-users), but it is far from certain that this lack of trust is in any way related to a low level of political awareness or engagement. Another possibility is that there is a positive feedback loop between online engagement and offline involvement: the same people are active in both places because participation is its own reward (self-selection). If this is the case, the Internet may reproduce well-known patterns of social and political engagement. But, as Putnam (2000: 179) points out: '... it is a fundamental mistake to suppose that the question before us is computer-mediated communication versus face-to-face interaction' (Putnam's analysis, however, is largely based on this distinction). The crucial test for any communication system, then, is its effectiveness in overcoming barriers against social communication (and face-to-face interaction is not very effective in doing that as it seems to foster bonding rather than bridging social capital).

Concerning horizontal connectedness, it is probably true that the Internet is not a substitute for face-to-face community but it can make a sense of community possible where face-to-face interaction is difficult or impossible to achieve. Instead of just looking at how ICTs facilitate horizontal connectedness, as Putnam does, it is just as important to understand how these systems change the basic conditions for vertical connectedness—how people relate to political, civic and state institutions. One possibility here is that intermediaries (parties, associations, interest groups, mass media, etc.) are bypassed: the interactions between citizens' and state institutions, for instance, are individualized and privatized due to the widespread use of customer relationship management software.

Paradise Lost?

The argument of this article has been that constructing technology is one important way of building society: a way largely ignored by political scientists. This lack of interest in the interaction between technical development and social change is unfortunate in an age of high technology. But there are exceptions: Robert D. Putnam and the cyberlibertarians are probably right in pointing out that modern ICTs—digital network systems like the Internet—will change how people relate to each other. But rather than replacing face-to-face interaction, the Internet may facilitate more interaction 'on top' of real-community environments. The failure of the dotcom companies, for instance, is probably due to their misreading of the importance of 'click and mortar' integration: companies that are built on nothing but software code are not real enough to make most people trust them with their. wallets. And the reason for the local orientation that the Internet seems to give rise to must, I think, be explained by it's basic characteristic: entrenched flexibility. By putting the users in command of a global communications system, it is likely that the users will exploit the system to strengthen established relationships—and most of those relationships are local. The Internet may therefore foster horizontal connectedness but, at the same time, weaken vertical connectedness: people may grow more concerned with their small-scale worries and less preoccupied with matters of large-scale importance. But by taking part in shaping digital social environments, people may also aquire social and political skills that are transferable to the offline world. If so, large-scale civic engagement may not be something that the old-timers—those who, by their own account, campaigned their way through the 1960s—view as a 'paradise lost'. This new form of civic engagement, however, is likely to be of a different kind: short-term, intense, issue specific and result oriented.

Notes

1. Researcher, the Rokkan Centre, University of Bergen, Norway.
2. The social constructionist perspective is also problematic because of the way the distinctions between, for instance, the technical and the social, actor and structure, are deconstructed: by resorting to 'concept fetishism'—introducing new labels that are supposed to encompass 'unproper' analytical distinctions (these relabeling exercises are, as a rule, based on limited empirical evidence). The main problem, however, is that social constructionists (and postmodernists) seek to combine unfettered relativism and grand generalizations, which makes the theory so abstract and fuzzy that it is hard to pin down exactly what is explained and how (and to get a grip on the political relevance of it all).
3. A counter argument may be made here: you can watch television, but a television set may also be redesigned for other purposes—a fish bowl, for example. Sensible use, therefore, is context-dependent—it all depends on how you interpret your needs in relation to technology. But technology is first and foremost infrastructure, and the infrastructure is often transparent (television infrastructure, for example, is made up of head-end stations, bandwidth (frequencies), transmission systems, regulatory institutions, etc.). You may be free to use your television set as a fish bowl, but that does not mean that you have any control over the technological system that television sets are only the most visible part of. At any rate, it is silly to buy a television set instead of a fish bowl if you are planning on getting a goldfish.
4. See, for instance, Sunstein (2001); Lessig (1999); Nardi and O'Day (1999); Raymond (1999); Hill and Hughes (1998); Kelly (1998); Tsagarousianou, Tambini and Bryan (1998); Hagel and Armstrong (1997); Negroponte (1996); Kelly (1994); Harasim (1993); Rheingold (1993). These lessons are also based on personal observations.

References

Abbate, J. 1999. *Inventing the Internet.* Cambridge, Massachusetts: The MIT Press.

Arthur, B. W. 1994. *Increasing Returns and Path Dependence in the Economy.* Ann Arbor: University of Michigan Press.

Bijker, W. E. 1995. *Of Bicycles, Bakelites and Bulbs. Towards a Theory of Sociotechnical Change.* Cambridge, Massachusetts: The MIT Press.

Bijker, W. E. and Law, J. (eds.) 1992. *Shaping Technology/Building Society. Studies in Sociotechnical Change.* Cambridge, Massachusetts: The MIT Press.

Bijker, W. E., Hughes, T. P. and Pinch T. J. (eds.) 1987. *The Social Construction of Technological Systems. New Directions in the Sociology and History of Technology.* Cambridge, Massachusetts: The MIT Press.

Brand, S. 1999. *The Clock of the Long Now. Time and Responsibility.* New York: Basic Books.

Collingridge, D. 1980. *The Social Control of Technology.* London: Frances Pinter.

Dyson, E., Gilder, G., Keyworth, G., and Toffler, A. 1994. 'Cyberspace and the American Dream: A Magna Carta for the Knowledge Age.' Release 1.2. The Progress and Freedom Foundation, Washington, D.C. Available at *http://www.pff.org/position.html*

Ellul, J. 1980. *The Technological System* (translated by Joachim Neugroschel). New York: Continuum.

Ellul, J. 1964. *The Technological Society* (translated by John Wilkinson). New York: Vintage Books.

Fernback, J. and Thompson, B. 1995. 'Virtual Communities: Abort, Retry, Failure?' Paper presented at the annual convention of the International Communication Association, Albuquerque, New Mexico, May 1995.

Gilder, G. 1994. *Life After Television.* New York: W.W. Norton.

Hafner, K. 1997. 'The World's Most Influential Online Community (And It's Not AOL)'. *Wired 5.05.*

Hafner, K. and Lyon, M. 1996. *Where Wizards Stay Up Late: The Origins of the Internet.* New York: Simon & Schuster.

Hagel, J. and Armstrong, A.G. 1997. '*Net Gain. Expanding Markets Through Virtual Communities.*' Boston, Massachusetts: Harvard Business School Press.

Harasim, L. M. (ed.) 1993. *Global Networks: Computers and International Communication.* Cambridge, Massachusetts: The MIT Press.

Hill, K. A. and Hughes, J.E. 1998. *Cyberpolitics. Citizen Activism in the Age of the Internet.* Lanham, Maryland: Rowman & Littlefield.

Jasanoff, S. et al. (eds.) 1995. *Handbook in Science and Technology Studies.* Thousand Oaks: Sage Publications.

Kelly, K. 1998. *New Rules for the New Economy. 10 Radical Strategies for a Connected World.* New York: Viking Penguin.

Kelly, K. 1994. *Out of Control: The Rise of Neo-Biological Civilization.* Reading, Massachusetts: Addison-Wesley Publishing Company.

Lebow, I. 1995. *Information Highways and Byways: From the Telegraph to the 21st Century.* New York: IEEE Press.

Lessig, L. 1999. *Code and Other Laws of Cyberspace.* New York: Basic Books.

MacKenzie, D. and Wajcman, J. 1985. *The Social Shaping of Technology: How the Refrigerator Got Its Hum.* Milton Keynes: The Open University Press.

Micheletti, M. 2000. 'Shopping and the Reinvention of Democracy. Green Comsumerism and the Accumulation of Social Capital in Sweden.' Paper presented at the ECPR Joint Sessions Workshop: Voluntary Associations, Social Capital and Interest Mediation: Forging the Link. Copenhagen, 14–19 April 2000.

Mumford, L. 1971. *The Pentagon of Power.* London: Secker & Warburg.

Nardi, A. and O'Day, V.L. 1999. *Information Ecologies. Using Technology with Heart.* Cambridge, Massachusetts: The MIT Press.

Negroponte, N. 1996. *Being Digital.* London: Hodder & Stoughton.

Norris, P. 1996. 'Does Television Erode Social Capital? A Reply to Putnam'. *Political Science & Politics* 29 (3): pp. 474–80.

Putnam, R. D. 2000. *Bowling Alone: The Collapse and Revival of American Community.* New York: Simon & Schuster.

————. 1995a. 'Bowling Alone: America's Declining Social Capital'. *Journal of Democracy* 1: pp. 65–78.

————. 1995b. 'Tuning In, Tuning Out: The Strange Disappearance of Social Capital in America.' *Political Science & Politics* 28 (4): pp. 664–83.

————. 1993. *Making Democracy Work: Civic Traditions in Modern Italy.* Princeton, NJ: Princeton University Press.

Raymond, E. S. 1999. *The Cathedral and the Bazaar: Musings on Linux and Open Source by an Accidental Revolutionary.* Sebastopol, CA: O'Reilly.

Rheingold, H. 1993. *The Virtual Community: Homesteading on the Electronic Frontier.* Reading, Massachusetts: Addison-Wesley.

Schwarz, M., and Thompson, M. 1990. *Divided We Stand. Redefining Politics, Technology and Social Choice.* Philadelphia: University of Pennsylvania Press.

Selle, P. and Øymyr, B. 1995. *Frivillig organisering og demokrati. Det frivillige organisasjonssamfunnet endrar seg—1940–1990.* Oslo: Det Norske Samlaget.

Sunstein, C. 2001. *republic.com.* Princeton: Princeton University Press.

Tanenbaum, A. S. 1996. *Computer Networks.* Upper Saddle River, NJ: Prentice-Hall.

Tsagarousianou, R., Tambini, D. and Bryan, C. (eds.) 1998. *Cyberdemocracy: Technology, Cities and Civic Networks.* London: Routledge.

Tranvik, T., Thompson, M. and Selle, P. 2000. 'Doing Technology (and Democracy) the Pack-Donkey's Way: The Technomorphic Approach to ICT Policy', in Christoph Engel and Kenneth H. Keller (eds.), *Governance and Global Networks in the Light of Differing Local Values*. Baden-Baden: Nomos Verlagsgesellschaft.

De Tocqueville, A. 1990. *Democracy in America*. New York: Vintage Books.

Winner, L. 1986. *The Whale and the Reactor. A Search for Limits in an Age of High Technology*. Chicago: Chicago University Press.

Winner, L. 1977. *Autonomous Technology. Technics-out-of-control as a Theme in Political Thought*. Cambridge, Massachusetts: The MIT Press.

Internet Sources

www.pewinternet.org
www.netvalue.com
http://catborg/~esr/jargon/html/
http://www.netslaves.com/weblogs/

About the Editors and Contributors

The Editors

Sanjeev Prakash is Senior Researcher at the Centre for Development Studies, University of Bergen, Norway. He has earlier been a Member of the Advisory Committee on International Development Policy, Norwegian Ministry of Foreign Affairs (2001–2003), and Guest Professor and Researcher at the Norwegian Centre for Research in Organization and Management, Bergen. Sanjeev Prakash has extensive management and consultancy experience with development, poverty and environmental policy issues in India, East Africa and Scandinavia, and has written or edited numerous publications dealing with these issues.

Per Selle is Professor in the Department of Comparative Politics, University of Bergen, Norway. He has previously published *Cultural Theory as Political Science* (with Michael Thompson and Gunnar Grendstad) and *Government and Voluntary Organizations: A Relational Perspective* (with Stein Kuhnle). Professor Selle is a Member of the Norwegian Global Change Committee, and was part of a group set up by the Norwegian Government to study Power and Democracy in Norway (1998–2003).

The Contributors

D. Douglas Caulkins is Earl D. Strong Professor of Social Studies at Grinnell College, Iowa, USA. Caulkins first began his research on organizational society in western Norway in the 1960s. He is currently researching aspects of identity among the Welsh diaspora and the organizational cultures of British heritage sites. Among his recent research papers are *Grid-Group Analysis, Social Capital and*

Entrepreneurship in North American Immigrant Groups (with Christina Peters, *Cross-Cultural Research 36*, 2002) and *Consensus, Clines and Edges in Celtic Cultures* (*Cross-Cultural Research 35*, 2001).

Paul Dekker is Head of the Participation and Government Research Group at the Social and Cultural Planning Office of the Government of Netherlands, and part-time Professor of Civil Society at the Globus Institute, Tilburg University. His most recent publications include *Social Capital and Participation in Everyday Life* (co-edited with Eric Uslaner, 2001) and *The Values of Volunteering: Cross-Cultural Perspectives* (co-edited with Loek Halman, 2003).

Mario Diani is Professor of Sociology at the University of Trento in Italy. Among his recent books are *Green Networks: A Structural Analysis of the Italian Environmental Movement* (Edinburgh University Press, 1995) and *Social Movements* (with D. Della Porta, Blackwell, 1999). Diani is co-editor of *Studying Collective Action* (Sage, 1992), *Beyond Tocqueville: Civil Society and the Social Capital Debate in Comparative Perspective* (University Press of New England, 2001), and *Social Movements and Networks* (Oxford University Press, 2003) as well as being European editor of *Mobilization*.

Axel Hadenius is Professor of Political Science at Uppsala University, Sweden. His works include *Democracy and Development* (Cambridge University Press, 1992), *Democracy's Victory and Crisis* (ed., Cambridge University Press, 1997) and *Institutions and Democratic Citizenship* (Oxford University Press, 2001).

Anirudh Krishna teaches Public Policy and Political Science at Duke University, USA. He was educated at the Delhi School of Economics and Cornell University. He is the author of *Active Social Capital: Tracing the Roots of Development and Democracy* (Columbia University Press, 2002) and co-author of *Reasons for Hope: Instructive Experiences in Rural Development* (Kumarian Press, 1997). He has written numerous papers on rural development, poverty and social capital.

Bo Rothstein is August Röhss Professor of Political Science at Gothenburg University in Sweden. Among his publications are *The Social Democratic State: The Swedish Model and the Bureaucratic Problems of Social Reforms* (University of Pittsburgh Press, 1996) and *Just Institutions Matter: The Moral and Political Logic of the Universal Welfare State* (Cambridge University Press, 1998). Rothstein is a regular contributor to public debates about politics, the welfare state and labour policy in Sweden. He has been visiting scholar at Cornell University, Harvard University, University of Bergen, Pittsburgh University, the University of Washington in Seattle and the Russell Sage Foundation.

Susanne Hoeber Rudolph is William Benton Distinguished Service Professor Emeritus of Political Science at the University of Chicago. Together with Lloyd I. Rudolph she is the author of *In Pursuit of Lakshmi: The Political Economy of the Indian State* (University of Chicago Press, 1987), *Gandhi: The Traditional Roots of Charisma* (University of Chicago Press, 1983) and *The Modernity of Tradition: Political Development in India* (Orient Longman, 1967). She is also editor of *Transnational Religion, the State and Global Civil Society* (with James Piscatori, Westview Press, 1997) and *Education and Politics in India* (with Lloyd Rudolph and Paul Brass, Harvard University Press, 1972). Rudolph is President of the American Political Science Association, 2003–2004.

Dietlind Stolle is Assistant Professor of Political Science at McGill University, Montreal, Canada. She has published widely on the themes of social capital and trust in journals and books. Stolle is co-editor of *Generating Social Capital: Civil Society and Institutions in Comparative Perspective* (Palgrave, 2003) and *Politics, Products, and Markets: Exploring Political Consumerism Past and Present* (Transaction Press, 2003).

Tommy Tranvik is Researcher at The Rokkan Centre, University of Bergen, Norway. His primary research interests are the relationship between national sovereignty and modern information and communication technologies, Internet-based forms of civic engagement and the implications for democracy with the use of modern information technologies by local governments.

Gaute Torsvik is Professor of Economics at the University of Bergen, Norway. Among the research themes that interest him are the interaction between formal and informal credit institutions in developing countries. He has published several articles and papers on the structure and effects of economic incentives in social interaction.

Dag Wollebæk is a PhD candidate at the Institute for Comparative Politics, University of Bergen, Norway. His research focuses on social capital and the voluntary sector, a subject on which he has written (with Per Selle) several books and articles. One of his recent papers (with Per Selle) won an award for best contribution in 2002 to the *Nonprofit and Voluntary Sector Quarterly*.

Index